THE
WORK
RELATED
CURRICULUM

14.95

rb act

NEW DEVELOPMENTS IN VOCATIONAL EDUCATION

Series Editors: Peter Funnell and Dave Müller

THE WORK RELATED CURRICULUM

Challenging the Vocational Imperative

JERRY WELLINGTON

KOGAN PAGE

London • Philadelphia

First published in 1993

Kogan Page Limited
120 Pentonville Road
London N1 9JN

© 1993, Jerry Wellington and named contributors

British Library Cataloguing in Publication Data

A CIP record for this book is available from the British Library.

ISBN 0 7494 0601 1

Typeset by DP Photosetting, Aylesbury, Bucks
Printed and bound in Great Britain by
Biddles Ltd, Guildford and King's Lynn

Contents

Series Editors' Preface

Vocational education is increasingly shaking off its 'Cinderella' status to take its place at the forefront of social policy issues internationally. The widespread recognition of the essential link between effective vocational education and economic and social development is resulting in a range of strategies and approaches within individual nations – and supra-national bodies such as the European Community – to educate, train and retrain the current and future workforce in response to increasing global competition.

In response, vocational education in the UK has experienced substantial change in recent years in terms of its curriculum delivery and organization. In recent years it has faced the implications of a demographic downturn and the need to extend the range of its provision to meet new demands, whether from relatively new areas such as the adult unwaged or areas of professional, industrial and commercial updating, or its more traditional clients. New central-government-initiated curriculum initiatives have emerged at a bewildering pace requiring substantial changes in teaching and learning practice. In the same period it has become necessary to respond positively to the challenge of the Single European Market and wider structural changes, both in Europe and across the globe, within a context which recognizes that, historically, the UK has failed by Western industrial standards to provide the education and training necessary to meet the needs of the economy. Measures have been taken to increase significantly the participation rates of those aged 16 and over while also recognizing that some 80 per cent of the UK workforce of the year 2000 are already economically active.

The 1990s will witness the continuation and heightening of these processes and the generation of new opportunities and challenges for those responsible for providing vocational education. This process and these opportunities and challenges will emerge internationally with the pattern of delivery and the balance of responsibility for action varying between the individual, the employer and the state.

This series of books focuses on the opportunities and challenges facing vocational education. The aim of the series is to provide contemporary texts which focus on newly emerging issues, with an emphasis on innovation and comparative analysis. More specifically, the series will seek to influence and inform practice by focusing on the application of new and original ideas. In this way, texts in the series will be at the interface between theory and practice with the explicit intention of enabling policy-makers, practitioners and managers to apply new educational ideas and philosophies. The books are designed for those engaged professionally in vocational education and will provide information on, and critical analysis of, new developments. The contemporary and applied nature of this series will, we hope, make it a valuable source of material on important current issues which builds into a library to support the application of good practice.

Within this context, *The Work-Related Curriculum* makes an important contribution by bringing together critical analysis from a number of prominent contributors to explore current vocational education provision for the 14–19 age group. The book combines theoretical argument with an analysis of policy formation and operational practice, and makes explicit and challenges the ideological and economic assumptions which underpin the expansion of vocational education. By doing so the book raises fundamental questions about the place of education in society and the relationship between compulsory education and the supposed 'needs' of the economy. Critically, the book challenges the 'common sense' notion that a greater level of vocationalism in the curriculum has value within the workplace. As such the book offers a range of alternative insights to those dominant in current practice which will be of value to policy-makers, teachers and educational managers.

We hope you enjoy this and other texts in the series.

Peter Funnell
Dave Müller
Ipswich, Suffolk 1993

A Note on the Contributors

Wilfred Carr is a Reader in Education at the University of Sheffield. He has published extensively in the areas of philosophy of education and curriculum studies and is the executive editor of *Curriculum Studies: A Journal of Educational Discussion and Debate*.

David Finegold is a Research Fellow at the RAND corporation in California and a Visiting Fellow at the Centre for Education and Industry at the University of Warwick. David is one of the co-authors of the influential publications on the British Baccalaureate and HE reform from IPPR.

Ian Jamieson is currently Professor of Education at the University of Bath. He was previously Head of Sociology at Ealing College of Higher Education, an evaluator with the Schools Council and Reader in Business and Management Studies at a business school. He is the author of numerous books and articles on aspects of work and schooling, and the editor of the *British Journal of Education and Work*.

Maggie MacLure is Lecturer in Education at the University of East Anglia. Her research interests and publications lie in the areas of curriculum analysis, language education and research methodology.

Val Millman is currently Education Adviser for Equal Opportunities with Coventry City Council. She has been interested in the work-related curriculum since she was a secondary school careers teacher and has been involved in a number of research and curriculum development projects on gender equality and the work-related curriculum.

William Richardson is Senior Research Fellow at the Centre for Education and Industry, University of Warwick. His research interests are divided between religious policy in sixteenth-century England and education and labour policy in twentieth-century national economies. His most recent book, co-edited with David Finegold and John Woolhouse, is on the reform of post-16 education and training in England and Wales.

Ian Stronach is Professor of Education at the University of Stirling. He has published extensively on the subject of vocationalism. His other interests include evaluation and research methodology.

Jerry Wellington taught in Tower Hamlets before joining Sheffield University, where he is now Senior Lecturer in Education. His main research interests are in science education and the links between education and employment, particularly in the area of information technology (IT).

Foreword

The belief that education should attempt to meet the needs of employers and employment is by no means a new one, as later chapters discuss. The vocational imperative has been around for a long time. A term that is relatively new, however, is the 'work-related curriculum'. The main aim of this book is to take a close look at the work-related curriculum and more generally at the notion that education and schooling should somehow be related to the world of work and the so-called needs of employers. It would be impossible to examine all of the ideas and initiatives that have made up the growth of the 'new vocationalism' and subsequently the enterprise era and the current work-related features of the new, post-1988 curriculum. What this book is intended to do, however, is to address certain questions through the writing of different authors and to concentrate on a small number of initiatives, some of which were born in the 1980s and lived until the 1990s. The book will also concentrate largely on the education and training of 14–19-year-olds, although much of the argument and discussion will relate to a broader spectrum. The various chapters, contributions and case-studies will address the following questions:

- What are the major initiatives which have influenced vocational education since 1976?
- Are these initiatives related to each other?
- Has there been a pattern or have they been a haphazard set of events?
- What effects have demographic and employment/unemployment patterns had on the bond between education and employment?
- Can and should education attempt to meet the 'needs of industry'?
- Does the notion of the needs of industry have any real, ie. descriptive as opposed to emotive, meaning?
- What valuable research evidence is there on the needs of employers?

- What is the vocational significance of new technology and, in particular, information technology?
- What does the notion of the work-related curriculum entail?
- Is there anything new about the work-related curriculum?
- What identities are created for pupils by the 'new' curriculum?
- In what way should education respond to changing patterns of employment and economic forces in the future?
- If we are really entering a post-industrial society, what approach should education in the future take?
- Should education be shaped by a vocational imperative?
- What is the role of education in contemporary society?

The concept of the 'work-related curriculum' will be examined in this book but it is recognized from the start that it is a problematic one. There is no single meaning for the term 'work-related' (let alone the term 'curriculum') and it is unlikely that one could ever emerge. As Saunders (1991) notes, there are many and varied ways of interpreting what 'relatedness to work' means. Equally, the issue of what counts as work is of vital importance, as Watts (1983) and others have discussed. Do we include solely paid employment or should the broad concept involving voluntary work, unpaid work generally, community work, the informal economy, and other forms of work be considered? The distinction between work and labour is also an important one and is discussed by more than one contributor in this book. Finally, from a very practical, curriculum perspective there may be various models for a work-related curriculum. It may be viewed as a part or a sub-set of the entire curriculum of a school or college. It may be seen solely as an addition or 'bolt-on' to the main curriculum, or at the other extreme as coterminous with or identical to the entire curriculum. It may be seen, less strongly, as something which permeates the curriculum.

All the issues and questions posed above will be discussed in the chapters below.

Acknowledgements

My thanks are due to all the people who have contributed to this book – not only the authors but also the teachers, pupils, schools and City Technology Colleges who have been involved in the various case-studies. Special thanks are due to my former teaching colleague in Tower Hamlets, Pat Ainley, for his comments on early drafts of several chapters.

J.J. Wellington

References

Saunders, L (1991) 'Education, work and the curriculum', *Policy Studies*, Summer, **12**, 2, 13–26.

Watts, A G (1983) *Education, Unemployment and the Future of Work*, Milton Keynes: Open University Press.

SECTION 1

The Evolution of the Work-related Curriculum

The vocational imperative, ie, the demand that education should be more responsive to the needs of industry, the requirements of employers and the health of the economy, is not new. Its basic premise is that future education should include better preparation for work and should therefore lead to improved economic performance and wealth creation. This imperative has manifested itself not only in official documents, politicians' speeches and polemic literature but also in bar-room discussion and the popular press. The *Mail on Sunday* provides an excellent example:

> For years the major industrialised nations have seen their competitive edge eroded by low-wage economies in the newly developing states. Every year we lose more jobs to such countries. Unskilled, even semi-skilled work, is shrinking relentlessly.
>
> Hence the importance of positioning Britain as a skills and ideas nation renowned for our excellence in innovative science and possessing a workforce with unique technical know-how.
>
> The tragedy of the past few decades is that even while we were losing low-skilled jobs to the Third World, our education system was doing nothing to build the basis for a changing Britain.
>
> (*Mail on Sunday*, 13 September 1992, p.20)

How should those in education respond to this vocational imperative? How should the role and purpose of education and the structure of the curriculum be conceptualized in the remainder of this century?

These are the central questions of this book, which are introduced in Section 1. Chapter 1 starts the discussion by tracing some of the allegations and landmarks which have contributed to the vocational imperative. It goes on to consider the spate of initiatives which have been a response to the perceived need to relate education more closely to employment. The chapter identifies the various contexts for those responses: employment patterns; economic factors; technological development; political and social change. The changes of the 1980s formed part of the so-called new vocationalism of that era. Following the 1988 Education Reform Act we are now into a new era in which the terms of vocationalism have been joined by the language of enterprise and competence. This chapter, and the discussion with Watts which follows in Chapter 2, considers the new discourse in education and training – a discussion followed up by Carr in Chapter 11.

In Chapter 2, Watts considers the concept of the work-related curriculum and its meaning. He discusses the range of vocational initiatives from 1976 to 1992 which led to the present status of work-related teaching and learning. Watts considers the future status of such activity given the new emphasis on market forces in education and the introduction of a National Curriculum – this is a point examined at length by Jamieson in Chapter 10. Watts concludes by pointing out the many issues about education and the future of work which remain unresolved but often ignored.

Both Chapters 1 and 2 point out that the variety of initiatives involved in shaping the work-related curriculum have not always pulled or pushed in the same direction. There has been inevitable conflict. Finegold, in Chapter 3, analyses one of the underlying reasons by a detailed examination of the conflict between and within institutions. He illustrates the critical role played by institutional factors in shaping education and training policy by considering the case of TVEI. He describes how TVEI was a response, influenced by the distinctive institutional capacities of the Manpower Services Commission (MSC), to the problems of rising unemployment and alleged skill shortages. Finegold discusses the unique role of the MSC in developing the contract culture referred to in Chapter 1 as a means of effecting and managing educational change – in Finegold's terms, the contract-compliance mechanism. He goes on to discuss the undermining of the work of TVEI by subsequent Education Acts, a theme returned to fully in Section 4. This undermining process also illustrates the tensions between institutions such as the MSC and the DES at that time. Finally, he considers the factors outside this vocational initiative's remit, such as the strength of the academic examination system and the realities of the labour market, which inevitably reduced its impact.

The latter is yet another example of a general theme which is introduced in this section and followed up in subsequent chapters.

1 The Growth of the Vocational Imperative: Initiatives, Trends and Language Games

J J Wellington

Tracing the history of the vocational imperative

The function of schooling has been open to question and debate ever since schools began. There are a number of interesting historical accounts on the purpose of education and its links with employment and I will not attempt to improve upon them here. Authors on the history of education in this field seem to take great delight in going back as far as possible to show that vocationalism is not new. Williams (1961) for example, talks of the vocational education provided by the monasteries of the sixth century. Others talk of periods, eras or waves in attempting to conceptualize the history of the debate on the purpose of education and its links with the 'outside world'.

Reeder (1979) talks of three periods in a 100-year time span in which employers and governments have attempted to influence the education system. The first occurred in the 1880s and 1890s when efforts were made to extend science education in schools and universities, and to promote technical education (see also Jenkins, 1979; McCulloch *et al*, 1985). The second, Reeder claims, occurred in the 1920s when a flurry of complaints and comments by industry and employers led to the publication of key official reports such as the Malcolm Report (HMSO, 1928). The third period developed from the 1960s and the 1963 Newsom Report (Central Advisory Council, 1963) in which employers complained that teachers did not 'know or understand' the world of industry and 'consciously or unconsciously' influenced pupils against industrial careers. This period extends to the 1970s and in particular a series of official Green papers, a Yellow book, HMI reports (a series usefully listed by Beck, 1981) and of course the Callaghan speech of 1976. James Callaghan's speech is seen by many as something of a landmark in the rise of vocationalism. The speech contained an attack on falling standards in the basics of education and linked this fall with 'progressive' methods, but principally it criticized the lack of economic relevance in education, the anti-industrial attitudes of graduates, and the failure of schools to provide young leavers with the basic skills required by industry.

Ainley (1988) talks of three 'forms' of relationship between education, training and work from 1944 to 1987. He calls them 'tripartite' (in which, from 1944 to 1964, education, knowledge and consequently labour supply were divided in three), 'comprehensive' (in which, from 1964 on, the wholesale introduction of comprehensive schools led to a new connection between education and work, mortally wounded by the Callaghan speech of 1976) and finally, 'vocational'. This period was ushered in by the belief – unsupported by evidence – that the transition from school to work was problematic. It led to the period of vocationalism and the well-known spate of initiatives which Ainley argues were ultimately a failure by 1987 and were replaced by a policy of free-market competition between schools for academic success based on a 'grammar-school' National Curriculum.

Periods, forms, eras – Brown and Lauder (1991) also talk of 'waves', rather in the style of Alvin Toffler, the paperback prophet of the 1980s (Toffler, 1980). They look forward to a 'third wave' of education-economy relationship in which an emphasis on 'collective intelligence' will replace the emphasis on the individual of the current period, and self-direction, control and the acceptance of responsibility will characterize both education and work.

The analysis given by all of these authors deserves full attention, not least because they attempt to provide a framework for the events and initiatives which have led to the present situation, and thereby provide possible look-out posts from which we can view the future.

Common remarks and complaints

The complaint about products of the education system which now seems to provide tabloid fodder, material for after-dinner speeches and a platform for certain employers is not a recent phenomenon. The remark that 'England is the worst educated country in Europe' was made not in 1992 but in 1840 by Brougham (Harris, 1991). A similar comment that:

> Britain's workforce is under-educated, under-trained and under-qualified ... and that a third of school-leavers have no useful qualification to show for at least eleven years in full-time education

was made 170 years later (Harris, 1991) and by the CBI (1989) in *Towards a Skills Revolution*. In the interim period there have been numerous reports outlining the weaknesses of schooling, loud statements by industrial bodies or individuals, and of course politicians' speeches, most notably from Callaghan in 1976.

It is not easy to perceive any great pattern in the comments of recent years, which is hardly surprising since they come from such a variety of sources and with varying degrees of support from reliable evidence. However, certain themes do emerge, some of which have become accepted wisdom only in certain quarters, while others have received broad consent from a variety of people and political perspectives. They are presented and briefly discussed below.

1. The 'falling standards' allegation

This usually concerns literacy and numeracy and has a long history, certainly as far back as Plato's moans about the youth of Athens. Complaints of this nature preceded the 1928 Malcolm Report, as did those in the years before the 1944 act which talked of 'deplorably low standards in elementary arithmetic' (discussed in Reeder, 1979). In 1975 a typical example occurred in an MSC document (1975) *Vocational Preparation for Young People*, which criticized the standards of school leavers and pointed to a need to provide 'young workers' with basic literacy and numeracy. A more recent attack from a royal quarter received vast publicity in the tabloid press when Prince Charles was quoted as saying 'they can't bloody spell' in generally bemoaning the illiteracy of youth.

2. The 'negative attitudes of teachers to commerce and industry' complaint

This surfaced in the evidence of the Employers' Confederation to the Newsom Report (1963) but has been aired many times before and since.

3. The 'negative attitudes of school, college and university leavers to work' criticism

This is often coupled with the conviction that the transition from school to work is a particularly problematic one for young people, a view again for which there is little evidence.

4. The 'academic bias' allegation

This surfaced in the Callaghan (1976) speech which referred to 'the preferences of our best-trained students ... to stay in academic life or to find their way into the Civil Service'. It was further popularized by Wiener's (1985) account of the 'decline of the industrial spirit' in English culture, said to be one of the long-standing causes of Britain's economic plight. The vocational/ academic divide concern, as in the phrase 'what we must do is break down the academic/vocational divide' has now become coupled with this allegation.

5. The 'education is not meeting the needs of industry' allegation

This is similar to the first allegation and is coupled with the 'skills shortage' argument, which at times may be attributed to deficits in education and at other times to demographic trends. This notion is discussed at length in a later chapter.

These common complaints and remarks are listed above, somewhat tongue-in-cheek, as outcries which will be familiar to many readers. The rhetoric, the publicity, the hype all appear to be a perennial part of the education-industry interface. One of the arguments throughout the book is that these exchanges are partly dictated by the social, economic and political contexts in which the exchanges occur.

Kushner (in Fiddy, 1985) presents a more rigorous framework for considering how the education-industry relationship often works in terms of apportioning blame and offering solutions. He refers to 'deficit models' as a useful analytic tool. Such a model has three stages. First, a shortfall is identified in the outcomes of education or training, eg, literacy as in point 1 above. Second, blame is established and a culprit identified, eg, the attitudes of teachers as in point 2 above. Third, a remedy is designed to ease the identified shortfall or problem, eg, teacher placements, new maths syllabuses to replace 'modern maths'. This model of *shortfall, blame, solution* is an interesting one and fits many of the situations and initiatives discussed later in this book. Kushner goes on to identify three emphases in deficit models: student deficit, school deficit and culture deficit. Within the school, the deficit can be seen either in terms of the curriculum or the teachers, which Kushner further analyses. In addition, teachers blame pupils and parents – pupils and parents blame teachers.

Contexts for change in the vocational imperative

There has always been an education-employment interface (Ainley, 1988; Kushner, 1985; Reeder, 1981; Williams, 1961). What does change, to state the obvious, is the context for that interface. The social, economic, technological and political context for education in the sixth century monasteries referred to by Williams (1961) differs from that which gave rise to TVEI in the 1980s (discussed by Finegold, Chapter 3, this volume). The various contexts in which the education-employment relationship is shaped are outlined briefly below, as a prelude to the discussions in later chapters. Six inter-related contexts can be classified as follows.

Unemployment

Many analysts argue that one of the principal influences on the education-industry interface is the unemployment situation, particularly youth unemployment. In times of high unemployment the 'implicit promise' (Watts, 1983) in schooling is undermined and the bond between education and employment is (ironically) tightened (Marshall, 1963). My own summary of this process is shown in Table 1.1.

Table 1.1 *The effects of high unemployment on education: 4 stages*

---

1. The implicit promise in schooling (ie, 'work hard at school to get a job after it') is undermined.
2. The direction and traditional function of schooling and education are questioned.
3. Education, training, and 'pre-vocational education' are increasingly seen as an instrument to respond to youth unemployment.
4. The bonds between education and employment are tightened.

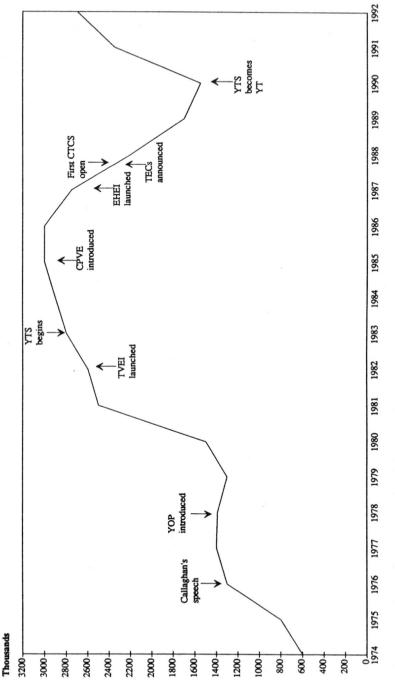

Figure 1.1 *Unemployment trends in the United Kingdom 1974–92*
Source: *Employment Gazette, 1992*

Table 1.2 *Unemployment rates by age (per cent) January 1992*

Age	Male	Female	Both
18–19	19.5	12.8	16.4
20–24	19.9	9.2	15.2
25–29	15.8	6.5	12.0
30–39	12.3	3.8	8.8
40–49	9.3	3.5	6.7
50–59	11.2	4.7	8.5
60+	5.5	0.1	3.9
All ages	12.6	5.2	9.4

Source: Employment Gazette, March 1992, p. 525.

Clearly, the implicit promise in education was undermined by the rapid growth in unemployment in the 1980s shown in Figure 1.1.

The year of introduction of various initiatives is also shown in this figure, although I am not suggesting that there has been any overall pattern to their introduction with respect to unemployment. It is also worth noting that unemployment has affected different age groups to varying degrees and this situation still exists. Current unemployment rates by age group are shown in Table 1.2; clearly, the age groups of 20–24 for men and 18–19 for women are the most seriously affected. There are interesting gender differences in these figures at all age ranges; the issue is discussed by Millman in Chapter 8.

Employment patterns and practices

I have looked closely elsewhere (Wellington, 1987) at the connection between employment patterns and their implications for education. My suggestion then was that the goals of education should be modified in the light of rapidly changing patterns of employment and, in particular, should avoid a narrow, specific-skill-based approach at any level. The rapid changes in employment patterns examined then have continued at a similar rate. The notion of the pace of change and the move to a 'post-industrial society' (both discussed in that article) are still supported by the data. Table 1.3 shows the actual changes and the rates of change in employment by sector from the year of the TVEI launch (1982) to the start of the present decade.

To some extent those figures speak for themselves but I would

Table 1.3 *People in employment by SIC sector: the change from 1982 to 1990*

SIC sector	1982	1990	% change
Agriculture, Forestry and Fishing: 0	361,600	298,000	−17.5%
Energy and Water Supply: 1 (including coal)	661,800	443,000	−33.1%
Other mineral and ore extraction: 2	833,100	721,000	−13.5%
Metal goods, engineering, vehicles: 3	2,632,300	2,301,000	−12.6%
Other manufacturing industries: 4	2,146,200	2,053,500	−4.3%
Construction: 5	1,005,500	1,052,700	+4.7%
Distribution, hotels, catering, repairs: 6	3,955,800	4,743,800	+19.9%
Transport and Communication: 7	1,318,200	1,361,400	+3.3%
Banking, Finance and Insurance: 8	1,702,600	2,697,600	+58.4%
Other Services eg, defence, education, health, R&D: 9	5,868,700	6,625,600	+12.9%

Source: Employment Gazette, January 1992, p. 513.

highlight the radical changes in two sectors: first, the startling downward trend in sector 1, energy and water supply, explained partly by the fact that this includes coal extraction – this is true more generally of the primary (extractive and agricultural) sector as a whole; second, the huge rise in sector 8, banking and finance, over the period of TVEI (Technical and Vocational Education Initiative). Both changes suggest that the notion of 'technical education' as a vocational element of the curriculum is linked to employment and the 'working world' (the phrase used at the launch of TVEI) more by rhetoric than by reality. This notion and the so-called technological bandwagon, particularly in relation to IT (Information Technology), are considered in Chapter 6.

My point here is that any examination of vocational education should be based on a consideration of actual working practices, employment patterns, and trends in demand for labour, with due regard for the rapidity of change.

Economic contexts

Some authors argue that the history of vocational education can be viewed as a series of recurring cycles of concern which are stimulated largely by worries over economic competitiveness (Keep and Mayhew, 1988). My view is that this is just one of a number of important contexts, albeit a central one, linked vitally with the others outlined here. The launch of TVEI, for example, can be seen as a government response to the recession of the early 1980s (Merson, 1992) as can the introduction of YOP and YTS.

Technological change

The importance of the technological context in shaping the vocational curriculum has been stressed since the Crowther Report (1959), and no doubt before then:

> A boy (sic) who enters industry today will not retire until well into the next century. In that time, the odds are that he will see at least one complete technological revolution in his industry (Chapter 5).

The Crowther Report went on to argue for the development, through education and training, of a quality described as 'general mechanical intelligence'. Interesting comparisons and contrasts between Crowther and the launch of TVEI can be drawn (see for example, Layton's 1984 discussion of Crowther's 'alternative road', combining the practical and the academic). But the notions of technological revolution, preparation for the 'technological era' and skills obsolescence have permeated many of the other initiatives of the 1980s. The list would include City Technology Colleges, Compact, the Youth Training Scheme amongst many others. These will be considered in later chapters.

One theme which was generated as a response to awareness of the rapidity of change was the growth of the notion of transferable or generic skills. Again, this will be considered in a later chapter, but it can be said now that this is an idea which infiltrated almost every vocational initiative in the 1980s, particularly those promoted by the MSC and later the Training Agency. It led to what has been termed the 'Manpower Services model of education' (Jonathan,1983), based on core and generic skills, which underpinned not only YTS but also subsequent developments in schools such as the growing emphasis of social and life skills. The notion is based on the belief that, as a result of technological change, the half-life of training and acquired skills is vastly reduced ('half-life' being defined as the time taken for half of an individual's skills or training to become obsolete). Hence, the argument runs, the emphasis for the future should be on transferable, generic skills and the development of 'learning cultures' in organizations.

To sum up then, many aspects and features of the vocational imperative can be seen as being driven by the technological context, either real or perceived (discussed fully in Section 3 of this volume).

Societal changes

Changes and trends in society obviously play an important part in shaping education. In addition, education itself plays an important role in shaping society (see Reeder, 1979, for example, on education as a critical force). One area of increased awareness, if not of direct action, has been the green movement, which has grown perhaps more as a result of informal education and media attention than the formal curriculum. The belated realization that continued growth and consumption of finite, non-renewable resources cannot continue indefinitely has yet to have a major impact on formal education (despite the half-hearted introduction of 'Environmental Education' as a cross-curricular theme). But surely the notion that our only future, in both employment and education, is through sustainable growth must be a central principle of curriculum planning. This notion is clearly not compatible with the belief of the 'New Right' that the problems of society (including education) can be resolved by unbounded market forces (Watts, 1991).

Other changes in society which must have an impact on education policy would include: changes in family structure and the 'typical family'; working patterns in terms of age, gender, structure of the working day, job-sharing and home-working (see Handy, 1985, on the future of work); possible shifts in attitudes towards gender and the role of women in the workplace; and the growing list of new demands placed upon schooling such as drug and sex education, foreign language learning, financial counselling, first aid and so on.

Perhaps the most documented change is the so-called 'demo-

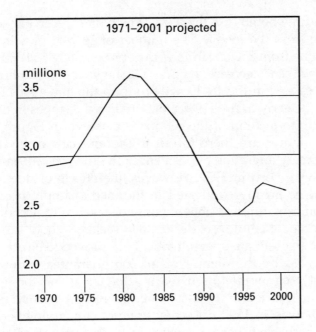

Figure 1.2a *Changes in the UK population aged 16–19 until the end of the century*
Source: CSO (1992)

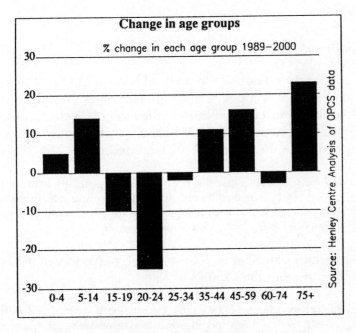

Figure 1.2b *Predicted changes in age groups until the end of the century*
Source: CSO (1992)

graphic time-bomb' in the UK, which has received so much attention from the media. The number of 16-year-olds in the UK will decline from 850,000 in 1987 to approximately 500,000 in 1993, ie, a 41 per cent decrease. Figure 1.2a shows more graphically the trough reached in the 16–19 age group in the mid-1990s from the peak in the early to mid-1980s; the predicted changes in other age groups up to the end of the century are shown in Figure 1.2b.

These figures are there for all to see and cannot be disputed (barring mass migration or pestilence): the 16-year-olds in the 1995 trough were born in 1979. However, the effects of demographic trends were greatly overstated in the media simply because the other contexts outlined above were not taken into account. Talk, for example, of employers desperately seeking school leavers and of an end to graduate unemployment has proved to be empty. This is illustrated by the demise of the job guarantee feature of the Compact programme (discussed in Chapter 5) and the figures of AGCAS (Association of Graduate Careers Advisory Services) which showed in 1992 the worst graduate unemployment for 25 years. These have been largely due to the impact of economic trends, ie, the recession of the 1990s, and the general increase in staying-on rates. In short, the influence of one context in considering vocational education cannot be divorced from any other.

The political context

Last, but far from least, is the political context in which change in education occurs and policy making takes place. In the past it has surfaced in its most blatant form in the kind of 'keep the people in their place' pronouncements. Williams (1961), for example, cites the Justice of the Peace from 1807 who declared:

> It is doubtless desirable that the poor should be generally instructed in reading ... that they may read the scriptures. As to writing and arithmetic, it may be apprehended that such a degree of knowledge would produce in them a disrelish for the laborious occupations of life.

Similar remarks are said by Ranson (1984) to have been made by a senior figure more than 150 years later:

> There may be social unrest but we can cope with the Toxteths. But if we have a highly educated and idle population we may possibly anticipate more serious social conflict. People must be educated once more to know their place (p. 241).

It is not clear whether the latter statement is a plea for more vocational education or less; the speaker in question went on to argue for more central intervention in education.

For those who have lived and taught through the 1980s the principal and most obvious change (I will suggest later that there are other, less noticed changes) is towards a market-led or market-driven system. Education has been inextricably linked to national prosperity and industrial competition, despite the lack of evidence that there is a clear connection, let alone a causal relationship (*Oxford Review of Economic Policy*, 1988, especially Fonda and Hayes). The language of producers and consumers (be they parents or employers) has now replaced the 'social justice' perspective on education of the 1970s (Weiner, 1989). This is linked with the new emphasis in education on 'bureaucratic' rather than 'professional' modes of working within education (Lawton and Chitty, 1987). The bureaucratic approach is said by Lawton and Chitty to be concerned with 'the efficiency of the whole system', with controlling what is taught in schools, and generally making teachers more accountable to central authority. In contrast, the professional approach focused on 'the quality of the teaching process and the needs of individual children'.

Autonomy has been replaced by accountability in the space of a decade. This change has taken place, in my own experience, largely as a result of what can be called the 'biddable curriculum', itself a key feature of what has been termed 'the new vocationalism'. As a result of the initiatives of the 1980s, not least TVEI and Compact, many of the activities pursued by teachers are direct results of bids for funding. This includes the act of bidding itself, which certain individuals in education have developed into a fine art, and also the activities of reporting, responding and auditing which form part of the accountability attached to the biddable curriculum. It might be the case that teachers pursue activities and follow curricula which have not been influenced by the need to bid for funding over the last ten years. More realistically, teachers I have interviewed (see Chapter 5, this volume) believe that the activities they carry out which are supported by funded initiatives are activities which they would have done anyway; the funds have simply been a help to them in promoting or speeding up those pursuits. My suspicion is that those teachers use this as a justification or an excuse for appearing mercenary. Either way, it cannot be denied that bidding and resultant reporting and accounting are an everyday feature of the 1980s and 1990s curriculum which was not present in earlier decades. We have entered what has been called the 'contract culture'.

A more subtle change, and one perhaps less likely to have been noticed by the teachers who lived through the changing political climate of the 1980s, has occurred in the language of education (see Carr's discussion, Chapter 11, this volume). I have mentioned above the shift towards the language of market forces, producers and consumers. Few teachers in the 1970s would have predicted that they would be immersed in such language, in meetings, documents and press reports, in the 1980s and into the 1990s. They may, however, have noticed such shifts because, at least in some cases, they have been able to take a detached view of them. But other shifts in language have been more subtle and have entered the teacher's vocabulary. Thus we hear of 'delivery' of a 'curriculum package', largely as a direct result of the 1988 Education Reform Act. Teachers are seen, and in their more depressed moments see themselves, as deliverers or intermediaries between curriculum and policy-makers, the National Curriculum Council (NCC) and the 'consumers', ie, the pupils (Weiner, 1989).

The difficult position of the work-related curriculum in relation to an imposed National Curriculum is discussed by Jamieson in Chapter 10, this volume. He argues that the future of a work-related curriculum in compulsory schooling is threatened by the very 'market forces' which may at one time have underpinned it. In Chapter 9 of this volume, MacLure and Stronach discuss the effects of vocationalism and the National Curriculum on pupil identities; they point out the various attributes and virtues in pupils which seem to be implicated in the language of the National Curriculum. Identities such as 'pupil as middle manager' and 'pupil as producer and consumer' are, it is argued, to be found in the NCC documents of the post-1988 era. The accountability of teachers to the other two groups of consumer, ie, the parents and employers, has grown largely as a result of the 1988 Education Reform Act and the vocationalism of the 1980s. The language of education is now akin to the language of the retail industry. Other subtle shifts in the language which now permeates education are discussed in a later section; they involve the language of skills and 'competences', and the hi-jacking (Avis, 1991) of the 'progressive' language ('student-centred', 'negotiated', 'active', 'experiential') of the 1960s by the vocationalism of the 1980s (discussed by Watts in Chapter 2, this volume).

These important changes have all occurred in the political

context of that period. Of growing importance in the next period will be the international perspective on both education and employment at the end of the 20th century, a factor discussed by Richardson in Chapter 12, this volume.

From vocationalism to enterprise and competence

Changing contexts produce changing initiatives, re-formed attitudes and new language games. The above section has summarized six key contexts in which changes in vocational education and policy generally can be viewed. This section will consider briefly the range of initiatives spawned by the changing contexts of the 1980s and 1990s, and the consequent shifts in the language used to describe education and training.

National programmes, local interpretations

A chronology of the main recent landmarks in vocational education is given in Chapter 2. These include: the launch of TVEI in 1982 and its extension (before full evaluation) in 1987; the import of the Compact scheme; the development of YOP into YTS then YT; the plans for City Technology Colleges in 1986; the establishment of the National Council for Vocational Qualifications in the same year; and the introduction of the idea of Training and Enterprise Councils (TECs) in 1988. These must be seen alongside the build up to the 1988 Education Reform Act and the subsequent changes through the National Curriculum, local financial management, and the consequent growth of market forces in education such as 'parent power', and further developments as a result of the 1992 Education Act.

It would take more than one book to describe them in detail. Fortunately, with the benefit of hindsight in a new decade, several important features can be seen to be shared by these initiatives when viewed together.

The difficulty of evaluating the effect of any one initiative

Many of the initiatives have been characterized by the evaluation which was 'built into' them. However, none of the changes can be seen in isolation, particularly in the context of the secondary school. This has made the concept of evaluating a particular initiative an impossible one in practice. A concrete example of this is given in the case study of Compact in Chapter 5 of this volume.

The difficulty of evaluation is exacerbated when national initiatives receive many and varied interpretations at local level (Bates, 1989). The emphasis in evaluation is then often on process rather than products or outcomes (Jessup, 1991) which is notoriously more difficult to identify, quantify or place performance indicators against.

Diverse sources and ad-hocery

The various initiatives which shaped education, particularly in the field of school-industry links, have come from a range of sources, with a diverse range of agents and champions, with a variety of goals and purposes. This suggests that any allegation of 'conspiracy' in considering the vocational programmes of the 1980s is well wide of the mark. As Ainley (1990) puts it:

> What many had regarded as the consequence of a conspiracy, was in fact the result of a succession of ad hoc measures to deal with an uncontrolled and uncontrollable crisis (p. 24).

Confusion rather than conspiracy seems to have been the overriding feature. This has sometimes resulted in potential conflict, eg, between TVEI and the National Curriculum for the 14–16 range and between the DES and MSC/TA in the management of change (discussed by Finegold in Chapter 3, this volume).

Phases in programmes

Some, if not all, of the programmes can be seen as having gone through phases which depend largely on the institutional, political and economic context of the time. Thus the Compact programme in its first form in this country was seen as a means of securing jobs for inner-city school-leavers. Then, in the late 1980s, as the so-called 'demographic time bomb' began to bite, many employers saw it as a way of securing the personnel they needed (see Wellington, 1989a, and Bynner in Banks *et al.*, 1991). Now in the 1990s, as the economic recession undermines recruitment once again, it seems that employers can no longer fulfil their job guarantee and the programme's aims have become vastly more modest in certain instances (see Chapter 5, this volume).

A similar analysis of phases has been carried out by Merson (1992), who talks of the four ages of TVEI. The first consisted of a popular, exploratory phase (1983 to 1985). This phase allowed diversity which the second phase, labelled 'containing diversity'

(1985 to 1986), attempted to contain, particularly through the efforts of the DES in limiting diverse curricular provision. The third phase is described by Merson as 'controlled expansion' (1986 to 1987), following the 1986 White Paper announcing the extension of the programme. Finally, a phase of marginalization and transmutation of TVEI is said to have occurred from 1988 to the present, as schools were:

> deflected by the demands of a spate of new initiatives and the DES went into the ascendancy on the back of the 1988 Act, whilst the MSC disappeared step-by-step into the Department of Employment (Ainley and Corney, 1990).

My general point, illustrated by the two cases above, is that most of the initiatives in vocational education can be seen as going through a series of phases, depending on the prevailing contexts categorized earlier.

National plans, local versions

The blueprints for change may have been national; the reality has been local. At ground level, Bates' comment (1989) that there are 'wide variations between sites' is an understatement. Commentaries and evaluations of TVEI have shown repeatedly the wide variations in local interpretations of the programme (Saunders *et al.*, 1991). There is an extensive literature on this feature of TVEI and some interesting explanations for it (not least the 'take the money and run' story of school folklore). Other programmes show the same characteristic, though the literature may be less extensive. Versions of YTS, for example, are shown to have important local variations (Coles and Macdonald, 1990), which is hardly surprising given the wide differences in local context.

The key point is that local versions and variations are likely to be a common feature of any new central programme or initiative. This will be true of the TECs, the CTCs, and possibly even the National Curriculum. This is part of the growing adeptness of teachers to use funding linked to national programmes to promote and enhance work in their own setting which they claim 'to have been doing, or planning to do, anyway'. It is in many ways a heartening and very human feature of a market-led education system.

New blueprints, new language games

As new programmes and initiatives have entered the education and training arena, new language has infiltrated along with them. The language of educational discourse has shifted from the endless talk of skills which was central to the vocationalism of the early 1980s to the language of competence and its development which underpins the enterprise response of the early 1990s.

I have analysed the growth of skills discourse elsewhere (Wellington, 1989b). One interesting language game which will be summarized briefly here is the take-over of the language of progressivism and child-centred education (which could be traced back to Plowden, 1967, and earlier) by the advocates of the new vocationalism, not least through TVEI. Phrases and heralds of new thinking such as active learning, learner autonomy, negotiated curricula, collaboration and flexibility have all been adopted, at one time or another, by the 'new' vocationalism of the 1980s. An excellent analysis of this 'hi-jack of progressivism' or rather, the language of progressivism, is given by Avis (1991). He draws largely upon documents from the Further Education Unit (FEU) in the 1980s, but examples could be taken equally well from elsewhere. His main point is that:

> ... the paradox of progressivism is that it faces both ways and can be appropriated by both left and right in attempts to use it for quite different political purposes (p. 116).

My own summary of the comparison between the language of progressive education and vocationalism, and their deliberate contrast with 'traditional education', is given in Table 1.4.

The move from vocationalism to enterprise

One of the shifts mentioned above was the move from vocationalism to enterprise. This has been documented, with the benefit of hindsight, by a number of authors (Coffield, 1990, provides one of the most readable analyses).

The characteristics of vocationalism have been described usefully by Dale (1985) as:

- limited to the 14 to 18 age range, and the low two-thirds of the ability spectrum;
- aimed at adjustment of attitudes and expectations of young people to work (and non-work);
- continuing to generate and legitimate inequalities in gender and race (although this was an incidental outcome, not an implicit aim);

Table 1.4 *The language of progressivism, vocationalism and traditional education: contrasts and comparisons*

Aspect	Progressivism	Traditional education	'New' vocationalism
Pedagogy	Experiential learning Child/centred Learning not teaching Playing	Teacher-centred Subject-centred Pursuit of knowledge 'Passive' learning Memorising	Learner autonomy, self-reliance, student-centred, Out-of-school learning, Experiential, active learning, Doing
Teacher/pupil interaction	Teacher as facilitator and guide Discursive Listening teacher Pupil participation	One-to-many relationship Lecture style, didactic Teacher 'as' and 'in' authority Teacher as subject expert	Meeting for profiling and monitoring Counselling and guidance Teacher as fellow learner
Curriculum	Process-based Topic-based Integration Concrete, immediate Negotiated	Content-based Segregated Forms of knowledge (determined by objective criteria) Abstract, second-hand Imposed	Skills emphasis (transferable) Modular integration Negotiated Social and life skills/techniques
Timetabling	Flexible Child-centred Planning flexible	Rigid blocks of time Institution-centred Lessons programmed	Flexible Modular
Assessment	Teacher- and pupil-based Continuous Processes/skills assessed	Examination-based Narrowly accredited No self-assessment Only content assessed	Profiling Credit accumulation Records of Achievement New forms of accreditation
Location	Class, field, environment, workplace	Classroom- and institution-based	Field and workplace (not just classroom)
Organization and Ethos	Team work Cooperative groupwork	Individual work Competition essential	Collaboration, team work
Relevance	Relevant to the pupil	Relevance not an issue	Relevant to employers and future workers

- contested by several groups of people, despite its support at high levels (which was also true of 'academic approaches').

How do the features of enterprise initiatives and programmes differ from these? First, the introduction of 'enterprise' in all its forms has not been limited to an age or ability range. Thus we now have a massively funded enterprise programme for undergraduates in universities and polytechnics (the Enterprise in Higher Education Initiative). At the other end, we have Young Enterprise and mini-enterprise events and initiatives. We also have the Training and Enterprise Councils. The move has been from 'vocationalism for some' to 'enterprise for all' (Coles and Macdonald, 1990). A second feature of the shift to enterprise has been the increased emphasis on the individual and the development of individuals' enterprise qualities. Thus Coles (1988) argues that the eclipse of the new vocationalism came in 1987 with the shift of the pressure for reform from the collective consumers of education (the employers) to the owners of individual products (parents and students). ·

The emphasis in 'enterprise' has certainly been towards the individual and away from the so-called culture of dependency, with the rhetoric focusing on preparation for the age of flexibility, small business and entrepreneurship. However, there has never been any agreement on what enterprise actually is (Coffield, 1990). The enterprise elements of YTS, which included displaying initiative, making decisions, displaying drive and determination, and influencing others were to form part of the National Record of Vocational Achievement (NROVA), but other initiatives defined the term 'enterprise' for themselves. This was particularly true for higher education with the EHEI, where polytechnics and universities in their bids for Training Agency funding created their own meaning, including terms such as 'risk-taking, flexibility, problem-solving, leadership and hard work'. The resulting mixture of conceptual all-sorts thus included personal qualities, attitudes, aptitudes, dispositions, and even the generic skills of the recent past. Clearly this represents another example of national programmes developing local versions.

In practice there has been no consensus on the meaning of the term 'enterprise'. This is stated more strongly by Coffield (1990) who concludes that 'we are not dealing with a tightly defined concept but a farrago of hurrah words'. The language shift in the move from vocationalism to enterprise is put forward in Table 1.5; these issues will be returned to in later chapters.

Table 1.5 *Contrasting language in the aims and rhetoric of vocationalism and enterprise*

Vocationalism	Enterprise
Pleas for 'relevance'	Self-monitoring, self-reliance
Improved attitudes to work and industry	Risk-taking
	Decision-making
Transferable skills, core skills	Flexibility and creativity
Social and life skill	Displaying drive and determination
Preparation for 'rapid technological change'	Promoting initiative, independence and autonomy
ie *Preparation emphasis, Collective emphasis*	Taking responsibility, leadership
	ie *Personal, individual emphasis*

The education-employment relationship

The key point discussed in this chapter, and extended by Carr in Chapter 11, this volume, is that the education-employment relationship is a complex one, determined by a range of contexts. There is not a simple causal relationship between education and industry, and certainly no proven link between education and economic performance. Education shapes industry and employment as well as being shaped by it. In Reeder's (1979) terms it is both a critical and an adaptive force. In its critical role, education can shape and monitor social and economic developments; in its adaptive role it attempts to match and react to these developments. The contrast is rather like Piaget's notion of assimilation and accommodation in the learning process. Thus education can assimilate the developments of the 'outside world'; it can also accommodate them. It also relates to Dewey's (1916) dream of an education system which will first alter the existing industrial system and then ultimately transform it. In short, education should be both productive and reactive. The concept of pegs connecting with holes is a less accurate and useful analogy

EDUCATION   INDUSTRY/EMPLOYMENT

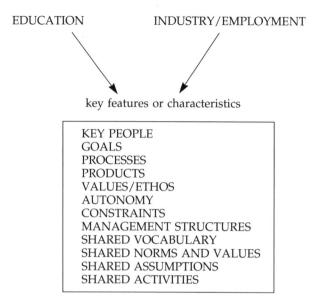

key features or characteristics

KEY PEOPLE
GOALS
PROCESSES
PRODUCTS
VALUES/ETHOS
AUTONOMY
CONSTRAINTS
MANAGEMENT STRUCTURES
SHARED VOCABULARY
SHARED NORMS AND VALUES
SHARED ASSUMPTIONS
SHARED ACTIVITIES

Is the education–employment interaction like this ...

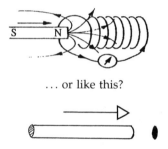

... or like this?

What kind of interaction takes place between the two? Is the 'peg and hole' metaphor appropriate or is it more like an interaction between two magnetic fields – a mutual influence?

Figure 1.3 *Relating education to industry; the key characteristics*

than the idea of two mutually interacting magnetic fields (see Figure 1.3).

A further point which follows from Reeder's (1979) discussion is that education and industry are independent, autonomous social systems and have, over a long period, developed as such. They are separate organisms, each with a life of their own, involving different professional groups having different (though sometimes overlapping) occupational interests and goals. The essential features which characterize the two systems are shown in Figure 1.3.

Education and industry differ in their goals and moreover in the level of agreement on what those goals might be. In education there is probably less agreement on aims and goals than in industry, despite the fact that industry is a less unitary entity, covering all sorts of human activities from digging holes to fingering keyboards.

Education and industry differ also in their processes and products and the emphasis placed on each. The values and ethos of the two may well differ, as will the degree of autonomy and constraint on each. Finally, the key people and the management of those people and the resources differ between the two 'systems'. There will, of course, be important differences in the key features between organizations within industry and within education. This aggravates the problematic nature of the education-employment relationship still further. The purpose of this book, in the chapters which follow, is to examine that relationship from a number of different perspectives.

References

Ainley, P (1988) *From School to YTS: Education and Training in England and Wales 1944–1987*, Milton Keynes: Open University Press.

Ainley, P (1990) *Training Turns to Enterprise: Vocational Education in the Market Place*, London: Tufnell Press.

Ainley, P and Corney, M. (1990) *Training for the Future: The Rise and Fall of the MSC*, London: Cassell.

Avis, J (1991) 'The strange fate of progressive education', in Education Group II, *Schooling and Training and the New Right Since 1979*, London: Unwin Hyman.

Banks, M, Bates, I *et al* (1991) *Careers and Identities*, Milton Keynes: Open University Press.

Bates, I (1989) 'Versions of vocationalism: an analysis of some social and political influences on curriculum policy and practice', *British Journal of Sociology of Education*, **10**, 2, 215–31.

Beck, J (1981) Education, industry and the needs of the economy', *Cambridge Journal of Education*, **11**, 2, 87–106.

Brown, P and Lauder, H (eds) (1991) *Education for Economic Survival*, London: Routledge.

Brown, P and Lauder, H (1991) 'Education, economy and social change', *International Studies in Sociology of Education*, **1**, 3–24.

Burchell, H and Millman, V (eds) (1989) *Changing Perspectives on Gender*, Milton Keynes: Open University Press.

Bynner, J (1991) 'Contexts and issues', in Banks, M and Bates, I *et al* (eds), *Careers and Identities.*

Callaghan, J (1976), 'Towards a national debate', *Education*, 22 October, 332–3.

Cathcart, G and Esland, G (1983) 'Schooling and industry: some recent contributions', *British Journal of Sociology of Education*, **4**, 3, 275–83.

CBI (1989) *Towards a Skills Resolution: a Report of the Vocational Education and Training Task Force*, London: Confederation of British Industry.

Central Advisory Council (1963) *Half Our Future: The Newsom Report*, London: HMSO.

Coffield, F. (1990) 'From the decade of the enterprise culture to the decade of the TECs', *British Journal of Education and Work*, **4**, 1, 59–78.

Coles, B (ed.) (1988) *Young Careers: The Search for Jobs and the New Vocationalism*, Milton Keynes: Open University Press.

Coles, B and Macdonald, R. (1990) 'From new vocationalism to the culture of enterprise', in Wallace, C and Cross, M (eds), *Youth in Transition*, Lewes: Falmer Press.

Crowther Report (1959) *15–18: A Report of the Central Advisory Council for Education*, London: HMSO.

CSO (1992) *Social Trends 22*, London: HMSO.

Dale, R (ed.) (1985) *Education, Training and Employment: towards a new vocationalism?* The Open University: Pergamon Press.

DES (1967) *Children and Their Primary Schools*, London: HMSO.

Dewey, J (1916) *Democracy and Education*, New York: Macmillan.

Edgley, R (1977) 'Education for Industry', *Educational Research*, **20**, 1, 26–32.

Fiddy, R (ed.) (1985) *Youth, Unemployment and Training*, Lewes: Falmer Press.

Fiddy, R (1986) 'Education for employment and unemployment: is this the age of the trained?' in Wellington, J J (ed.), *Controversial Issues in the Curriculum*, Oxford: Basil Blackwell.

Gleeson, D (ed.) (1987) *TVEI and Secondary Education: A Critical Appraisal*, Milton Keynes: Open University Press.

Handy, C (1985) *The Future of Work*, Oxford: Basil Blackwell.

Harris, M (1991) *Schools, Mathematics and Work*, Lewes: Falmer Press.

Holt, M (ed.) (1989) *Skills and Vocationalism: The Easy Answer*, Milton Keynes: Open University Press.

Jenkins, E (1979) *From Armstrong to Nuffield*, London: John Murray.

Jessup, G (1991) *NVQs and the Emerging Model of Education*, Lewes: Falmer Press.

Jonathan, R (1983) 'The Manpower Service model of education', *Cambridge Journal of Education*, **13**, 2, 9.

Keep, E and Mayhew, K (1988) 'The assessment: education, training and economic performance', *Oxford Review of Economy Policy*, **4**, 3, i–xv.

Kushner, S (1985) 'Vocational chic: an historical and curriculum context to the field of transition in England', in Fiddy, R (ed.), *Youth, Unemployment and Training*, Lewes: Falmer Press.

Lawton, D and Chitty, C (1987) 'Towards a national curriculum', *Forum*, Autumn 1987, **30**, 1.

Layton, D (ed.) (1984) *The Alternative Road: The Rehabilitation of the Practical*, Leeds: The University of Leeds.

Malcolm Committee (1928) *Education and Industry*, London: HMSO.

Manpower Services Commission (1975) *Vocational Preparation for Young People*, London: HMSO.

Marshall, T H (1963) 'Citizenship and social class', *Sociology at the Crossroads*, London: Heinemann.

McCulloch, G, Jenkins, E and Layton, D (1985) *Technological Revolution? The Politics of School Science and Technology in England and Wales Since 1945*, Lewes: Falmer Press.

Merson, M (1992) 'The four ages of TVEI', *British Journal of Education and Work*, **5**, 2, 5–18.

Oxford Review of Economic Policy (1988) *Education, Training and Economic Performance*, **4**, 3, Oxford: Oxford University Press.

Ranson, S (1984) 'Towards a tertiary tripartism', in Broadfoot, P (ed.), *Selection, Certification and Control*, Lewes: Falmer Press.

Reeder, D (1979) 'A recurring debate: education and industry', in Bernbaum, G (ed.), *Schooling in Decline*, Macmillan, 115–48.

Saunders, L (1991) 'Education, work and the curriculum', *Policy Studies*, Summer 1991, **12**, 2, 13–26.

Toffler, A (1980) *The Third Wave*, London: Pan Books.

Watts, A G (1983) *Education, Unemployment and the Future of Work*, Milton Keynes: Open University Press.

Watts, A G (1991) 'The impact of the "New Right": policy changes confronting careers guidance in England and Wales', *British Journal of Guidance and Counselling*, **19**, 3, 230–45.

Weiner, G (1989) 'Feminism, equal opportunities and vocationalism', in Burchell, H and Millman, V (eds), *Changing Perspectives on Gender*, Milton Keynes: Open University Press.

Wellington, J J (1987) 'Employment patterns and the goals of education', *British Journal of Education and Work*, **1**, 3, 163–77.

Wellington, J J (1989a) *Education for Employment – The Place of Information Technology*, Windsor: NFER-Nelson.

Wellington, J J (1989b) 'Skills for the Future', in Holt, M (ed.), *Skills and Vocationalism: The Easy Answer*, Milton Keynes: Open University Press.

Wiener, M (1985) *English Culture and the Decline of the Industrial Spirit*, Harmondsworth: Penguin.

Williams, R (1961) *The Long Revolution*, Harmondsworth: Penguin.

2 Connecting Curriculum to Work: Past Patterns, Current Initiatives and Future Issues

An Interview with Tony Watts

Introduction

This chapter of the book is based on a discussion with Tony Watts, Director of the National Institute for Careers Education and Counselling (NICEC). In the field of the work-related curriculum he is well known through the many books he has edited and written, including *Work Experience and Schools* (ed. 1983), *Education, Unemployment and the Future of Work* (1983b) and *Rethinking Work Experience* (with Miller and Jamieson, 1991). Watts is also the author of numerous articles in refereed journals and has been involved in developing curriculum materials in this field for over a decade. His perspectives and comments on the rise and fall of 'vocationalism', the meaning of the 'work-related curriculum' and new initiatives in this area are therefore both important and most welcome in this introductory section.

Watts picks up many of the themes introduced in Chapter 1. The discussion begins with the notion of the work-related curriculum and recent developments which may have enhanced or restricted it. It then goes on to look at the spate of initiatives from 1976 to 1992 which had an impact in this area. Although not suggesting that there was any clear pattern in their introduction, Watts does suggest that there were three rather different periods in that time. The discussion then goes on to the ubiquitous notions of 'enterprise' and 'personal transferable skills' which gained such currency during the 1980s, and considers their importance for people from a number of viewpoints. Finally, the conversation moves on to three current initiatives of different magnitude – action planning, National Vocational Qualifications (NVQs), and the TECs. All will play some part, and raise important questions, in the debate about the future of education and training for employment, the central issues of which are still alive and unresolved.

The material which follows is presented in the conversational style in which it was spoken and recorded, with the minimum of interference during transcription and subsequent editing. The comments and questions of the interviewer (Jerry Wellington) have not been included.

What is the work-related curriculum?

I suppose the work-related curriculum covers two really quite different strands. There obviously are links between them, but they are, I think, conceptually really quite different. Both are cross-curricular themes in the National Curriculum: one is Economic and Industrial Understanding; the other is Careers Education and Guidance. I do see these as being distinctively different from one another. It seems to me that the notion of Careers Education and Guidance is designed to help individuals, in their role as potential future *workers*, to have a base on which they can make decisions and transitions that will determine their own working lives. Whereas Economic and Industrial Understanding is concerned with their role as *citizens*: wherever they themselves personally may end up, they need to have some understanding of the way in which the world of work is structured – the role of work in relation to the national economy and the structure of society, and so on. Obviously, work experience, for example, can feed both of these areas in a very rich way. Students don't learn in two distinct segments. But conceptually, in terms of curriculum planning, I do think the bases of those two areas are quite different. On top of that, of course, there are also the areas to do with socialization into work, preparation for work and selection for work, as well as the wider possibilities for learning *through* work. I suppose these too can be viewed as part of the work-related curriculum, but I personally tend to see it primarily in terms of the two cross-curricular themes.

Recent developments: enhancing or restricting the work-related curriculum?

Broadly, I think that GCSE has clearly been important in permitting a much wider range of things to happen in the curriculum, particularly in its emphasis on coursework assessment and project-based work. GCSE allowed much more of the work-related curriculum to come in, and TVEI gave all of that a great fillip. On the other hand, within the National Curriculum – I know these are all terrible generalizations – it seems to me that the cross-curricular themes are extremely weak in structural terms. They have very little purchase in the system. I know that they are covered within the Act, but it's framed so vaguely I don't see how schools can be pinned down on it. It seems to me, in broad terms, that it is TVEI that has kept these areas of the curriculum in place, because of its contractual basis. But now TVEI is on the downward slope: it's going to come to an end fairly soon, in the next five years or so. With Ian Jamieson, I've recently written an article for *Education* ('Is there life beyond TVEI?'). Our basic argument is that at the moment all the drive is elsewhere. Local management of schools, league tables based on exam results, attainment targets, reducing the amount of course-work – none of these things are conducive to the work-related curriculum and only TVEI is keeping it in place. Once TVEI goes, I am very concerned about whether it will survive. Of course it will in some schools, because individual teachers care about it. But this will be against the drift of policy currents rather than being supported by them.

Take work experience, for example. Work experience takes up a lot of time. In Key Stage 4, the most crowded period, a two-week work experience programme consumes 3 per cent of curriculum time: a big investment. You can say, 'Well of course it can feed many of the Attainment Targets across the curriculum'. But whether, when the dice are down, schools will see it as cost-effective – cost being the time, and effectiveness viewed in these narrowly conceived terms – seems to me highly questionable. I fear that a lot of schools will say: 'We can't do it; it was a nice thing to do when times were better, but no longer'. Some schools may say, 'This is what we're about: the league table we want to be in is not the academic one, it's the job placement one'. But I think that it will be very difficult to hold any kind of student entitlement to work experience in place. So that's why I see TVEI as being very important and why its end is potentially troubling for the future unless it's replaced by some other significant government initiative.

The NCC itself doesn't seem to be enormously interested. It has done very little on the cross-curricular themes for some time now. The weakening of the inspectorate is also very worrying. The running of the work-related curriculum has been made very largely by the Employment Department and the MSC in its various mutations, and that now is being reorganized and eroded. DTI have been pulling out. The main action is with TECs now, and the future is seen as lying with Education–Business Partnerships. How strong are they? How much muscle are they going to exert? In some areas of the country they may prove to be strong and influential, but elsewhere they will barely exist, one suspects.

This comes after 15 years in which there's been a real bandwagon rolling. The political origins are very interesting. The first chapter of *Mirrors of Work* (Jamieson *et al.*, 1988) makes the point that the Ruskin speech attacked two main targets. One was the anti-industrial ethos in education and the lack of links between education and industry; the second was progressive education. The fascinating thing is the way in which the ethos of the schools-industry movement has encouraged active, student-centred and experience-based learning – all aspects of progressive education. So, ironically, the first of Callaghan's attacks has encouraged a huge resurgence of the object of his second attack, particularly in secondary education but even to some extent in primary education. The notion used to be that industry was anti-educational: antipathetic to the things people in education cared about. But for the last 15 years it's been seen as being an ally in terms of keeping together some models of progressive education which have been under severe attack elsewhere. You can link this politically with the different wings of the 'new right'. On the one hand there are the social conservatives – the Hillgate Group and so on – who want to preserve traditional subject-based methods, etc. On the other side there are the economic liberals – the enterprise movement. Many of the items they have promoted – records of achievement, action planning, experience-based learning about work – are actually (although the government would probably hate to think of it in those terms) learner-centred notions.

Language shifts and language games: has student-centred language been hijacked?

I'm always very interested by the question of 'who is seducing whom'. Some people take the opposite stance: they say 'TVEI was hijacked by the educationalists'. Certainly it started as a highly political intervention, with direct support from Thatcher, to re-introduce tripartism in secondary education. That was what it was all about initially as I understand it. It was then, in a sense, hijacked by the educationalists who converted it into progressive education. That's the other way of looking at it. I don't know who hijacked what and who seduced whom. Perhaps to actually look at it in only *one* way is too limited. Certainly, I think to say 'we allowed progressivism to be hijacked by those awful Employment Department people' is a very narrow way of looking at it.

What is interesting is the way in which different ideas came together in a way in which they were able to gain energy from each other. The notion that really progressive education should have remained unalloyed by these 'awful things to do with the world of work' is appalling. I'd want to be quite careful about this notion of hijacking. Much of it comes from a narrow, para-Marxist kind of approach, which in the end, I think, becomes terribly repetitive and doesn't actually illuminate very much. There has been a lot of writing about education and work from that perspective, and I have been interested by some of it, but I felt a lot of it actually missed the heart of what was occurring and didn't seem grounded in what was actually happening in the schools. It missed the potential in what was happening because it was only concerned with its particular ideological lens as a way of analysing it. I think in the end I have tried to escape that: to use it but then go beyond it. Does that make any sense?

Education for employment – chronology

1974 MSC established by Employment and Training Act
1975 MSC publishes *Vocational Preparation of Young People*
1976 Callaghan's Ruskin College speech
1978 Youth Opportunities Programme (YOP), until 1983
1981 *New Training Initiative* (NTI) – White Paper and MSC
        Document
1982 TVEI launched
        DES proposal for CPVE
1983 14 TVEI pilot projects begin
        One-year Youth Training Scheme (YTS) launched
1984 *Training for Jobs* White Paper
1985 'Mini Enterprise in Schools Project' (MESP) launched by the
        DTI

1985 CPVE introduced
      TVEI now running in every LEA
1986 National Council for Vocational Qualifications (NCVQ)
          established
      CTC plans announced by Kenneth Baker
      Two-year YTS introduced
      GCSE introduced
      'Enterprise in YTS' launched by MSC
1987 TVEI extension
      MSC launches EHE programme
1988 Compact initiative launched nationwide
      Education Reform Act (ERA)
      First CTCs open
      MSC re-absorbed into Department of Employment
      MSC becomes Training Commission
      TECs announced in White Paper, *Employment for the 1990s*
1989 LECs launched in Scotland
      'Enterprise Awareness in Teacher Education' (EATE) project
          begins
1990 YT (Youth Training) replaces YTS
1991 NCVQ completes its review

Conspiracy or ad-hocery? Is there a conspiracy or pattern, or any links between the initiatives of 1976–92?

They're very different kinds of things. YOP, for example, came from a very different set of problems than TVEI. YOP and the other things that happened around that time in the post-school scene were of course initially responses to youth unemployment. Maybe you could say that the whole thing was to some extent triggered by a kind of moral panic which youth unemployment stimulated. There is some truth in that, although in fact it goes right back to the Ruskin speech, and even further back to reports like *The Vocational Preparation of Young People* (MSC, 1975). The precursor of the MSC originally produced that document, and Callaghan then gave their analysis a big boost. It might be worth looking back at that early period, but certainly it pre-dated the massive growth in youth unemployment. Nevertheless, the rise in unemployment was important. In those days, the notion was that if the government allowed unemployment to go over a million, there was no way it would ever be re-elected. So there was a huge scare about it, although actually, by modern standards, the figures were still quite low. I think in large measure it started with that and with the sense of disjuncture which that produced.

Conspiracy theories, I think, are of limited value. The notion that there is some power-group which has a very clear, well-defined strategy and the power to implement it in a consistent way over a sustained period of time is often a fantasy. Certainly Thatcherism influenced what happened, but it covered so many different strands, which didn't actually hang together terribly well because they came from different ideological stables and different pressures at different times. So I don't buy the conspiracy theory too much.

At the same time it's a bit more than ad-hocery. I think you can see some kind of emerging strategy which develops, modifies and responds to different things over a period of time. I suppose one of the interesting things is the way in which some of those early things are based very much on narrow considerations. YOP was essentially about providing something for unemployed young people to do: it was therefore largely about early leavers, with little in the way of skills development. TVEI started as being about introducing a new stream, so it was about segmenting groups. A lot of later ones were actually about comprehensive education. It is fascinating that things like TVEI, CPVE and GCSE were introduced by a Conservative administration. It was GCSE that actually brought together the comprehensive secondary curriculum, because the old CSE/GCE split it apart. Yet it was a Conservative administration under Thatcher that brought it in, whereas it was Callaghan who started the assault on liberal education. There are so many ironies in all of this. GCSE is very important, it seems to me, because it established the notion of a common curriculum and because the way in which it was set up permitted things to happen which were project-based and had links with the world of work, whereas the old O-level model had made that extremely difficult. GCSE made it possible for the academically bright kids to do some of this as well as some of the less-bright kids. So I do see GCSE as having been extremely important.

Work experience is a good example. The survey which the DES did on where work experience was integrated into the curriculum, showed that almost entirely it was in English. This is partly because English can use any experience, but also the fact that English was 100 per cent (in many cases) continuous assessment meant that it could use all the schools-industry stuff really well, and English teachers latched on to it in a big way. Now they're being told to reduce drastically the amount of continuous assessment, so I fear it will all become much more difficult. But

GCSE did permit it and therefore supported some of these other things that happened, TVEI in particular.

If we look at the chronology in broad terms, I think you could see the period from 1976–82 as being about responding to the needs of a particular group (whether the unemployed, or those kids who were missing out because they weren't GCE O-level kids), based on a segmented model; then a 'comprehensive' period, which was largely about implementing the work-related curriculum on a comprehensive model; and then a market-based period, from 1988. It seems to me there is some broad clustering of ideas in these three periods, from 1976 to the early 1990s.

The work-related curriculum and 'enterprise' for all abilities

'Enterprise' is an interesting word of course. I wrote a piece in the *Times Higher Education Supplement* (Watts, 1989) which was about the EHE programme (a kind of higher education TVEI) but I think it was a broader analysis really. The basic outline was that the power of the word 'enterprise' lies in bringing together two different notions which have quite a wide purchase, and does so through a third concept which is much narrower but has a lot of political appeal. This third concept is entrepreneurship (see Figure 2.1) – people setting up on their own – which obviously applies only to a small minority. There are all sorts of questions

Figure 2.1 *The power of the ambiguity in the term 'Enterprise'*

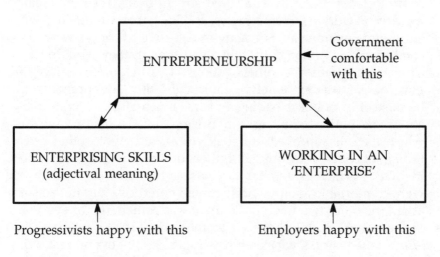

(After Watts, 1991)

about entrepreneurship in terms of the significance of its overall impact on the economy, but it had enormous purchase in terms of political power under Thatcher. This meant that anything labelled 'enterprise' had a head-start. But beyond that there are two really rather different ideas. One is about enterprising *skills*, which are skills that can be used in all sorts of contexts, not only in employment but also the community, politics, and in all sorts of ways. The other is the notion of working in 'enterprises', as a noun, and the skills you require for employment. There are real tensions between these two notions. Whether employers really want employees who are enterprising is highly questionable, it seems to me. Some do, but some certainly don't because enterprising people rock boats, they ask too many questions, they don't fit in, they're not always good team members – and some employers don't want that.

So there is much tension between those two things. But the notion of entrepreneurship, while very thin on its own, brings them together, subsumed under this conveniently ambiguous word 'enterprise'. It's a very potent political combination which can then be unpacked and used for all sorts of different purposes. You can see why there was a time when it seems that anything that came out which had the 'enterprise' label on it would get funded. The label meant many different things to many different people, and this was extremely useful. For example, the progressive education movement is interested in enabling people to be 'enterprising'. It's about encouraging people to be creative, in control of their own lives, all that sort of thing. It's not actually focused on working in enterprises, and it's got no strong links with entrepreneurship at all. So, many progressive educators were very comfortable with one definition, even though they wouldn't feel comfortable with the other notions. On the other hand, the government was extremely comfortable with 'entrepreneurship' because of its political loading, but was much more uncomfortable about the notion of being enterprising in relation to values of which they disapproved. It usually never quite got to that point, though of course they put the shutters down on political education in YOP – which is another fascinating topic. Again, employers were comfortable about 'working in an enterprise' but not so sure about the other two notions. So there was something for everyone in the notion of 'enterprise'. It therefore provided a rich base for education–business partnerships supported by government, with each putting the frame they preferred around it. That shows the power of language. If you can find words which have that degree of ambiguity, you can form alliances which you wouldn't be able to form otherwise, building upon that ambiguity. If we had been working with words that had single usages and precision, a lot of what has happened probably wouldn't have happened. Ambiguous language can be enormously influential.

The value of personal transferable skills in non-vocational areas

One of the things about personal transferable skills is that, especially at a higher education level, they provide a support for traditionally non-vocational parts of the curriculum which otherwise would be very threatened by vocationalism and by the notion that education must be justified by its utility. What it does is to transfer the emphasis from *content* relevance, where areas like philosophy, history and the pure sciences find justification difficult, to *skill* areas. The content of history, for example, may be of limited vocational use unless you are going to teach it, but from studying history you can also acquire skills which are highly transferable. Our higher education system has always incorporated that notion, without making it explicit. We've always viewed graduates as being broadly employable (over 40 per cent of graduate vacancies do not specify subjects). That's not true in any other European country; tracking there is far, far stronger. So we do have a belief in what we have thought of as a liberal education which makes you broadly employable. 'Personal transferable skills' provides a modern language acceptable to a hard-nosed government (which likes to think of itself as being very hard-nosed and rather anti-liberal, in social though not economic terms). I think the notion of personal transferable skills has actually been very useful in that way.

Current initiatives

(For this conversation we selected just three)

Action planning

I have done some recent work on action planning, mainly based in schools (Watts, 1992). I tried to distil some of the underlying issues in relation to the concept of action planning, recognizing that there was a wide range of notions that it pulled together (as with so many of these things, there are lots of different threads). At one level it's about career planning; at another, it's about management of learning.

There are also some basic issues about the relationship between the process and the product: whether it's really the process of action planning, and the skills involved, that we're concerned with, or whether our concern is really the actual action plan – which is a public not a private document, used as a basis for awarding credits and that kind of thing, in which case it's a totally different kind of animal. It's much the same with Records of Achievement where you can have a formative process and a summative process but you mustn't pretend they're the same thing – although they can reinforce each other.

There is also the question about who owns it – who owns the process, who owns the product? Action planning could be a tool for manipulating young people into declaring intentions which are then used as sticks to beat them with, i.e. talking the language of empowerment but actually using it for control. On the other hand, in principle, it is potentially about recognizing that the student owns the learning process and about giving them some tools to do so. This has huge implications for curriculum design. So, although it's a small thing in itself (coming in again, of course, with Employment Department blessing and given a big boost by TVEI) it does bring into focus all of these tensions, as so many of these initiatives do.

NVQs

I suppose I'm ambivalent about NVQs in the sense that I feel that the model for them is a narrow technicist one ... but at the same time I think they have potential in terms of opening up barriers to access within the labour market. The notion of increasing flexibility is a way of raising people's aspirations and expectations in terms of what they can actually do, which I think is potentially very empowering. I know from personal experience from secretaries in our own offices that they can be very empowering in this way. And they do challenge vested interests within occupational structures, in a way which potentially brings into question power bases within those structures. So I think there are virtuous aspects of them.

In terms of their implications for education, I am concerned about their emphasis on narrow instrumentalism and their narrow notions of behaviourally-defined outputs, which are potentially very restrictive. So I do have a resistance to them as a model of education. At the same time, in terms of their impact on continuing learning, particularly work-based learning, they are potentially a benign force.

The TECs

Who knows where the TECs will go? The fact is they have been given an extremely *broad* remit, but they have been given *funding* for an extremely *narrow* remit. The devolutionary policy underlying TECs has also produced a 'splintering' effect, which means a lot of interesting, exciting innovation but very patchy implementation. If TECs want to attract high-level people from industry, as they say they do, then they can't just be concerned with implementing government programmes. You're not going to sustain the involvement of any high-level people from industry just on that basis. So as soon as you have significant decision-making devolved to that level, you're going to have patchiness – you'll have some flowers blooming and quite a lot wilting.

It's ironic that at the very time when LEAs are being eroded, we're setting up a structure of geographically similar kinds of units, and yet eroding the natural partners in education which might provide a really effective way of bringing things together. Another rich irony. Where you do have LEAs and TECs working together, they can be extremely powerful partners. But LEAs are being seriously undermined and whether they have a future at all is very much in question.

Issues for the future: education, unemployment and the future of work

There are underlying issues about the nature of work and its future which haven't gone away. But I think the issues have gone away from *education* partly because, at the youth level, YT has provided schools with a buttress against reality. The fact is, on leaving school, all kids are now, in theory at least, guaranteed something. Therefore, schools don't have to bother about what happens beyond that. YT provides an illusion of full employment which means that schools don't have to confront the grimmer reality which lies beyond it. It's YT and other TEC-managed programmes that have to confront it – or not do so, as the case may be.

The government, of course, has controlled the debate about

those matters very firmly. I wrote a document in 1985, entitled *Adult Unemployment and the Curriculum* (with Knasel). After writing that document I was summoned to a meeting at the DES with two ministers, the Permanent Secretary and four other top civil servants. The document was seen as subversive because it talked about the possible causes of unemployment and suggested that high unemployment was a result not of individual inadequacies but of economic forces and political responses to those forces. The ministers and officers at the meeting were unable in the end to sustain any serious argument against the statements we had made, but it demonstrated the political sensitivity of the issue, and the government's concern to try to control the debate. Then of course there was that extraordinary government statement that in YTS schemes 'There shall be no consideration of issues relating to the wider society' (quoted in Watts, 1983b). This also showed the government's attempts at thought-control, in a way which is discreditable in a society that claims to be open and democratic.

But I think the issue of the future of work, and the discontinuity and fragmentation of people's working lives, are still basic issues which are not going to go away. There's now far less debate about them in education, particularly in secondary schools, for the reasons I've mentioned. And in a way that's a pity for education – particularly in terms of links with the *reality* of the world of work, rather than with some illusion of what it should be like.

The issues of what we mean by employment, how far it can be guaranteed, whether we need broader concepts of work, and what these are to be: all of these things are still open to debate. In the 1970s and early 1980s the issues were addressed and debated quite widely but, interestingly, I don't see them as having been anywhere near as influential in the more recent period. And yet we're now beginning to talk about whether this actually is a long recession or whether it's something more enduring. I fear it's because we've had a government that's been in power for so long that it's been able to control the way people think. They've managed to constrict the area of public debate.

References

Jamieson, I, Miller, A and Watts, A G (1988) *Mirrors of Work: Work Simulations in Schools*, London: Falmer Press.

Manpower Services Commission (1975) *Vocational Preparation for Young People*, London: HMSO.

Miller, A, Watts, A G and Jamieson, I (1991), *Rethinking Work Experience*, London: Falmer Press.

Watts, A G (ed.) (1983a) *Work Experience and Schools*, London: Heinemann.

Watts, A G (1983b) *Education, Unemployment and the Future of Work*, Milton Keynes: Open University Press.

Watts, A G (1989) 'In tune aboard the bandwaggon: enterprise in higher education', *Times Higher Education Supplement*, 7 April.

Watts, A G (1992) 'Individual action planning: issues and strategies', *British Journal of Education and Work*, **5**, 1, 47–63.

Watts, A G and Jamieson, I (1992) 'Is there life beyond TVEI?' *Education*, 22 May.

Watts, A G and Knasel, E G (1985) *Adult Unemployment and the Curriculum*, London: FEU.

3 The Importance of the Institution: The Case of the Technical and Vocational Education Initiative

David Finegold

The Technical and Vocational Education Initiative (TVEI) was the most significant attempt at educational change undertaken by the Thatcher government prior to the Education Reform Act. At the time of its launch, TVEI marked the most direct intervention ever by central government in what was taught in secondary schools and colleges. With the backing of its originator, MSC Chairman David Young, the Initiative grew extremely rapidly, from 14 local pilot projects in 1983 to the start of a nationwide, £1 billion extension just four years later. Both the stated purpose of this Initiative – specifically to improve the preparation of 14–18-year-olds for the workplace – and the unprecedented nature of the reform strategy – an attempt by central government to devise a new means of altering curriculum, pedagogy and educational organization – make TVEI an ideal case for studying the state's capacity and the constraints which it faces in elevating skill levels.

A large literature already exists on TVEI, most of it written by and for educationalists. The majority of TVEI case-studies feature some combination of evaluation and description, reflecting the agendas of the two major groups concerned with the Initiative: the government and educational practitioners. Fuelled by the generous evaluation funding which was built into each stage of the programme by the MSC, researchers have produced numerous accounts of the content of TVEI in local authorities throughout

54

Britain, identifying problems which pilot schemes have faced and disseminating best practice in areas such as curriculum development, equal opportunities, education-industry links and modular assessment (Training Agency, 1988).

The study in this chapter can be distinguished from the bulk of that research by using TVEI to study the policy, rather than the educational process; hence, the purpose will be to test the applicability of an institutional form of analysis to decision-making within TVEI rather than evaluating the educational merits of the Initiative. In this way it will seek to avoid one of the problems common to many of these case studies of local practice: the inability to generalize from the details of a specific case. This recurring difficulty with case-study methodology is exacerbated when looking at TVEI due to the extreme degree of variation among the pilot schemes (Dale *et al.*, 1990, p. 2). Examples can be found which substantiate conflicting interpretations of the Initiative; for example, some have cited TVEI as a next step toward a truly comprehensive curriculum (Pring, 1985), while others see it as an effort to reestablish a separate technical track (Dale, 1985b). By concentrating not on the divergent content of particular pilot programmes, but on the distinctive TVEI policy process and the institutional factors which shape it, this study will attempt to analyse a new mechanism for educational change and identify the constraints on central government reform.

Pressed to do

As Lord Young's initial description and subsequent references to TVEI made clear, the Initiative was conceived as a direct response to many of the factors which combined to trap Britain in a low-skill equilibrium. Like the NTI (New Training Initiative, 1981) and other programmes launched during the second phase of Thatcherism, TVEI was driven by the perceived need to close the supply-side skills gap that was hindering industrial performance. Young stated that TVEI 'will play a vital part in raising technical training in Britain to the level of our best overseas competitors' (Young in McCulloch, 1987, p. 27). It was designed to act as a complement to YTS, addressing many of the problems within the educational system: the failure to motivate the majority of individuals in the education system who were not going on to A-levels; the need to bridge the institutional divisions between compulsory and post-compulsory education; and the need to improve the attitudes and skills of young people so that they would be better equipped to find employment (Young, 1982; 1984b). By confronting these issues, TVEI was responding to the same long-standing British problems that Callaghan had identified in his Ruskin College speech and that numerous previous reform efforts (Bryce, Spens and Crowther Reports) had tried and failed to solve (McCulloch, 1987, p. 23).

In addition to these longer-term pressures for change, TVEI was a response, if less direct, to the same external pressure that had led to the development of YTS: rising youth unemployment. When asked why the government had launched the Initiative without consultation and allowed less than a year to have it operating in schools, Young (1982, p. 4) replied:

> Next summer, nearly half a million school-leavers will be coming on to the labour market, and every year that passes brings still more young people unprepared for the world of work on to the job market.

Want to do

The timing and precise nature of the government response to these pressures for reform that was manifested in TVEI was dictated by Young's arrival at the MSC. He came to the Commission with well-defined views about technical and vocational ET based on his work as a trustee for the Jewish charity ORT (Organisation for Rehabilitation through Training), which set up independent schools that provided a mix of general education and job-specific training to students from the age of 14 (Hofkins, 1984, p. 180). Young (1982b, p. 386) summarized TVEI's main objective:

> The curriculum in English schools is too academic and leads towards the universities. What I am trying to show is that there is another line of development that is equally respectable and desirable which leads to vocational qualifications ...

When analysing the many changes which TVEI has undergone, however, it is critical to keep in mind that Young, while the Initiative's originator and key proponent, was only one of the policy-makers involved in the programme. At each stage of TVEI's development different actors took part, each with his or her own view about what the Initiative was designed to accomplish (Sikes and Taylor, 1987). The way in which the Initiative was constructed, and the pre-existing institutional structure, affected how much each of these individuals or groups could influence TVEI developments. As with any ET (education and training) policy, the further removed TVEI became from central government, the less control ministers could exercise over the programme.

Able to do

The challenge for the government was to devise a means of retaining influence over TVEI as it was put into practice within schools, given the historical weakness of the central educational state apparatus. The choice of the MSC to run TVEI and the strategy which the Commission developed will be shown to represent a new means of governing education that can be contrasted both with traditional British reform models and the subsequent market-based paradigm developed by the Thatcher government. It is as a novel strategy for managing educational change or a new ET reform process, rather than a lasting shift in educational practice, that TVEI may have had its most significant impact (Dale *et al.*, 1990, p. 3).

At each stage in the development of this new reform strategy, TVEI was shaped by the surrounding institutional context. These institutional factors took two forms: first, the organization of the ET state, both the MSC's internal structure and its relationship with other government departments; and second, those institutions outside the ET system that influence the decisions of students and hence the capacity of TVEI to alter low skill equilibrium.

Inception: the dawn raid

The origins of TVEI, or 'The New TVEI' as it was first called, marked a radical break with the consensual approach to British ET policy-making. The Initiative was conceived totally by politicians – Young in cooperation with Tebbit and Joseph (Young, 1990, p. 89). It was launched, in what Young called 'a dawn raid on education' (ibid), by Mrs Thatcher on 12 November 1982 in response to a planted parliamentary question, with no prior warning or consultation with educational interest groups (*Hansard*, 1982, pp. 269–70). The pilot scheme was broadly defined as: 'new institutional arrangements for technical and vocational education for 14–18 year-olds, within existing financial resources, and, where possible in association with local authorities' (ibid), with Young (1982c, p. 10) suggesting that the MSC might set up separate schools if LEAs did not cooperate.

This surprise announcement caused consternation in the education world, with some teachers' unions and the Inner London Education Authority deciding to boycott the scheme (see, for example, Chitty, 1986, p. 84; Garner, 1984). Their opposition was based not only on the absence of consultation and the threat of central government-run schools, but also on what was perceived as a more general attack on comprehensive education through a return to secondary technical schools (Dale, 1985a, 41). This concern was enhanced by the decision that the MSC, which previously had focused solely on training and work creation programmes for school leavers, should administer a project which would intervene in the compulsory education sector.

The main reason for choosing the MSC rather than the DES, aside from Young's personal involvement, was the Commission's greater institutional capacity to deliver reform. The MSC had the ability to target spending on specific measures which the DES's grant system lacked (Harland, 1987, p. 40); this ability was increased by the fact that the MSC was not responsible for the oversight of the entire system, but could concentrate on specific projects, and that, unlike the DES, it could spend money first and then account for it to ministers instead of seeking prior approval. Also, it had the cash available to finance the pilot from unfilled places on the first year of YTS. The MSC could also deliver programmes with greater speed, since it was not required to consult on its proposals and it had a 'technocratic or commercial' rather than bureaucratic mode of operation (Dale et al., 1990, p. 15); as Young (1982b) said in an interview a week after TVEI's launch: 'If we had gone through the normal machinery it would have been the end of the decade before anything happened'. Finally, the Initiative fitted broadly under the MSC's charter to improve the skills of the workforce, so that no legislation would be required at a time when the Parliamentary agenda and budget were under extreme pressure (Chitty, 1989; Salter and Tapper, 1985; Young, 1990). The last reason shows the role which unintended or previously unutilized institutional capacity can have in shaping ET reforms, since it was, according to Young, careless drafting of the MSC's charter in the 1973 Act that gave the Commission the power to intervene in education and even set up its own schools (Young, 1990, p. 93).

The initial stage of TVEI not only showed the key role which institutional structures play in shaping policy, but also demonstrated the changing role of the Commission under the second phase of Thatcherism. It was not just educationalists who were surprised by the Prime Minister's announcement; neither the MSC's board nor its staff were given prior warning of TVEI, with Young informing only Geoffrey Holland, the MSC's Director, beforehand (Young, 1990, p. 94; MSC, interviews). As the next stage of TVEI's development made clear, however, while the MSC was no longer an independent source of new policy, it did have significant scope for shaping the content and structure of the Initiative.

Development of the pilot

By announcing TVEI without prior consultation, locating the Initiative outside the educational establishment and proclaiming that it would be up and running in less than ten months, the Conservatives created a potential problem, as Moon and Richardson (1984, p. 25) observed: '... at first sight there appears to have been unusually little concern, as the policy-makers formulated their ideas, for their implementability'. In order to gain the cooperation of practitioners required to make TVEI work in such a short period of time, the MSC had to create a new way of governing the educational system.

To develop this new approach, the MSC set up a National Steering Group (NSG) which, in addition to the Commission's normal tripartite membership, drew heavily on the educational expertise of DES and HMI (MSC, 1983c; MSC, interviews). While the NSG was responsible for the broad definition of TVEI, the detailed plans were left to a new, small (six–seven people) Unit set up within the MSC that reported directly to Holland and Young. The TVEI Unit was a departure from normal MSC procedure in two respects: it was directed by John Woolhouse, recruited by Young from outside the civil service, and it was based in London, set apart from the rest of the MSC's bureaucracy. The latter step was taken in order to facilitate communication with the DES and other educational interest groups (Woolhouse, 1989), but as we shall see later, it was to have more far-reaching effects on the relationship between TVEI and other MSC programmes.

Through these new institutional mechanisms, the MSC adopted a strategy designed to overcome some of the initial resistance to TVEI and gain broad educational support for the Initiative. The crucial first step in this process was the drawing up of the aims, criteria and guidelines for TVEI (MSC, 1983b). The NSG and TVEI Unit defined TVEI in a way that removed the threat of establishing separate schools, as well as leaving scope for LEAs to design projects tailored to local circumstances within the broad TVEI guidelines. This approach was fostered by the number of LEAs who had expressed an interest in the Initiative following the PM's announcement. Running TVEI through local authorities and existing schools and colleges was a strategy that was cheaper, quicker, less politically controversial and more likely to produce replicable change than building new institutions (*Education*, 1982, p. 1; Woolhouse, 1989).

The MSC sent an invitation to all 104 LEAs on 28 January 1983 to submit proposals for five-year TVEI projects that would 'explore and test ways of organising and managing the education of 14–18 year old young people across the ability range' (MSC, 1983b). The objectives of the TVEI projects were to: increase individuals' 'qualifications/skills which will be of direct value to them at work'; ensure 'more emphasis is placed on developing initiative, motivation and enterprise as well as problem-solving skills'; begin 'the construction of the bridge from education to work' before age 16 through varied work experience; and encourage closer collaboration between LEAs and industry. Each was also meant to include the possibility of replication, equal opportunities and 'four-year curricula, with progression from year to year'.

The proposals were due back in just five weeks. Despite the short time-frame, 66 LEAs submitted bids (four for two projects each) of which 14 were eventually approved. The political nature of the selection process became apparent when the final list of 10 pilots agreed by the NSG was increased to 12 by Young, and then 14 by Employment Secretary Norman Tebbit (Woolhouse, 1989); the additions were made in the interest of 'geographical diversity', with the last two pilots bordering on the constituencies of Tebbit and his Employment Minister, Peter Morrison (*TES*, 1983).

The use of bidding, or competitive tendering, to determine which LEAs won the prize of pilot funding was a second strand in the TVEI governance strategy. While the bidding process represented a new funding mechanism for the education system, for the MSC it was an adaptation of the contractual model that had proved successful for YOP and YTS (Woolhouse, 1989). The LEAs, however, were far more independent, both in terms of resources and autonomous policy-making capacity, than the training agents that relied heavily on YTS funds; hence the need for the MSC to allow greater flexibility in the TVEI criteria. Despite this independence, however, the LEAs, which had in the past blocked central government's efforts to reform the curriculum, could not resist the enticement of generous funding – equivalent to £3,226 per pupil for the first pilot schemes (Keep, 1986, p. 29) – following the tight budgets of the previous phase of Thatcherism (Dale, 1985a). The MSC ensured that these funds were not diverted into general educational spending, by formalizing the LEA proposals into a detailed contract which the authorities were legally obliged to deliver and then following up on the progress of the pilots through a process of planning, monitoring and evaluation (Cohen, 1989; Harland, 1987).

The lure of resources was also influential at the individual level in mobilizing support for TVEI. At a time when LEAs were coming under growing pressure to reduce the size of their staff, TVEI offered education professionals a rewarding new career path. This personal development aspect of TVEI was enhanced by what Harland (1987, p. 46) has dubbed 'the Fidelio effect', as technical and vocational teachers who had 'led rather isolated and low-status professional lives' were liberated by the extra funds and training that the Initiative provided.

A final factor that was critical in gaining LEA acceptance of TVEI was the TVEI Unit's success in recruiting well-respected, senior educationalists as advisors for the initiative (Cohen, 1989; Curtis, 1990; Woolhouse, 1989). The advisors, eventually organized on a regional basis, played a key role in the TVEI structure, acting as intermediaries between groups of LEA pilots and the MSC. They gave TVEI immediate credibility in educationalists' eyes, ensuring that the narrow view of 'vocationalism' and clash of institutional cultures that characterized the MSC's first contacts with education during TOPS, UVP and YOP was minimized.

Taken together, these elements of TVEI – broadly defined aims and criteria, locally designed bids for central funding, an emphasis on personal development and reliance on trusted intermediaries – represented a new means of generating and managing change within the education services (Cohen, 1989; Howieson, 1989). While never explicitly stated in the MSC guidelines, the TVEI Director saw the Initiative as a 'planned and funded innovation – a more systematic approach to the equivalent of R & D in education through a new form of action research' (Woolhouse, 1991). The relationship between the TVEI Unit and LEAs was analagous to shifts in the structure of corporations that are seeking to foster innovation, while coping with rapid changes in the competitive climate. Companies have found that the Fordist or 'control' model of organization, where central office formulates strategy and then implements it through rigid hierarchies, was not flexible enough to survive in the new environment. What TVEI attempted to put into place was a 'commitment' model of organization, where the centre seeks to foster innovation by giving local actors a sense of ownership over the design of TVEI, within broad guidelines, and providing the resources and planning structure needed to support reform. In choosing this mode of governance, however, the MSC relinquished its ability to dictate the specific content or operation of TVEI pilots, thus allowing them to depart further from Young's original vision. This led some analysts to conclude that LEAs 'took the money and ran', spending it on activities they would have done anyway (see, for example, Fiddy and Stronach, 1987; National Audit Office, 1991, pp. 14–15; Yeomans, 1990).

The pilot phase

The first pilots were still busy designing courses and buying equipment for the students that would arrive in September 1983, when TVEI was declared a success. In December 1982, Young had told a House Select Committee that the MSC had no intention to expand TVEI (*Education*, 1982, p. 1); six months later, the government announced that a second round of bidding would be conducted, offering 40 more LEAs (eventually increased to 48, including Scottish authorities for the first time) the chance to receive TVEI funding for five-year projects to start in 1984–5 (DE, 1983). Like the first round of TVEI, the initial year of the new pilots was to be financed primarily through virement of unspent funds within the MSC's existing budget (Curtis, 1990, p. 8). In contrast with the first round of pilots, however, these projects, and subsequent ones, were strictly limited to £2 million over five years.

This pattern was repeated in subsequent years with 103 LEAs eventually introducing pilot projects at an estimated cost to the MSC of £228 million. While the TVEI guidelines allowed for a great deal of variation among the pilots, it is possible to construct a composite outline of the average scheme: a pilot typically featured eight or nine schools and/or colleges joined together in local consortia; in some cases, a special TVEI facility was constructed to serve as a focal point for the Initiative's activities. These might consist of a range of new 'work-related' courses (eg business studies, information technology) that were used to supplement the curriculum of the 250 students in each year's TVEI cohort, new equipment (usually computers) and other provision such as enhanced guidance and work experience placements. The time spent on TVEI courses rose from an average of about 30 per cent at age 14 to up to 70 per cent of the timetable for those 18-year-olds who remained in the scheme. Each TVEI pilot was managed by a coordinator, appointed by the LEA, who was responsible for liaising with the MSC.

The success of TVEI as a vehicle for implementing education reform was demonstrated in 1985 when the DES asked the MSC to administer the new arrangements for teachers' in-service training which that Department had announced in the White Paper, *Better Schools* (DES, 1985). The DES still lacked the MSC's capacity to target funds to particular programmes (it later acquired this power through legislation) and saw the TVEI as a way of achieving its objectives (Curtis, 1990, p. 10). In order for these funds (£25m from 1985–7) to be channelled through the MSC, the programme was christened 'TVEI-Related In-Service Training' (TRIST) and the courses provided had to be nominally tied to the world of work.

The effect which TVEI had on the reform process, however, must be distinguished from its impact on educational outcomes. Although TVEI has probably been evaluated more extensively than any other British educational reform, these studies (eg, HMI, 1990; NFER, 1988; NAO, 1991) have not demonstrated any improvements in individual attainment or preparation for work as a result of the Initiative. The national evaluations have been funded and disseminated by the MSC, which has a clear interest in the Initiative's success, while local evaluators (each project had to spend at least 1 per cent of its budget on evaluation) often saw their role as developmental – supporting and disseminating best practice – rather than as independent assessors (Cohen, 1989; Dale *et al.*, 1990, pp. 9–10; Hopkins, 1986).

The few independent studies which have attempted to evaluate TVEI have faced the severe methodological difficulties common to most educational research, compounded in the case of TVEI by the large variation among the pilots. Any attempts to measure the effect of TVEI on student attainment or qualifications have been hindered by the fact that TVEI students were not chosen on a random basis; hence, assessments of the effects of TVEI on individuals' decisions lack an adequate control for self-selection bias (Fitz-Gibbon, 1988). In addition, it is not possible to isolate the effects of TVEI from the numerous other education reforms (most notably, GCSE) that were introduced during this period. As a consequence, the MSC's own internal review of the Initiative concluded that there was no proof that TVEI had had a positive effect on staying-on rates, examination success or career opportunities (MacKay, 1986).

In the absence of any hard evidence of TVEI's benefits, MSC officials have relied on softer measures of the Initiative's success. They cite the large number of LEAs who wished to take part and surveys of TVEI participants which show the enthusiasm of students, teachers and employers for TVEI activities (MSC, 1985; Young, 1984a). They also point to process indicators, such as the NFER's findings that TVEI has improved the relationships between schools and colleges and their links with industry (Saunders and Stradling, 1991; Stoney et al., 1985).

Most researchers, however, have been far more sceptical about the ability of TVEI to achieve its original objectives (Dale et al., 1990; Raffe and Tomes, 1987; Sikes and Taylor, 1987). Part of the problem was created by the very nature of TVEI as a pilot programme. The first HMI report on TVEI found resentment toward the Initiative's generous funding was created at a number of levels: among the LEAs that lost out in the bidding; within successful LEAs in the majority of institutions that received no funding; and within TVEI schools, where the majority of teachers and students were not part of the Initiative (Jackson, 1985). This gave rise to what Saunders (1986) described as TVEI 'enclaves', where participants – both teachers and students – were isolated from their peers. The justification for this pilot structure began to crumble as it became apparent that the TVEI cohorts could not be properly evaluated and that pilots would not be replicated in their existing form, thus leading many LEAs and schools either openly or surreptitiously to make TVEI resources available to a greater number of students (Curtis, forthcoming).

The main difficulties which TVEI faced in achieving Young's objectives, however, were caused by the institutional context – both within the education and training state and external to it – in which the Initiative was formed. While the MSC mode of policy-making was successful in getting the Initiative into place quickly, the sheer speed with which TVEI developed, both within each LEA and nationally, created planning problems. Not only was the quality of the first round pilots reduced relative to later bids (MacKay Report, 1986, 5.11), but it also meant that some of the Initiative's initial aims were de-emphasized. In particular, LEAs did not have the time to design a coherent offering for 14–18-year-olds, but rather struggled to get a programme up and running for the first cohort, before turning their attention to the 16–18 phase (ibid, 5.5; Gleeson and Smith, 1987).

This short-term approach to policy-making, combined with the Thatcher government's refusal to address certain issues (A-levels and regulation of the youth labour market) also meant that those involved in TVEI were forced to take a number of the elements in Britain's low-skill equilibrium (Finegold and Soskice, 1988) as a given. In a memo written after TVEI had been operating for one year, Young identified four obstacles beyond the Initiative's immediate control which had hurt pilots' efforts to elevate the status of technical and vocational studies:

1) Universities and employers are generally conservative in their approach to new kinds of qualifications and accreditation. Unless they are fully aware of TVEI-type developments and support them (and make practical adjustments in entry requirements and further training/education programmes), such developments may lose their impetus. 2) Employers have a key part to play and are not yet properly organised to play it. 3) The expansion of technology education in schools is limited by the number of specialist technology and design teachers qualified to teach the modern subject and a prospective continuing shortage of supply; and 4) The examination system is regarded as a mess ... (Young, 1984a, author's numbering).

The TVEI pilots attempted to solve the last problem by working with examination boards to develop new forms of qualification, but the conservatism of HE and employer recruiting practices (factor 1) meant these new qualifications were devalued relative to traditional, academic examinations (*TES*, 1985). The examination system also institutionalized the break at the age of 16, making it impractical to design coherent curriculum packages and encouraging a high percentage of students on TVEI to leave after only two years; this forced pilots to recruit new students to make up the numbers for their 16–18 phase. The incentive for young people to leave halfway through TVEI was further reinforced by another of the MSC's own programmes, YTS, which provided individuals with a weekly stipend and, in some cases, access to jobs that were not available if they remained in education. Raffe argued, based on his analysis of the Scottish Young Peoples Survey, that the institutional *context* in which TVEI was introduced would take precedence over the *content* of the Initiative in determining TVEI's ability to meet its original objectives (Raffe, 1984, pp. 180–6; Raffe and Tomes, 1987, p. 31). This was subsequently confirmed in his and others' analyses of the early pilots (Fitz-Gibbon, 1988; Raffe, 1989), which compared the outcomes for the TVEI cohort with a control group possessing similar characteristics. They found that TVEI, despite the large injection of extra funds, had had no measurable effect or in some cases even a negative impact, on participation rates, attainment levels and the ability of young people to find a job.

The decision to extend TVEI

Given these ambiguous evaluation findings and the way TVEI in practice appeared to differ substantially from what Lord Young and his political colleagues had initially envisaged, why did the Conservatives decide to devote almost £1 billion to the national extension of TVEI in 1986? This question became even more perplexing when the government announced two major reforms – City Technology Colleges (CTCs) and the Education Reform Act – which conflicted with major aspects of TVEI. As previously undisclosed MSC internal documents and interviews with key MSC staff reveal, there was significant opposition within the government to extending the Initiative to all the secondary schools in the country. The story of how this opposition was overcome illustrates how timing and the preferences of key individuals interact with institutional factors in shaping the outcomes of the ET policy process.

The idea of a national TVEI extension was proposed by Young, who had by this time become Secretary of State for Employment, in a letter to the relevant cabinet ministers (DES, DTI, Treasury, Scotland and Wales) and the PM in February 1986 (MacKay Report, 1986, Annex 1). Young argued that the enthusiasm which LEAs had shown for the Initiative, combined with the demands from the initial round of pilot projects to know what would happen when their funding ran out in 18 months' time, meant that the government should start planning now for a national extension of TVEI. He proposed spending £600 million over ten years on extension and setting up an inter-departmental working group, to be chaired by the MSC, which would draw up detailed plans for extension. This proposal was strongly endorsed by Joseph at the DES, but was criticized by the Treasury's Chief Secretary (ironically, the critical letter came from John MacGregor who would later become what many regarded as Mrs Thatcher's most pro-education Secretary of State at the DES). MacGregor expressed serious reservations about extending TVEI, when the first pilots were still not complete, and about the cost of the programme, suggesting it should be halved:

I appreciate the importance you attach to TVEI but we cannot accept that we should now agree to a plan costing £600 million which you describe as a 'gesture of faith' ... I would need some persuasion that we should commit ourselves to expenditure on a national scheme prior to detailed and convincing evaluation results from the existing pilots, particularly in view of the priority you attach to enterprise and employment measures which have a direct impact on unemployment levels (MacKay Report, 1986, Annex 1).

Allied to these seemingly legitimate doubts about the speed and scale with which Young wished TVEI to proceed were questions regarding what the Conservative leadership thought this large sum of money would be spent on and what this expenditure would achieve. Tebbit, one of the scheme's original architects along with Lord Young, was obviously disappointed with the way the Initiative had evolved:

My idea that this should include a few entirely new schools in inner cities funded through the MSC was eroded until the TVEI became simply part of the curriculum in some comprehensive schools. It was a great opportunity sadly missed but now being taken up by City Technology Colleges (Tebbit, 1988, pp. 192–3).

The Extension Working Group reviewed the preliminary evalua-tion results of the first pilot, finding them inconclusive but far from encouraging, with no significant improvements in examination results or staying-on rates for the TVEI cohorts (MacKay Report, 1986, Annex 7). And yet the government not only approved the national extension of TVEI, but also increased the funding of the Initiative from the £600 million Young first proposed to the £900 million that was eventually announced in the White Paper, *Working Together – Education and Training* (DE/DES, 1986).

One critical factor in explaining this decision was the timing of Extension. If it had come just a year later, when the DES had regained the educational initiative from the MSC through the Education Reform Act, then Extension would have faced far greater difficulties. As it was, TVEI was the Conservatives' highest profile education initiative in the run-up to a general election and, thus, not an area where the government wanted to be perceived as withdrawing funding, particularly given the wide support the Initiative was now receiving from virtually all segments of the educational service.

The support from the educational sector, however, is unlikely, itself, to have had a major influence on the Conservatives' decision regarding TVEI. It was the way this support was channelled through an allegiance between Lord Young and the MSC that secured TVEI Extension. Young, at this time one of Mrs Thatcher's closest Cabinet colleagues, ensured that the Initiative he had created would be presented in a favourable light by selecting the composition of the Extension Working Group so that the representatives of the MSC and their allies from HMI out-numbered the Treasury. The Group's Report conceded that it was too early to quantify the benefits of TVEI, but argued that it was a success if measured by the reaction of 'institutions, teachers and students involved' (MacKay Report, 1986, 2.6) and that it was essential to maintain and extend the Initiative's momentum if the government was to deliver its pledge in recent White Papers (DE/ DES, 1985; DES, 1985) that 'all young people in school should have the opportunity of following a more relevant and practical curriculum' (MacKay Report, 1986, 2.1). The MSC also countered the criticism of lack of evaluation results by observing that the Extension was sufficiently different from the pilot that the findings would be largely irrelevant and pointing to qualitative indicators of success (Woolhouse, 1991). While the Treasury's proposal for a £300 million pound Extension was included in the final report, the majority opinion was that 'it would not be sufficient to secure the effective delivery of a national extension across the great majority of authorities'; the Report came out in favour of more generous funding, going beyond Young's original directions to conclude that ' ... around £900 million would be more likely to ensure the achievement of the aims of the extension in the most cost-effective manner' (MacKay Report, 1986, 2.15–16).

Even with the support of the Working Group, TVEI Extension still had to compete with other departments' bids for government funds before it could be implemented. As with the pilot, however, though it was a large sum in aggregate, the way the funding was phased over a ten-year period meant that the first year of Extension would not actually require any new resources. Young proposed to finance the extension of the first 14 schemes through a redirection of the MSC's existing budget (ibid, Annex 1). In this way, the government received the publicity of a £1 billion educational initiative (see, for example, *TES*, 1986) without paying for it until its third term.

National extension

The institutional divisions within the British state's ET bureau-cracy which have contributed to a short-term approach to policy-making were clearly demonstrated when TVEI began the transition from a pilot to a nationwide Initiative. The MSC had just secured the funds for Extension and begun to implement it when the government, through the DES, introduced radical new education reform proposals that conflicted with both the content and mode of governance of TVEI. In response to these reforms, the MSC was forced to redefine TVEI.

Even before the onset of these changes, TVEI Extension was designed to differ substantially from the pilot phase, most notably in its scope. In place of the pilot's 'enclaves', Extension was intended to reach every LEA, school, teacher and 14–18-year-old student in the country over its ten-year phase-in period. As a consequence of this broader remit, the resources for each institution were spread much thinner, with insufficient funds to invest in expensive equipment, facilities or large numbers of new staff as occurred in some pilot schemes. Instead, the TVEI Unit initially targeted funding at the theme which had been implicit in the pilot – enhancing the education system's capacity to manage change. It sought to embed TVEI in the overall provision of 14–18 education by involving LEAs and their advisory staff more directly in the design and running of Extension (Cohen, 1989; Sims, 1989, p. 30). It also required for the first time that each educational institution create a development or strategic plan to show how it would deliver TVEI targets and that each authority set up consortia of schools and colleges and education-employer panels to improve the flow of information and coordination of ET provision for the 14–18 age group (Saunders and Stradling, 1991).

As the first Extension projects began to operate in 1987, TVEI came under threat from the DES. The initial conflict came when Kenneth Baker announced his plans to create 20 CTCs. The CTCs, a throwback to Young and Tebbit's ORT-inspired vision of separate vocational institutions outside LEA control, were an anathema to the way TVEI was attempting to spread the work-related curriculum across all secondary schools and colleges. The danger posed by CTCs, however, was minimized by the failure of the government to attract the anticipated industrial support to build these new institutions, with less than a dozen set up by 1991 (Green, forthcoming).

The major challenge to TVEI came in 1988 with the passage of the Education Reform Act (ERA). The DES's mode of governance, combining greater central control with the use of market forces in education, ran directly counter to the MSC's approach for gaining local commitment to TVEI. Rather than fostering cooperation among schools and colleges, as occurred in TVEI consortia, the Act encouraged greater competition between institutions through opting out, local management of school budgets and removing large colleges of further education from LEA control. TVEI's efforts to bridge the historical divide between academic and vocational subjects and encourage inter-disciplinary project work were undermined by the introduction of the National Curriculum and assessment organized around traditional subjects. The National Curriculum not only threatened to crowd TVEI work out of the timetable, but it also became the immediate priority for all the practitioners involved in or planning for Extension (Dale *et al.*, 1990; Yeomans, 1990).

In response to this shift in the government's education strategy, Anne Jones, who had replaced Woolhouse as Education Programmes Director at the end of 1987, drafted a controversial TVEI 'Focus Statement' (Curtis, 1990, Annex 8). It proposed to concentrate TVEI activities in five areas (eg, records of achievement, careers guidance, work experience), all directly related to the world of work and to concentrate more heavily on planning and provision for 16–18-year-olds, which was beyond the National Curriculum's remit. 'The number of different local developments was over the top', Jones (personal interview) recalled. 'Things were getting too complex. And many of the new courses didn't fit within the National Curriculum framework'. She was also responding to pressures from within the government bureaucracy:

> I was having serious trouble justifying to the Treasury what was distinctive about TVEI. There was a danger that the Initiative had become too educational, not work-related enough to fit within the Department of Employment.

Putting the Focus Statement into practice, however, proved a difficult task because of the mode of governance which TVEI had established. The commitment model that had been used to gain LEA and practitioner support for TVEI relied on their sense of ownership over the Initiative. These local actors did not share the TVEI Unit's need to satisfy the Treasury, nor did they want to stress the work-related elements and discreteness of the Initiative (Dale *et al.*, 1990, pp. 176–7; also Chapter 4, this volume); on the contrary, they saw TVEI's main virtue as offering a vehicle for integrating the numerous other national reforms they were being asked to implement. As Jones conceded two years after the Focus Statement was first circulated: 'It required a great deal of effort to get this message through to the people in the field and we're still working on it'.

Ironically, it was in the delivery of the National Curriculum – antithetical to TVEI's philosophy and not part of the Focus Statement – that TVEI Extension may have made its great contribution. Like all education and training reforms of this period, the National Curriculum was designed and implemented at a rapid pace; schools and teachers, already suffering from 'initiative fatigue', were given little time to prepare for the new courses. 'Teachers didn't have a crumb of support for change', observed Jones (ibid). 'The National Curriculum would collapse without TVEI; take the Initiative away and it's nothing more than a 1957 grammar school curriculum'. The benefits gained from using TVEI structures to support and plan for DES reforms, however, were neither included in the Department of Employment's remit nor easily quantifiable for the Treasury.

Conclusion

This brief review of TVEI, from its inception through pilot and the early stages of national extension, has shown the critical role which institutional factors, both within and external to the government bureaucracy, play in shaping policy. Institutional factors, however, can never provide a complete explanation of the policy process for, while they provide incentives and structure the behaviour of actors within the system, they do not determine who these actors are or eliminate the differences in individuals' preferences.

TVEI emerged from outside the normal ET bureaucracy, conceived by Young as a response to the issues dominating the second phase of Conservative ET policy: rising unemployment and supply-side skill problems. As we have seen, the subsequent development of TVEI was strongly influenced by the MSC's distinctive institutional capacities, explaining the decision to place TVEI, and later TRIST, within the MSC rather than the DES, and the creation of the TVEI targeted-funding model – a case of organizational learning based on the Commission's experience with YOP and YTS (Heclo, 1974). The contract-compliance mechanism was part of a new, broader strategy for managing educational change that the MSC developed in order to secure the commitment of LEAs and teachers to TVEI in the short time available. As a consequence, however, the Initiative departed significantly from Young and his Conservative colleagues' original vision.

This study of the TVEI policy process has also highlighted some of the constraints on the British state's ability to break out of the low-skill equilibrium. The short-term approach to policy-making was evident at each stage in TVEI's development: from the inadequate time for initial planning, through the proclamation of the pilot as a success without adequate evaluation, to the national extension of the Initiative that was then undermined by the ERA, which represented an entirely different approach to the content and governance of education. The last point was also an indication of the conflicts that existed within the government bureaucracy, not only between the MSC and DES, but also within the MSC over TVEI and YTS. TVEI's deliverers attempted to overcome some of these organizational tensions by using the Initiative to bring together separate programmes for the 14–18 age group. Their efforts to improve individuals' motivation and attainment of qualifications, however, were further constrained by the institutional context in which TVEI was introduced. Factors such as the academic-dominated examination system, employer and HE recruiting practices and the operation of the youth labour market were all treated as beyond TVEI's remit, yet limited the Initiative's ultimate impact.

References

Bell, C and Howieson, C (1988) 'The status of vocational education and training: the case of TVEI', paper presented to ESRC/DE Workshop on Employment and Unemployment, London, 29 January.

Chitty, C (1986) 'TVEI: the MSC's trojan horse', in Benn, C and Fairley, J (eds) *Challenging the MSC on Jobs, Training and Education*, London: Pluto Press.

Chitty, C (1989) *Towards a New Education System: The Victory of the New Right?*, London: Falmer Press.

Cohen, G (1989) 'Managing change in education', *International Journal of Educational Management*, **3**, 3, 13–18.

Curtis, J (1990) *TVEI Review*, Sheffield: MSC.

Curtis, J (1991) personal interview.

Curtis (forthcoming) 'TVEI', Surrey University, Master's thesis.

Dale, R (ed.) (1985) *Education, Training and Employment*, Oxford: Pergamon Press.

Dale, R (1985b) 'The background and inception of TVEI', in Dale (ed.) op cit.

Dale, R (1989) *The State and Education Policy*, Milton Keynes: Open University Press.

Dale, R *et al.* (1990) *The TVEI Story*, Milton Keynes: Open University Press.

DE (1983) 'Support for more TVEI projects', Press Notice, 30 June.

DE/DES (1985), *Education and Training for Young People*, Cmnd. 9482, April, London: HMSO.

DE/DES (1991) *Education and Training for the 21st Century*, 2 Vol., Cmnd. 1536, London; HMSO.

DES (1985) *Better Schools*, Cmnd. 9469, March, London: HMSO.

De Ville, H G *et al.* (1986) *Review of Vocational Qualification in England and Wales – A Report by the Working Group*, London: MSC and DES, April.

Education (1982) 'Technical schools', 24/31 December, 1–2.

Fiddy, R, and Stronach, I (1987) 'Fables and futures: cases in the management of Innovation', in Gleeson, D (ed.), pp. 96–118.

Finegold, D, MacFarland, L and Richardson, W (eds) (1993), *Something Borrowed, Something Blue? A Study of the Thatcher Government's Appropriation of USA Education and Training Policy*, Wallingford: Triangle Books.

Finegold, D and Soskice, D (1988) 'The failure of British training: analysis and prescription', *Oxford Review of Economic Policy*, **4**, 3, Autumn, 21–53.

Fitz-Gibbon, C, *et al.* (1988) 'Performance, indicators and the TVEI pilot', *Evaluation and Research in Education*, **2**, 2, 49–60.

Garner, R (1984) 'Young in conference clashes over TVEI', *TES*, 24 February, 15.

Gleeson, D (ed.) (1987) *TVEI and Secondary Education*, Milton Keynes: Open University Press.

Gleeson, D and Smith, G (1987) '16–18: the neglected territory of TVEI provision', in Gleeson, D (ed.) op cit, pp. 177–94.

Green, A (forthcoming) 'Magnet schools, choice and the politics of policy borrowing', in Finegold *et al.* (eds).

Hansard (1982), 'Written answers to questions', 12 November, 269–70.

Harland, J (1987) 'The TVEI experience: issues of control, response and the professional role of teachers', in Gleeson, D (ed.) op cit, pp. 38–54.

Heclo, H (1974) 'Social policy and political learning', in Heclo, H (ed.), *Modern Social Politics in Britain and Sweden*, New Haven: Yale University Press, pp. 284–323.

Her Majesty's Inspectorate (HMI) (1990) *TVEI*, London: DES.

Hofkins, D (1984) 'ORT: confidence through skills', *Education*, 163, 5, 180, February.

Holt, M (1987) 'Vocationalism on the hoof', in Holt, M (ed.), *Skills and Vocationalism*, Milton Keynes: Open University Press, pp. 56–76.

Hopkins, D (ed.) (1986) *Evaluating TVEI: Some Methodological Issues*, Cambridge Institute of Education, Occasional Monographs on Evaluation Issues, No. 1.

Howieson, C (1989) 'The impact of the MSC on secondary education', in Brown, A and Fairley, J (eds) *The Manpower Services Commission in Scotland*, Edinburgh: Edinburgh University Press.

Jackson, M (1985) 'TVEI: very good and very bad', *TES*, 15 November, 15.

Keep, E (1986) 'A coherent vocational training system?', *Personnel Management*, August 28–31.

Kirkman, S (1985) 'Recruitment problems on TVEI', *TES*, 6 December, 9.

MacKay, P (1986) 'Report of the interdepartmental working group on TVEI development', (The Mackay Report) Sheffield: MSC, unpublished.

MSC (1983a) *Towards an Adult Training Strategy*, Sheffield: MSC.

MSC (1983b) *Aims of the Technical and Vocational Education Initiative*, London: MSC.

MSC (1983c) 'Group to oversee new education initiative', MSC press notice, 10 January.

MSC (1985) *TVEI Review*, Sheffield: MSC.

McCulloch, G (1987) 'History and policy: the Politics of the TVEI', in Gleeson, D (ed.) op cit, pp. 13–37.

Moon, J and Richardson, J (1984) 'Policy-making with a difference? The Technical and Vocational Education Initiative', *Public Administration*, **62**, Spring, 22–33.

Moon, J and Richardson, J (1985) *Unemployment in the UK*, Aldershot: Gower.

Moorhouse, H F (1989) 'No mean city? The financial sector and the decline of manufacturing in Britain – review article', *Work, Employment and Society*, **3**, 1, 105–18.

Morris, B (1990) 'America finds itself with an identity crisis', *The Independent on Sunday*, 25 March, Business section, 14.

Morris, J L (1988) 'New technologies, flexible work practices, and regional sociospatial differentiation', *Society and Space*, **6**, 3.

National Audit Office (1991) *The Implementation and Development of the TVEI*, London: HMSO, 22 October.

NFER (1988) *Perspectives on TVEI*, Slough: NFER, March.

Pring, R (1985) 'In defence of TVEI', *Forum*, **28**, 1, 14–17.

Raffe, D (1984) *Fourteen to Eighteen: The Changing Pattern of Schooling in Scotland*, Aberdeen: Aberdeen University Press.

Raffe, D (1989), 'Making the gift horse jump the hurdles: the impact of the TVEI pilot on the first Scottish cohort', *British Journal of Education and Work*, **2**, 3, 5–16.

Raffe, D and Tomes, N (1987) 'The organisation and content of studies at the post-compulsory level in Scotland', paper prepared for OECD, University of Edinburgh Centre for Educational Sociology, May.

Richardson, W (forthcoming) 'Employers as an Instrument of School Reform', in Finegold *et al.*

Salter, B and Tapper, T (1985) *Power and Policy in Education; The Case of Independent Schooling*, London: Falmer Press.

Saunders, L and Stradling, B (1991) *Clusters and Consortia: Coordinating Educational Change in the 1990s*, Slough: NFER.

Saunders, M (1986) 'The innovation enclave: unintended effects of TVEI implementation', Norwich: CARE, University of East Anglia, *TVEI Working Papers 1*, Spring, 1–10.

Sikes, P and Taylor, M (1987) 'Some problems with defining, interpreting and communicating vocational education', in Gleeson, D (ed) op. cit.

Sims, D. (1989) *Project Management in TVEI*, Slough: NFER, July.

Stoney, S *et al.* (1985) *The Management of TVEI*, Slough: NFER.

Tebbit, N (1988) *Norman Tebbit: Upwardly Mobile*, London: Weidenfeld and Nicolson.

TES (1983) 'MSC pilot project list increased to 14 on Minister's insistence', 1 April.

TES (1985) 'Job supremo in pledge over TVEI Extension', 25 October, 5.

TES (1986) 'TVEI to expand as option for all', 13 June, 1.

Training Agency (1988) *TVEI Developments, Series 2 and 5*, Sheffield: Training Agency.

Woolhouse, J (1989; 1991), Personal Interviews.

Yeomans, D (1990) 'TVEI: policy, practice and prospects', *British Journal of Education and Work*, **3**, 3, 5–16.

Young, D (1982a) 'Helping the young help themselves', *TES*, 26 November, p 4.

Young, D (1982b) 'Technical schools', *Education*, 19 November, p. 396.

Young, D (1982c) 'MSC' *Education*, 26 November, p. 19.

Young, D (1984a), 'Technical and vocational education: some personal reflections', NEDC paper, unpublished.

Young, D (1984b) 'Knowing how and knowing that: a philosophy of the vocational', London, Birkbeck College, the Haldane Memorial Lecture.

Young, D (1990) *The Enterprise Years: A Business Man in the Cabinet*, London: Headline.

SECTION 2

Education for Employment?

One of the driving forces behind the vocational imperative has been the belief, shared by many, that a satisfactory education should involve adequate preparation for employment and therefore contribute to improved economic performance. Indeed, Chapter 4 argues that the choice of many who follow an apparently academic route through education is in reality based on a highly instrumental view of education. The connection between education, subsequent employment and the economy is a highly problematic one, as later chapters (Chapter 12 in particular) discuss.

The main aim of Chapter 4 is to consider just what the needs of employers are. What do employers want from the education and training systems? Are there any clear messages? What useful evidence has been collected on the requirements of industry and employers? The chapter argues that certain clear messages have emerged but the situation is made more complex by employers' selection and recruitment processes which may contain hidden practices, criteria and requirements, some of which act against certain groups.

The role of qualifications – both academic and vocational – in gaining employment is also considered, ending in a summary of the main findings emerging from work such as that of Raffe (1988). Finally, the chapter considers a complex question which is often conveniently ignored in considering education as preparation for employment: the issue of transfer. Belief in transfer seems to be a cornerstone of vocational education and in particular the focus on generic, transferable skills which grew in the 1980s. What evidence is there to show that skills, abilities, knowledge and competence learnt in the education system will transfer effectively to the workplace, or more commonly now, workplaces?

The attempt to link education directly to employment has never been more direct than in the Compact scheme. In this scheme, as first conceived, students would be guaranteed a job – or at least training leading to a job – if they achieved certain goals during their compulsory education. Immediately attractive to many parents, pupils, teachers and employers, the scheme (having crossed the Atlantic) became a national project in 1989. What has become of it? Chapter 5 considers Compact in just two cases. Whilst not pretending that the data from these cases can be generalized, the chapter does exhibit a recurrent theme in this book: the way in which a well-intentioned initiative can be undermined by changing economic, political and educational contexts.

Reference

Raffe, D (ed.) (1988) *Education and the Youth Labour Market: Schooling and Scheming*, London: Falmer Press.

4   Fit for Work? Recruitment Processes and the 'Needs of Industry'

J J Wellington

Introduction

The aim of this chapter is to consider the function of education as preparation for work. The chapter addresses the following questions.

- In what sense can education be described as 'relevant'?
- What are the needs of employers with regard to education?
- How are personal qualities used by employers in recruitment – are they of equal value to qualifications or credentials?
- Do the skills and learning/thinking strategies of education and training 'transfer' to subsequent employment?

Relevance and instrumentalism

For many people, preparation for the world of work is, and has been for some time, a prime educational aim. In 1970, Entwistle reported that 90 per cent of parents in a Schools' Council survey felt that schools 'should teach things which would enable their child to get as good a job as possible' (Entwistle, 1970). Agreement with this view was reported to have been expressed by '86% of boys and 88% of girls'. Only the teachers, and particularly the head teachers, had a less instrumentalist view of education than this.

An instrumentalist view of schooling and education is still held by a majority of people from a range of backgrounds. The instrumentalism of many, however, is disguised. This is a feature of the attitude of many parents and students and may be defined as deferred vocationalism (Wellington, 1989b, p. 251). In this view, their instrumentalism is hidden, especially at school level, by their pursuit of an apparently 'academic route' and the adoption of subject choices which are seemingly 'irrelevant' and non-vocational. Such choices are not a symptom of some deeply felt need to follow a liberal, intrinsically worthwhile education but are the main aspect of deferred vocationalism. It has become clear, certainly to middle-class parents, that certain subjects have a high currency or exchange value either in securing a place in higher education or, in some cases, in impressing employers (a point explored later in a comparison between physics and technology as subjects). 'Relevant', vocational subjects may be useful and applicable but they have traditionally lacked currency – they have a low exchange rate.

Evidence and conventional wisdom on the needs of employers

The notion or the plea that education should meet the needs of industry, the needs of the economy, or the needs of employers is so commonplace that it would be impossible to list its many and varied sources here. Most famously in the recent past it formed the central theme of Callaghan's 1976 speech. Sixteen years later it formed a key element of TEED'S (1992) statement on National Training Priorities which included helping 'young people to develop the skills the economy needs'.

Before reporting on and considering the various attempts to determine such needs or skills it is worth clearing away at least some of the conceptual undergrowth (Locke, 1960) with two simple points. First, the words 'industry', economy and employment are often used (and read) as if they were interchangeable. Clearly, this is not the case. Many of the activities in which people are employed (see Chapter 1 for a summary of employment patterns) could not be called 'industry', even if that word is stretched beyond most people's common usage to include the service industries. In addition, the notion of 'employment' is a far broader one than the meaning usually associated with it – paid employment. As Watts (1983) and others have pointed out there are at least six meanings of 'work' and 'employment', including voluntary work and informal economic activity, which can be applied to current human activity. Thus the needs of industry, the needs of the economy, and the needs of employers may be at least three different things. Certainly, the needs of the economy in a national and global sense are likely to differ greatly from, for example, the individual and often selfish and short-term needs of some employers.

Second, the terms 'need' and 'want' have important differences and yet are often confused, and used interchangeably. Employers, for example, may often find it easier to state what they want of new recruits, but the business of discerning what they actually need especially in their long-term interest, is a far more difficult process, perhaps best done by an outsider or by the employees themselves.

There is a vast literature on the needs of employers/industry/ the economy and therefore only a small sample is included here. Some is based on extensive research, some on the sayings of a few employers, some on intuition and guesswork. Some is concerned with school-leavers, some with recruits from the 17–19 age range, some with graduates from higher education. With many other examples of reported work the level concerned is unclear.

An interesting starting point is reproduced as Table 4.1 from a Welsh survey into employers' needs carried out in 1987. This shows a mixture of attitudes, dispositions, skills, abilities, competences and credentials allegedly sought by employers – quite a conceptual mixture which inevitably arises from a survey which asks employers 'what they are looking for in school leavers'. The table provides an interesting contrast with an American study of 'What work requires of schools', published in 1991 (SCANS, 1991). The study involved in-depth interviews of job-holders and supervisors in 15 different occupations across a range of employment sectors. The outcome is the identification of five competencies, two sets of skills and a group of personal qualities which are described as the 'workplace know-how needed for solid job-performance' (see Table 4.2).

At the other extreme from these detailed surveys we have Raven's confident assertion that 'a series of studies have found that employers sought adaptability, enthusiasm, honesty, persistence, confidence, and ability to get on with others in their recruits' (Raven, 1984, p. 18). The series of studies is not listed but obviously pre-dates the two mentioned above, which raises the interesting issue of whether or not the 'needs of employers' vary over time. Raven's list overlaps with the Welsh and American study by including enthusiasm (fifth in the Welsh survey) and working in

Table 4.1 *Welsh survey into employers' needs*

	Very or quite important %	Important %	Not very important %
Reliability and trustworthiness	91	7	2
Punctuality	91	9	0
Willingness to learn	88	9	3
Ability to work as a member of a team	85	14	1
Enthusiasm	82	17	1
Clean and tidy appearance	78	20	2
Ability to work with minimum supervision	61	33	1
Initiative	59	34	7
Ability to work with figures	56	30	14
Ability to write clearly and concisely	52	38	10
Well organized	52	42	6
Ability to speak fluently/with confidence	51	40	9
Friendliness	44	44	12
Some qualifications related to job	35	22	43
Good 'O' level/CSE in academic subjects	30	31	39
Qualifications in vocational subjects	23	36	41
Good dress sense	23	38	39
Some general work experience	23	22	55
Creativity	22	46	34
Work experience related to job	21	16	63

Source: Recruitment & Training Research Unit, The Polytechnic of Wales, June 1987

teams (a 'competence' in the American study, ranked fourth in the Welsh survey).

An unusual study from 1979 which contrasts well with the above reports was carried out by the Industrial Training Research Unit (ITRU, 1979). Their report analyses the qualities of young people from the 'lower ability range' in their first job by taking groups of employers in South Wales (15) and East Anglia (39). Two types of employee were identified: A-type (improvers) and Z-type (non-improvers). The A-types had the attributes of 'versatility', 'pride in job', 'taking initiative' and 'good personal relations' as the four most important. The Z-types were described as: 'doesn't follow instructions', 'bad timekeeper', 'can't concentrate' and 'over-confident for ability'. It is interesting that only one of the improvers' attributes (initiative) overlaps obviously with the previous lists, although such general qualities as 'good personal relations' cover many of the features of the previous reports.

Table 4.2 *What does work require of schools?*

WORKPLACE KNOW-HOW

The know-how identified by SCANS is made up of five competencies and a three-part foundation of skills and personal qualities that are needed for solid job performance. These include:

COMPETENCIES – effective workers can productively use:

- **Resources** – allocating time, money, materials, space, and staff;
- **Interpersonal Skills** – working in teams, teaching others, serving customers, leading, negotiating, and working well with people from culturally diverse backgrounds;
- **Information** – acquiring and evaluating data, organizing and maintaining files, interpreting and communicating, and using computers to process information;
- **Systems** – understanding social, organizational, and technological systems, monitoring and correcting performance, and designing or improving systems;
- **Technology** – selecting equipment and tools, applying technology to specific tasks, and maintaining and troubleshooting technologies.

THE FOUNDATION – competence requires:

- **Basic Skills** – reading, writing, arithmetic and mathematics, speaking and listening;
- **Thinking Skills** – thinking creatively, making decisions, solving problems, seeing things in the mind's eye, knowing how to learn, and reasoning;
- **Personal Qualities** – individual responsibility, self-esteem, sociability, self-management, and integrity.

Source: The Secretary's Commission on Achieving Necessary Skills (SCANS), US Department of Labor, June 1991

Several studies referring specifically to graduates have been carried out and form an interesting comparison with the above. An AGCAS survey in 1985 reported that employers expect graduates to learn quickly; think constructively; work unsupervised; be literate and numerate; and have detailed knowledge of a specific subject. They were also seen as 'more mobile' than non-graduates. In the Expectations of Higher Education project, carried out between 1981 and 1984, it was found that personal attributes were valued highly, but that employers had a preference for university honours graduates, especially from Oxbridge. Another study in 1984 at North London Polytechnic (reported in *Business Education Journal*, October 1984) found that employers looked for a positive enthusiastic approach, good personality and willingness to work hard, in graduates. Finally, research based on five case studies of companies which recruit graduates, by Roizen and Jepson (1985) found that employers went for graduates partly because the degree was a handy screening process, a filter. They also sought people who can work under pressure, recruits with 'commercial awareness', a person who has mixed with a wide spectrum of people, and who has lived away from home.

This is just a sample of the research done on employers' expectations of graduates and their reasons for recruiting people with degrees. They compare and contrast interestingly with the other, more general survey data. For example, many of the personal qualities sought in graduates are also required of non-graduate recruits. This should not be seen, however, as implying that the two groups are interchangeable. There is strong evidence to show that employers recruit people from certain segments or strata of educational achievement. Personal qualities will be important *within* these strata but will not enable them to rise from one stratum to another. Other factors take priority. This is a point which will be returned to in a later section, and a later chapter.

Selection criteria and recruitment processes

There are various ways of attempting to determine what employers actually require of employees. We might simply ask them (as in some of the studies above); we might ask employers what their workers actually do; we might survey the workers themselves, either by interview or questionnaire (Harris, 1991). One interesting method is to analyse in detail the jobs actually carried out by different people, either by systematic observation or participant observation. Fitzgerald (1985), for example, carried out an ethnographic study of the mathematics involved in different jobs by in-depth observation in 29 companies. His findings do not easily relate to the studies above although they are of great interest in considering the role of new technology in education and will be examined in Chapter 6. Similarly, Stafford, Jackson and Banks (see, for example, Stafford *et al.*, 1982) used a 'Job Components Inventory' to analyse the skills involved in a variety of jobs. Again, their findings are interesting but highly specific – they found that the 'number of skills common to a wide range of jobs is limited' – and do not relate easily to the general research on the needs of employers.

One area which does relate to the research reported in the previous section is the study of employers' selection criteria and recruitment processes. This tends to reveal some of the implicit, as opposed to stated, requirements of employers, and also some of the more hidden practices in sifting and selecting.

An interesting piece of research carried out in 1985 using case-studies and interviews is reported by Jenkins (1986). From his studies he groups the selection criteria used by the employers into three categories: primary, secondary and tertiary, and scores each criterion. The results are shown in Table 4.3.

Jenkins' table of actual selection criteria contrasts with the surveys on the stated needs of employers. There appears to be little overlap, except perhaps in 'literacy' and 'personality'. This may be a reflection of the research itself which was clearly aimed at uncovering the less explicit requirements of employers, and indeed led to an important discussion of the more subjective aspects of recruitment such as gut feeling, speech style, appearance and the ability to 'fit in'. Jenkins discusses the implications of the concept of 'fitting in' as one of the requirements of employers, an issue which also emerged strongly in subsequent research (Wellington, 1989b). Jenkins and Wellington point out the extremely conservative influence of the 'fitting in' requirement, both in preserving existing working

Table 4.3 *Selection criteria used by employers: Three categories with ranking*

	Selection criteria	Score
1 Primary selection criteria	Appearance	62.5
	Manner and attitude	55.0
	Maturity	48.5
2 Secondary selection criteria	Manager's 'gut feeling'	36.8
	Labour market history	35.3
	Speech style	26.3
	Relevant experience	23.8
	Age and marital status (male)	23.8
	Literacy	22.3
	Personality, ability to 'fit in'	20.3
3 Tertiary selection criteria	English-language competence	18.5
	References	17.3

(After Jenkins, R, 1986)

practices and policies which may well be economically and technologically unsound, and in disadvantaging certain groups in society. This economically unwise and discriminatory practice is aggravated by the common practice which follows as a direct consequence: the use of word-of-mouth, grapevine and informal networks in recruitment. This practice had surfaced in earlier work. Carter (1962), for example, in a classic study, *Home, School and Work*, tells of an apprentice in a steel firm who was asked on his first day: 'Where does your father work?'

The other new apprentices were amazed when he told them that he had no relation in the firm. Carter went on to discuss the unfair practice of exercising 'influence', and its exclusion of new recruits with genuine merit (p.173). An almost identical finding and discussion is recorded 20 years later in Troyna and Smith (1983), who reported that discrimination is often hidden by the use of informal contacts and word-of-mouth recruitment which clearly disadvantages those who cannot or do not use informal channels.

Such findings help to suggest that the 'needs of employers' are complex and not always immediately tangible. Their needs may not always be in the best interest of their organization or the economy generally. Their statements of needs contain a conceptual mixture of attributes, qualities, dispositions, attitudes, competences and general skills, with very rare reference to specific skills (Wellington, 1989b). Their stated needs do not always coincide with their actual practices and selection criteria. To quote the Central Policy Review Staff (1980):

> There are quite serious difficulties about interpreting what the needs of industry are. Statements made by employers cannot always be taken at face value (para. 6).

And in a later paragraph:

> In many cases there is a conflict between the explicit statements made by employers and the implicit signals in the way that they select and recruit employees. We found these contradictions were widespread, at every level of recruitment, and that in most cases employers were unaware of them (para. 7).

Equally, 'employers' do not form a unitary category; in reality they may be the CBI, the directors, the supervisors or simply the personnel department. Thus, the notion of the needs of employers does not form a tangible, clear or unshifting foundation on which to build a coherent plan for education and training. This is not due to a lack of research. There is an inherent problem in determining the needs of employers, neatly summed up by Beck (1981):

...the determination of society's needs is a matter involving complex value judgements – it is not a simple empirical matter at all (p.88).

Diploma disease or qualifications game? Employers' use of credentials

If the determination of employers' needs forms an uncertain and value-laden interface between education and employment, then can the use of qualifications, standards and certification form a more reliable and less value-laden point of contact? Dore (1975) talked of the 'diploma disease', ie, an obsession with qualifications, which, in the mid-1970s, seemed to plague the connection between education and employment. Is this a fair assessment now? Which side, if any, is afflicted with it? How do employers use qualifications? More generally, what do they require of the 'products' of education and training?

An important study on the way in which employers use qualifications was carried out by Ashton and Maguire (1980). They identified five ways in which employers used qualifications in recruitment, ranging from qualifications as the dominant factor at all stages through to the situation in which educational qualifications actually performed a negative function. For brevity, their findings are summarized in Table 4.4.

Table 4.4 *The use made by employers of educational qualifications: a framework*

Academic criteria dominate			*Diverse range of non-academic criteria*	
I	II	III	IV	V
Academic qualifications dominate at all stages of selection	Educational qualifications used for shortlisting; final decision on non-academic criteria	Non-academic criteria begin to dominate; educational qualifications perform a focusing function only	All emphasis on non-academic criteria	Educational qualifications perform a negative function

(Based on work by Ashton and Maguire, 1980)

More than a decade later it would appear that Strategy V no longer operates and Strategy IV is increasingly rare. However, the emphasis on qualifications has certain unintended and unwanted side effects. This occurs especially when qualifications are used as a screening mechanism, a filter, particularly in the context of the high unemployment which has prevailed since Ashton and Maguire's research. Given a huge number of applicants for a small number of posts, any recruiting officer will be tempted to use qualifications which may bear no relation to the job involved but which serve as a useful means of reducing the size of the field. One side effect was superbly reported by Berg (1970) in his discussion of the 'great training robbery'. He talked then of the belief that 'education is the answer to the nation's problems' and the growing tendency for people to be in jobs that utilize less education than they have, which may lead, he claimed, to frustration with work and ultimately to those workers seeking jobs elsewhere. A similar problem was identified 16 years later by Mabey (1986) in a study of the recruitment and use of graduates in industry. He reported that high graduate turnover was often due to disenchantment through the underuse of their abilities. There was often a large gap between graduate expectations and the actual job carried out. A similar finding, particularly in the IT field, was reported in case-studies of companies by Wellington (1989b).

Below graduate level, Troyna and Smith (1983) report a study from 1979 which found that many workers were exercising less skill in their job than they did in actually driving to work. This is part of their general argument that the relationship between formal academic credentials and success in the labour market is taken for granted; in fact, the connection is an extremely problematic one. Their argument reaffirms the earlier suggestion that the complexity and inequality in the education-employment connection occur in the selection and recruitment process as much as in the education or training process itself. In short, 'Equality of educational attainment does not lead to equality of opportunity in the labour market' (Troyna and Smith, 1983, p.45).

In summary then, the use of qualifications in linking education to employment is a complex process. Equal qualifications will not ensure equal opportunity. Qualifications are used in different ways by employers in selection and recruitment. Personal qualities are important as an adjunct to qualifications, but only within strata pre-determined by other criteria, most notably academic achievement. In practice, verifiable credentials take priority over personal qualities.

General versus vocational?

One of the issues in the qualifications game is the question of general versus vocational in terms of efficacy in gaining employment. Again, this is an extremely complex question to unpack, not least because of an alleged gap between what employers say and what they do, and the distinction between relevance and hard currency (or use value and exchange value of qualifications). This is well illustrated by two examples from the Central Policy Review Staff (1980, p.4).

> One large and prestigious firm said that they thought university science courses tended to be too academic and should contain a practical element. However, because they aimed to recruit from the ablest graduates and the ablest graduates tended to be found on the more academic courses, in fact their recruitment policy reinforced the bias against practically oriented courses.
>
> In one area a group of teachers asked firms whether they preferred recruits to have taken O-level Physics or O-level Technology. The clear preference was for O-level Physics. However, when the firms were shown untitled syllabuses which were for the two courses, they chose the Technology syllabus as more relevant.

Many other commentators have since put forward the view that a general education, however defined, is favoured more highly than a vocational education. For example, Watts (1983) argued that:

> the overwhelming majority of industries are of the opinion that education given at school before the minimum school-leaving age is reached, should be general rather than vocational in character,

and that schools should not engage in offering 'some sort of vocational instruction which industry itself is much better qualified to give'.

In 1984, a wealth of written evidence to the House of Lords Select Committee on Science and Technology (1984, pp. 299–314) included the statement from the Royal Society that:

> ...the aim of education up to the age of 16 should be to teach basic skills, concepts and processes and should not be oriented towards any specific vocation.

Few in education would quarrel with this, but a statement in a similar vein in the same section of the report from Plessey plc reinforced the view that industrialists too require general skills rather than specific abilities in technology:

> The provision of microcomputers is to be encouraged but too much emphasis must not be placed on software and programming at the expense of literacy and numeracy (p.299).

An American study carried out by Wilms (1988), using 172 telephone interviews with personnel officers in Los Angeles, concluded that:

> Policies that continue to vocationalize public education at the expense of developing young people's literacy, work attitudes and abilities to compute and think will be a particular hardship for low-income students who are over-represented in vocational programs.

Oxenham (1988, pp.67–79), in a summary of 'what do employers want from education?', based mainly on Third World countries, concluded that employers seek a range of non-cognitive outcomes from schools, and value communication skills rather than skills geared to particular occupations. He suggests that schools should concentrate on giving a 'good education'.

From these studies, certain general conclusions on the uses of qualifications by employers and the relative value of vocational versus general education can be identified:

- Qualifications in academic subjects, not vocational subjects, are most strongly correlated with success in gaining employment.
- People's employment prospects are greatly helped by their access to informal networks.
- Employers recruiting young people do not value specific vocational skills very highly.
- Employers use educational qualifications as a *relative*, rather than an *absolute*, recruitment criterion. Qualifications are used to define strata, and personal qualities are only valuable *within* strata.
- Entry to vocational education is greatest in labour markets where employment opportunities and, paradoxically, the demand for vocationally-qualified students, are most limited.
- There is an inverse relationship between qualifications required and numbers applying for a job (Ainley, 1988). High unemployment leads to large numbers of applicants and a raised level of entry requirement. Full employment implies fewer or no applicants and a reduced level of qualifications required.
- Persistent problems for vocational initiatives such as TVEI are the low status of vocational education and employers' emphasis on traditional certification.

Preparation for work and the issue of transfer

A central issue in the debate on whether education should be 'general' or 'vocational' concerns the question of whether or not skills or abilities learnt at school or college will be of value, or will transfer to the workplace. An implicit belief in transfer forms a cornerstone of the justification of schooling as a preparation for work and the vocational curriculum. It is therefore useful at this point to take a short digression into a discussion of transfer as a feature of preparation for work.

Much of the rhetoric surrounding the new vocationalism and the pleas for education and training to provide skills for the future have hinged on the belief that there are such entities as 'generic, transferable skills'. Indeed, one element of the work-related curriculum is premised on the assumption that what is learned through schooling will transfer to other contexts after the student leaves. What evidence is there, however, that transfer of learning does take place? What are the conditions under which transfer occurs, if at all?

What is transfer?

Transfer is defined by Glaser (1962) as the ability to utilize one's learning in situations which differ to some extent from those in which learning occurs; alternatively, transfer may refer to the influence of learning in one situation or context upon learning in another situation or context (Ausubel and Robinson, 1969). This is a useful working definition. In addition, Annett (1989) separates *transferable* skills (which are skills learned in one context but readily used in others) and *transfer* skills (which are higher-order strategies that help a student to apply what has been learned to new situations, ie, to enable transfer to take place). There are several types of transfer. Two of the most important in this context are:

- Learning-to-learning transfer. Learning in one domain may enhance learning in another, eg, by learning Latin does it become easier to learn French, or vice-versa?
- Learning how to learn. The act of learning in one situation improves the ability to learn in another.

One, more general, way of classifying transfer is to describe it as either lateral, sequential or vertical (Ausubel and Robinson, 1969).

Lateral transfer occurs with learning at the same level as the initial learning but in a different context, eg, if skills or understanding taught at school are employed in a new context out of school. Thus the possibility of lateral transfer is particularly relevant in considering the vocational curriculum. Sequential transfer occurs if the skills, ideas or concepts taught in one context then have a relationship to the skills, etc. in the next learning situation. This type of transfer is particularly relevant for teachers in planning a course of study. Finally, vertical transfer occurs when learning at one level facilitates learning at a higher level. Again, this appears to have most relevance in the context of teaching a hierarchical subject such as maths or physics.

When does transfer take place?

The following summary presents the main points in the debate over transfer which appears to have been running for most of this century and probably longer (views on transfer are said to date back to the Ancient Greeks: Ausubel and Robinson, 1969):

- Rote learning is by definition unlikely to lead to transfer (Tomlinson, 1981), although training in memorization techniques can improve transfer.
- Transfer has been said to occur only where there are identical elements or common components in the original learning and the new task (Thorndike, 1924).
- Thorough mastery of the original learning task or material is necessary for transfer.
- Transfer is more likely to take place if widely varying examples of the concept, principle or strategy being transferred are used in the learning/teaching process and if the link is made consciously (Wolf et al., 1990), ie, a variety of instances is needed in the original learning.
- A conscious, meaningful approach to learning/teaching is required for transfer to take place, especially if the original learning contains over-learned, automatized sub-skills.
- 'Interference' (or negative transfer) in the application of original learning to new situations often arises.
- Transfer is likely to be greater the more intelligent a student is; with students of 'lower intelligence', longer and more detailed effort will be required to facilitate transfer.

Whilst there is some agreement on the seven points summarized above, the evidence in the literature seems to be problematic on the following issues:

- *Assessing the extent of transfer:* there is no easy way of assessing with any degree of confidence the extent of transfer from one context to another.
- *Motivation:* if teachers and trainers attempt to 'teach for transfer' by using general examples and a range of contexts, this may reduce the motivation of the learner, ie, the removal of training and education from a specific context in an effort to achieve generality may reduce the learner's motivation, for example, in teaching supposedly transferable skills such as problem-solving or planning. A delicate balance is needed between specificity and generality (Annett and Sparrow, 1985).
- *Transfer skills:* much work still needs to be done on the metacognitive skills and strategies which underly the ability to transfer. Little is known about how individuals succeed or fail to use higher order 'plans' to enable transfer (Annett and Sparrow, 1985).
- *Higher order transferable skills:* there is still little conclusive evidence to show that the very general skills and strategies such as 'learning to learn' and problem-solving really do transfer from one context or domain to another. Faith in problem-solving skills and approaches has now become accepted orthodoxy in curriculum statements and even in the mission statements of schools and colleges. Yet there is little evidence that there is a 'universal problem-solving ability', nor is there evidence that problem-solving transfers from one subject to another, let alone from school or college to the workplace. Are people who solve problems successfully in one domain successful in solving problems in another? Everyday experience and anecdote would certainly suggest not.
- *Change and transferable skills:* one of the driving forces behind the renewed emphasis in the 1980s and 1990s on generic and transferable skills has been the alleged rate of change of jobs, skill requirements and skill half-life in the workplace. This has been particularly strong in the case of technological change and the skills associated with new technology. Yet there is little concrete information on the skills required to handle new technology or whether they are transferable. This is a point considered more fully in Chapter 6 on IT and the notion of 'IT skills' which underpinned much of the vocationalism of the 1980s.

Lave (1988) provides a valuable critique of accepted wisdom on learning transfer and concludes that 'when we investigate learning transfer across situations, the results are consistently negative'. Even if skills do transfer within an educational context, it cannot be assumed they will transfer from the educational context to the world outside. Lave poses the question: 'Why have learning transfer theory and its functionalist underpinnings endured for so long?' Why have the 'widely distributed views which compose a taken-for-granted world of problem-solving and learning transfer' persisted? Why has the belief in transfer persisted? Lave (1988, p.71) suggests that:

> An important part of the answer surely lies in its key role in the organisation of schooling as a form of education and in justifications of relations between schooling and the distribution of its alumni into occupations.

In other words, implicit belief in transfer underpins the notion that the functions of education are to meet the needs of industry and to prepare young people for certain occupations through the selection, socialization, orientation and preparation functions of education (Watts, 1983). As suggested above, this implicit belief is problematic.

In what sense should education attempt to meet industry's needs?

This chapter has attempted to give an overview of available evidence on the 'needs' of employers, to relate these to employers' actual selection criteria and recruitment processes, and then to consider the use of qualifications in preparation and selection for employment. Two of the key questions in the debate on education for employment are the issues of general versus vocational education, and the perennial question of the transfer of skills and strategies from education/training to the workplace. There appears to be less agreement on the latter question than the former, yet an implicit faith in transfer underpins much of the talk of generic, transferable skills which grew in the vocationalism era of the 1980s and has been retained in the enterprise era of the 1990s.

The important messages for education from this discussion need to be carefully interpreted and unpacked. The importance of personal qualities, for example, is a common theme, but they should not be seen as a replacement for academic achievement in the actual selection practices of employers. There is strong evidence that personal qualities are important within strata but do not enable job-seekers to transcend strata. In addition, the growth in emphasis on 'social and life skills' in the curricula of education and training has helped to create the myth that the transition from school or college to work is a difficult and problematic one for young people. There is, in fact, little evidence to support this 'myth of transition', either now or in the past (see, for example, Carter [1961] and Roberts [1984]), although there may well be a problem of transition to unemployment.

Similarly, the notion of the needs of industry may have been valuable in certain speeches and statements in exhorting education to link more closely to employment, but it has little meaning in real terms, even when generalized to refer to transferable skills. It will also be dangerous and counter-productive for the economy if it leads to premature vocationalism and a neglect of the general education (including numeracy and literacy) which is clearly valued by employers. In short, the notion of the needs of industry or of employers generally does not provide a solid foundation on which a coherent plan for education and training can be built.

References

Ainley, P (1988) *From School to YTS: Education and Training in England and Wales 1944–1987*, Milton Keynes: Open University Press.

Annett, J (1989) *Training in Transferable Skills*, Sheffield: Training Agency.

Annett, J and Sparrow, J (1985) *Transfer of Learning and Training*, Sheffield: MSC.

Ashton D and Maguire, M (1980) 'The function of academic and non-academic criteria in employers' selection strategies', *British Journal of Guidance and Counselling*, **8**, 2, 146–157, July.

Ausubel, D and Robinson, F (1969) *School Learning: An Introduction to Educational Psychology*, New York: Holt, Rinehart and Winston.

Ball, Colin and Mog, C (1979) *Fit for Work? Youth, School and (Un)Employment*, London: Chameleon Books.

Beck, J (1981) 'Education, industry and the needs of the economy', *Cambridge Journal of Education*, **II**, 2, 87–106.

Berg, I (1970) *Education and Jobs: The Great Training Robbery*, Harmondsworth: Penguin Books.

Blagg, N (1991) *Can We Teach Intelligence?*, New Jersey: Lawrence Erlbaum Associates.

Carter, M (1962) *Home, School and Work*, Oxford: Pergamon.

Central Policy Review Staff (1980) *Education, Training and Industrial Performance*, London: HMSO.

Dore, R (1975) *The Diploma Disease*, California: University of California Press.

Entwistle, H (1970) *Education, Work and Leisure*, London: Routledge and Kegan Paul.

Fitzgerald, A (1985) *New Technology and Mathematics in Employment*, Birmingham: University of Birmingham.

Glaser, R (ed.) (1962) *Training Research and Education*, New York: John Wiley.

Griffin, C (1985) *Typical Girls? Young Women from School to the Job Market*, London: Routledge and Kegan Paul.

Hagger, E (1984) *Likely Trends in Graduate Employment*, London: Association of Graduate Careers Advisory Service.

Harris, M (1991) *Schools, Mathematics and Work*, Basingstoke: Falmer Press.

House of Lords Select Committee on Science and Technology (1984) *Education and Training for New Technologies*, London: HMSO.

ITRU (1979) *The A–Z Study: Differences Between Improvers and Non-Improvers Among Young Unskilled Workers*, Cambridge: Industrial Training Research Unit.

Jamieson, I and Lightfoot, M (1982) *Schools and Industry*, London: Schools Council/Methuen.

Jenkins, R (1986) *Racism and Recruitment: Managers, Organisations and Equal Opportunity in the Labour Market*, Cambridge: Cambridge University Press.

Lauglo, J and Lillis, K (eds) (1988) *Vocationalizing Education: An International Perspective*, Oxford: Pergamon.

Lave, J (1988) *Cognition in Practice*, Cambridge: Cambridge University Press.

Locke, J (1960) 'An essay concerning human understanding', in Woozley, A D (ed.), London: Fontana/Collins.

Mabey, C (1986) *Graduates into Industry*, Aldershot: Gower.

Maguire, M and Ashton, D (1981) 'Employers' perceptions and use of educational qualifications', *Education Analysis*, **3**, 2.

Oxenham, J (1988) 'What do employers want from education?', in Lauglo and Lillis (eds), *Vocationalizing Education: An International Perspective*.

Raffe, D (ed.) (1988) *Education and the Youth Labour Market: Schooling and Scheming*, Lewes: Falmer Press.

Raffe, D and Smith, P (1987) 'Young people's attitudes to YTS: the first two years', *British Educational Research Journal*, **13**, 241–60.

Raven, J (1984) *Competence in Modern Society: Its Identification, Development and Release*, London: H.K. Lewis.

Roberts, K (1984) *School Leavers and Their Prospects – Youth and the Labour Market in the 1980s*, Milton Keynes: Open University Press.

Roizen, J and Jepson, M (1985) *Degrees for Jobs: Employer's Expectations of Higher Education*, Windsor: SRHE and NFER-Nelson.

SCANS (1991), *What Work Requires of Schools: A Scans Report for America 2000*, Washington DC: US Department of Labor.

Stafford, E, Jackson, P and Banks, M (1982) 'School and Work: A Technique to Help Bridge the Gap', *Educational Research*, **24**, 4, 243–9.

TEED, (1992) *National Training Priorities*, Sheffield: TEED.

Thorndike, F L (1924) 'Mental discipline in high school studies', *Journal of Educational Psychology*, **XV**, 1–22, 83–98.

Tomlinson, P (1981) *Understanding Teaching*, Maidenhead: McGraw-Hill.

Troyna, B and Smith, D I (eds) (1983) *Racism, School and the Youth Labour Market*, Leicester: National Youth Bureau.

Watts, A G (1983) *Education, Unemployment and the Future of Work*, Milton Keynes: Open University Press.

Wellington, J J (1989a) 'Cradle snatching – attracting school leavers', *Times Educational Supplement*, 2 June.

Wellington, J J (1989b) *Education for Employment – The Place of Information Technology*, Windsor: NFER-Nelson.

Wolf, A, Kelson, M and Silver, R (1990) *Learning in Context: Patterns of Skills Transfer and Training Implications*, Sheffield: Training Agency.

Young, D (1985) *Knowing How and Knowing That: A Philosophy of the Vocational*, Birkbeck College, Haldane Memorial Lecture, 1984.

Young, M (1987) 'Vocationalising tendencies in recent UK educational policy', *Bildung und Erziekung*, No 40, 73–82.

5 Restoring the Implicit Promise in Schooling? Observations of Compact in Action

J J Wellington

Introduction

> Compacts are bargains between young people, employers, and schools or colleges. Young people work towards personal goals, such as improved attendance and higher attainment. In return, local employers provide a job with training, or training leading to a job, for those who achieve their goals (Government White Paper, 1991, *Education and Training for the 21st Century*).

The Compact idea came across the Atlantic from Boston, USA, where the Private Industry Council (one of the 'PICs', the forerunners to the TECs) had established a system of contracts with schools, by which students would receive work experience, counselling and priority in gaining jobs in return for meeting a series of goals such as literacy and numeracy, punctuality and attendance. The incentives for its development are said to be the race riots of 1975 (Davenport, 1989) and the fact that City firms were recruiting from the largely white suburbs of Boston, rather than the inner-city population (Wookey, 1986). In 1986 a group of people from what was then ILEA visited Boston and later decided to try a similar contract in East London involving employers in Docklands and the schools and colleges of Tower Hamlets and Hackney (Nash, 1987; Wright, 1988). The East London Compact produced personal goals for students, which included attendance, punctuality, completion of coursework and homework, satisfactory work experience and production of the 'London Record of

Achievement'. The employer goals were to provide permanent jobs with training to those who had achieved those goals, to take an active part in school-industry links and to ensure an equal opportunities approach in recruiting (Farley, 1988; Martineau, 1988).

Before the London scheme had been fully evaluated (DES, 1989; ILEA, 1988) the initiative was taken up at a national level by central government and announced in the Action for Cities document of April, 1988, though no mention was made of the East London initiative (Davenport, 1989). Funding was to be provided for Compacts in 30 Urban Programme Authority areas in England and Scotland totalling 2 million in 1989 and rising thereafter. Up to 100,000 each year for up to four years would be available for each Compact.

Central government support for the Compact idea led to a spate of new, glossy documents issued by the Training Agency in 1989. The leaflet for young people, entitled *How to Guarantee Yourself a Job*, began:

> Want to be sure of a decent job when you leave school or college? Your local Compact can guarantee you one, and the training to go with it.
>
> Finding it hard to get your act together and work well at school or in training – when you can't see the point of half the things you're asked to do? Being part of your local Compact will give you the incentive. It can guarantee you a good job with training, or training leading to a job – if you want one!

This was the message to the students – work hard at school or college to get a job after it: the restoration of the implicit promise (see Chapter 1). How far were these promises fulfilled? What effect did they have on pupils' motivation and diligence? Does the Compact provide the 'incentive' for the completion of coursework and homework, and the will to attend regularly and punctually? This is the subject of the case-studies which follow.

By 1992 the programme had been extended to 61 Compacts in Urban Programme Authority areas in England and similar priority areas in Scotland and Wales. The Employment Department had also commissioned the National Foundation for Educational Research (NFER) to carry out a four-year evaluation of the programme, due to end in 1994. The data presented below are clearly not as extensive as that study but hopefully will provide some insight, and raise some issues, which will complement it. Interestingly however, by 1991 the government was already convinced of the success of this initiative:

> The Compacts programme, which we launched in 1988 as part of our strategy to revitalise the inner cities, has been a success. Their success is such that we believe that employers, schools and colleges throughout the country should be able to adopt the Compact approach as a means of focusing attention and activity on the issue of individual attainment ... we want the Compact approach ... to spread across the whole country (White Paper, op cit., 1991).

Who needs an evaluation when you have conviction as strong as this?

The following case-studies are based on the three schools which joined the Compact scheme in one local education authority when it was first launched in one particular way there in 1989. Since then, the other comprehensive schools in the authority have joined the scheme. The benefits of focusing on these three schools are three-fold: first, it was possible with such a small sample to look in some detail at the scheme in action; second, the teachers involved had, by the time of the enquiry, acquired some experience and knowledge of Compact, albeit in one setting; third, in the summer of 1991 the schools had their first Compact graduates entering the job market in the region and therefore the 'job guarantee' aspect of the scheme could be considered.

As with any case-study report, one cannot pretend that the sample is in any way representative; however, one can say that these events and evaluatory comments came from three real settings, and it is hoped that readers can relate to this case-study material even if they cannot fully generalize from it. The material does at least pose some important questions about initiatives such as the Compact scheme as part of the vocational imperative.

The material below is based largely on interviews with the Compact co-ordinator in each school, supplemented by other data from documents and records.

Tightening the bonds between education and industry: three cameos of Compact in action

School A: City View

Background

School A is situated approximately two miles from the centre of the town, in an area consisting of mainly older established housing estates, some dating from before World War II and the rest built directly after it. Most of the pupils attending the school live within easy walking distance. The school caters for approximately 870 children aged between 13 and 17 years. School A was one of the original three schools that joined Compact in 1989. As a result of the publicity Compact received at its launch, this school managed to enrol nearly all the 240 pupils in the fourth year group who were eligible. There were one or two exceptions but these were the hard core disaffected pupils who were unlikely to finish their education at the school, for one reason or another.

The comments below come from the school's Compact co-ordinator (Teacher 1), an energetic and enthusiastic teacher who was also responsible for Records of Achievement, work experience, careers guidance and industry links generally in the school.

Positive effects

The first positive effect Teacher 1 felt Compact had was that it developed stronger links with parents, as a result of the parent evenings which are an integral part of Compact. Figures showed that attendance at the fourth year parents' evening increased from around 50 per cent to 78 per cent. He felt the parents had become more involved and interested in what their child was doing and what was going on at the school.

The introduction of Compact had also resulted in tutors taking a far more active role with their tutor groups. It had made them talk more to their pupils as now they had to regularly check with the student if the goals were being met. In the past it was felt that some tutors had not used tutor time to involve themselves with the children but for doing other things such as marking, etc. Compact had thus resulted in an increase in the work load of certain staff, which had caused some resentment towards the scheme in certain quarters. Teacher 1 felt the problem had been further compounded, in his school, as a result of Records of Achievement being launched at exactly the same time as Compact:

> The youngsters couldn't discriminate between Compact and Records of Achievement – because they were having so much paper pushed at them it worked against us. We learnt from that. Now we've managed to show pupils – and staff – that the two are very separate but complement each other.

The connection was the 'setting of targets', so the school has introduced staff training on one-to-one interviewing and counselling. The school has also introduced profiling across subjects, using a common format.

Teacher 1 felt that parental involvement and tutorial work generally had improved from Year 9 upwards:

The role of the form tutor has changed dramatically over three years. We now report 'effort grades' and publicize them. Form groups with the highest aggregate of effort grades receive a trophy sponsored by industry. Parents are invited to school to discuss and set targets, with all groups from Year 9 onwards, not just the Compact Years.

Teacher 1 was particularly insistent that the positive, often hidden benefits of Compact should be made clear:

The value of Compact is not in what it turns out at the end in terms of job-creation ... it's the process – the process of Compact is all important. It was really getting us to think about, and to do, the things that perhaps we ought to have done before ... and certainly it's still doing that.

He went on to sketch the 'invisible imports' of the scheme:

The wider aspect is the expertise that we're now drawing on from industry – the links that they (the pupils) get, the courses that are being run in conjunction with business and industry. It's, if you like, the 'invisible imports' through Compact that really are the spin-off and the benefit to the youngsters. And they don't normally see those – it isn't immediately apparent to them. It's only later on that they'll look back and see the benefits.

He was anxious that Compact should not be judged in terms of the job guarantee (examined later). Its importance was as a catalyst for change:

Compact was always about change – if you view it from that criterion, Compact has been an out-and-out success here.

Negative effects
Teacher 1 was asked what negative effects, if any, the school had experienced as a result of its involvement in the Compact scheme. As would be expected from the many positive comments above, his remarks were brief:

The introduction of Compact and Records of Achievement at the *same* time gave it (Compact) a bad name – the youngsters were sick and tired of filling in paper. We know we've got it right now.

He also made the very valuable point that it is currently almost impossible to single out one initiative and assess its impact:

It's difficult to know when it starts and finishes. We're trying to lose this tag, 'Compact' ... it's been totally subsumed by everything else we're doing. You can't see the gap between Head of PSE and me.

Meeting the Compact Goals

From the first batch of Compact students, only 170 of the original 240 pupils managed to complete their Compact goals and therefore graduated in 1991. The main reasons for students failing were given in order of importance as follows:

1. Attendance
2. Course work (either not completed or not handed in on time)
3. 'Attitude' of pupil, including 'communication' and 'self-presentation'.

Punctuality, Teacher 1 said, was no real problem as the pupils either arrived on time or not at all. He stated that the pattern of attendance for the pupils involved in Compact had increased, but the change was negligible. The feeling was that Compact had had little effect upon increasing attendance at the school. The hard-core non-attenders, who seemed to be ever-present in this school's fifth year, had not been motivated by Compact into attending regularly.

The school now sets its own goals, in line with those of Compact. Pupils' attainment of these goals is displayed in the staff room. This was seen as a 'major breakthrough':

> If we publish estimated grades to all youngsters, we tell them what their estimated grades are – now that is a major breakthrough for us ... directly as a result of Compact requiring us to do it – the Records of Achievement didn't. In terms of 'processing' (sic) youngsters, it was essential that youngsters know what their estimated grades were, as well as their effort grades. Now that is a major breakthrough really.

The job guarantee

Teacher 1 stated that 34 of the 170 graduates had applied for Compact jobs and of these he believed 6 or 7 had been taken on by firms but he was uncertain in what capacity, either job status or on a YT scheme. He felt it was very difficult for even Compact graduates to secure a position with a Compact firm. To illustrate this he quoted a Compact firm in the region which had one vacancy for a Compact graduate; 130 children had applied for it. All of these children had achieved all that had been asked of them, and many probably much more, but at the end of the day there would be 129 disappointed graduates.

He felt that Compact had helped to increase the number of children staying on at school post-16 or going on to further education elsewhere. This had come about as a result of their being made more aware of what was available by their tutors, and by the industrialists who had spoken to them on their Compact visits. This had led to an interesting situation:

> The people that employers are looking for are staying in school. You can't make them apply for jobs.

In conclusion

School A did seem to have a hard core of disaffected pupils upon which Compact had very little effect. The other problem which the school was now experiencing was that the pupils and parents were realizing that the initial promises Compact had made to them if they graduated were not being fulfilled. At the first launch of Compact the children and parents were given the guarantee of 'either a job with training or training leading to a job' if the pupil managed to achieve the Compact goals. It was plain for all to see, with the first group of graduates, that this was not the case. Teacher 1 said that the 'word soon gets around' as the school is based upon a community where brothers, sisters and cousins all attend the same school. This now makes his job and that of his colleagues more difficult when trying to motivate the children and when talking to parents.

However, there had been many positive aspects of Compact. It had accelerated the introduction of Records of Achievement and although the timing of its introduction could have been better, it was generally accepted that it provided a meaningful document to the teacher, pupil and the employer. It had stimulated the children in thinking and talking more about their futures, what job they would like to do and what qualifications they needed. They had taken a more active role in their education, having been involved with tutors on a more regular basis in discussing their progress and target-setting. The children, the school and the teachers had benefited from much better links with local industry. This has resulted in local firms sending people into school to talk to the children, children visiting local firms and work placements for both pupils and teachers. Teacher 1 felt the development of links with local employers had been one of the great benefits of the school's involvement with Compact. The final point mentioned was the positive spin-off from more contact with the children's parents. It was going a long way to break down the 'us and them' barriers, especially when a high proportion of the parents had attended the school themselves.

School B: Townedge

Background

School B is situated about three miles from the town centre on a split site. The catchment area is spread over a mixture of private and council housing estates which are within a two mile radius of the school. The school has a good tradition which it has maintained since its grammar school days, regularly producing some of the best examination results in the area. There are approximately 925 pupils at the school ranging from 13- to 17-years-old. It has by far the largest sixth form of the three pilot schools – approximately 210 pupils compared to School A's 120 and School C's 110. Despite the difference in size, proportionally School B has the best staying-on rate. In 1989, when Compact was launched, there were 206 students in Year 9 who were eligible to sign up for Compact; 199 of these 206 students actually signed up. The other seven did not because of 'parental objections'.

The comments below come from the school's Compact Coordinator (Teacher 2) who is also responsible for industry links and other vocational initiatives.

Positive effects

In contrast to Teacher 1, Teacher 2 had a limited number of positive points to make about Compact. She felt that it had improved links with industry ('we now have an industrial tutor scheme where employers come in once a month to work with a class') and liaison with parents to some extent. Punctuality rates had improved, more than attendance rates:

> Our attendance figures have not improved noticeably. I suppose you could say it helped about 10 children out of the whole year group.

However, in this respect, she revealed her surprise on one occasion:

> When the job guarantee was virtually withdrawn from this year's Year 11, the class I had said, 'Well, then there's no point in us coming to school – we've only been coming to meet our Compact goals'. I was quite surprised at that because I didn't think Compact was having any effect.

Teacher 2 certainly felt that record-keeping and tutorial group work had improved, although this may have resulted from the introduction of the Records of Achievement:

It's increased the contact between form tutors and their forms – it's strengthened relationships there ... but that's really the Records of Achievement part of it. It's given tutors experience of one-to-one counselling and reviewing ... and all staff have had some training in this.

Negative effects
When we went on to discuss the negative effects the mood changed:

> Don't mention Compact loudly in this staffroom, will you. (Teacher 2 laughs loudly.) We as a team would have liked to have packed it in when the job guarantee went ... we just felt that it had died a death. I think it will take just one to back off (one school) and they'll all go.

Compact had caused a slightly difficult situation with the parents which, it seems, the school had handled extremely tactfully:

> At first, right at the beginning, we had a hall full of parents for the big launch. But we didn't go for the big launch this year, really because we'd got our necks on the block because we'd offered job guarantees to the Year 10 (then) that we couldn't fulfil by the time they got to Year 11 ... the goalposts had changed. So we didn't want to go for this big show, you know.
>
> If we stood up there for the new Year 10 and had this big hype of a launch it may well be that a number of parents there had pupils from the year before ... and we'd end up with this slanging match, that we wanted to avoid.

Teacher 2 was particularly scathing about the financial aspect of the scheme in her school:

> All we've got to show for our Compact money is a portable display stand ... that cost about £800.
>
> It's been expensive in terms of administrative and secretarial time ... they do the recording of attendance and so on. We used Compact money to pay for that until it ran out. This year we've had £40.

Meeting the Compact goals
In total 98 pupils failed to achieve their compact goals – 49 per cent of all the pupils on the initiative. Teacher 2 was able to produce a detailed table illustrating the exact failure rates, in each form across the year. The following list is a summary of the reasons for failure:

1. Attendance   77 pupils
2. Coursework   42 pupils
3. Punctuality   37 pupils
4. Personal and Presentation Skills (PPS)   10 pupils
5. Work experience   4 pupils

Teacher 2 felt that the high failure rate was partly as a result of their rigour in applying standards. She felt that there had been a great inconsistency in applying Compact goals across schools. For example:

> I'm pretty certain that we were the only school which failed pupils on coursework alone. I can tell you that this year we shan't be failing anybody on just coursework. We also found out that 'coursework' in one subject is not coursework in another.

Thus there was a feeling in School B that there is a lack of standardization of Compact goals partly within, but especially amongst, the schools involved in the scheme.

Teacher 2 felt that her school should have fared much better than the other two judging by past external examination results. She had been in contact with Compact upon this matter but the responses received were vague and did not help to clarify things. If different standards are allowed in different settings, this could make the qualification meaningless.

The job guarantee

Of the 109 pupils who graduated, 28 had applied for 'Compact Jobs'. Of these, only one initially managed to secure a job with 'employee status', ie, they had a contract of employment. Eleven of the children had been taken on by firms, but on YT schemes. By September 1991 only 20 Year 11 leavers had got jobs of any kind – only five of these were Compact graduates. Teacher 2 said she was very disappointed with the number of children who had managed to find employment. As she said about the job guarantee promise: 'It's all a bit of a con really.' Why didn't it happen?

> I think really, the employers didn't change their attitude at all ... and I think you can understand it, really. They wanted the best person for the job ... which weren't necessarily the Compact graduates.

The other main reason was the local employment situation which had changed dramatically in just two years:

> When we started, firms were increasing their workforce, there was a lot of talk about expansion in the town and so on. And at the same time there was the falling rolls situation ... and it was very much, when we first started, 'the world's going to be your oyster in two years' time, people are going to be crying out for you'. Then over the next two year period — Ltd. lost 200 jobs, — cut about 500 jobs I think, — were in a stagnant position, and so on.

What had been the effect of the collapse of the job guarantee on the pupils and on their parents?

> I think pupils are more cynical now. The job guarantee element didn't feed back into the system ... it pulled the rug from under our feet.

The positive 'feedback' which a successful job guarantee *might* have had on motivation, however, was seen as no great loss:

> For the majority of our students Compact did not provide any motivation. Ninety per cent of our pupils would have done well with or without Compact. It is difficult to single out children that Compact really did help do better than they would have done in pre-Compact days.

What about the parents? Were they surprised or angry at the failure of the job guarantee?

> We've only had one parent who actually came up to the school to complain about the job guarantee. I thought they'd be queuing up down the school drive to complain, but they didn't. We say that the 'school's not in the real world' but the parents are ... they're losing their jobs as well, they know how difficult it is. And I think that perhaps we were a bit naive thinking this would work ... perhaps they *always* had reservations.

In conclusion

Despite the many critical comments above, Teacher 2 felt that Compact had helped to bring about some positive changes to the school in general, to the benefit of the children. She felt it had made the school look with a critical eye at their own systems and practices. As a result of this changes had occurred. Tutors were now more actively involved with their tutor group due to Records of Achievement and monitoring Compact goals. Links with local employers had been strengthened and developed, making the relationship more two-way and interactive: 'Compact could be a scheme for educating employers'.

Despite these benefits she felt that Compact as a 'scheme' had a bleak future:

> It's just limping along ... to be honest we're all pig sick of it ... so we go through the motions and try to be positive when we talk to the kids but privately we wish it would die its death. So, in school, we're playing down the Compact and playing up the industry links. We now call the Compact Steering Committee the 'Industry Links Committee'.

School C: Country Vista

Background

School C is situated in a small, pleasant town about nine miles from the centre of the metropolitan area. It originally developed as a market town but grew as a result of the local colliery, which was closed several years ago. Now there is a high level of unemployment in the area. The school has approximately 750 pupils on roll aged 13 to 18 years. In 1989 when Compact was launched, there were 240 pupils who were eligible to join in Year 9. The majority of these pupils signed up for the initiative, a total of 220 in all.

The careers teacher interviewed (Teacher 3) described the intake as 'skewed towards the lower ability', with the massive unemployment in the area lowering morale and causing lack of ambition: 'The kids are a bit aimless, but quite amiable'.

Teacher 3 was the most voluble of those interviewed – the remarks below are a brief distillation of a lengthy discussion.

Positive effects

Compact had achieved some positive effects in school C. It had accelerated the introduction of Records of Achievement, though the school was going in this direction already. It had greatly improved the school's links with industry with people coming into school to talk to the students and set up mock interviews, which had proved very useful. Perhaps the main effect was to improve record-keeping in the school and to 'highlight' certain basic goals:

> It made us tighter in terms of attendance and punctuality ... various goals that had to be met, we became a bit more vigilant about. It gave us that little bit of edge. It made us keep better records, just that little bit keener. It highlighted to the kids the need, perhaps, for good attendance, good punctuality, getting work in on time ... all the goals that are basic to any normal education system.

Negative effects

Teacher 3 was keen to talk at length about the negative effects of Compact: first of all, the attitudes of staff:

> I think it's had a negative effect on staff. They've become totally cynical because it's created a tremendous amount of work, a lot of paperwork, in monitoring, in making sure that all the records work out. Not only that, but just in promoting, establishing interest, keeping a track of goals and so on and making sure the kids have got assignments in. It's created a bit of work and the question is, for what? When you say 'for very little', the staff get very cynical. We don't need anything to make more work, unless there's a real plus to be gained.

He also commented on the changed attitudes of the students:

> I think the kids have gone very cynical. I'm a fifth year tutor this year with a Year 11 class and I just say to them 'Look, we're waiting for Compact jobs ... end of February the Compact Directory is out'. Do you know how many jobs there are this year? One hundred in total for seven schools.
>
> I just say to my Year 11, 'If anybody here is seriously looking for a job, if Compact comes up with the goods, it's a bonus, but it's not the be all and end all'.

Teacher 3 felt, as with the earlier cases, that the parents, coming from an area of high unemployment, were more realistic and sceptical about the Compact idea right from the outset:

> When we first launched Compact, the hall was full of parents ... and that's a rare thing here. It was for one simple reason: there was going to be a guarantee of a job. There were people that night who said: 'What? A real job ... a proper job?' ... and they just couldn't believe it. And, of course, they were right, ultimately ... it didn't happen.

The Compact experience seemed to have made the long-serving Teacher 3 very cynical himself about school-industry links in general:

> The problem with school-industry links is always the same. It's getting industries into school when you want them, to do what you want them to do. The number of times they say, 'I can't come to that meeting', which is fair enough. We're not a priority are we? Which I understand.
>
> We've had good school-industry links, quite good, but you have to be ever so careful. I don't want people coming and talking to the kids; that's the last thing I want. I want people to come in and work with the kids which we do quite a bit of from time to time. But it's an enormous job. We ran a technology week – we had all sorts of people in. What a workload. It was great for a week, but you can't do that week after week after week.

Meeting the Compact goals

It seems that just over 50 per cent of the pupils had completed their Compact goals, although there was some uncertainty over the exact figure. The main reasons for failure were attendance and punctuality, which had knock-on effects:

> Attendance and punctuality problems then lead to lack of completing assignments and that leads to a lack of cooperation with members of staff who are probably moaning at you all the time because you've not completed the assignments, then that leads to all the other issues. They're inter-linked. But the baselines, the easily quantifiable ones, are those two. We are now

looking, at the moment, at those who've not completed assignments and I know I can knock quite a few of those out. There's one or two others which are slightly less objective, like cooperation. One or two are definitely going to go out on that. Personal presentation skills – not many go out on that actually, and that's the bit that probably is where we are totally at odds with employers because we probably won't knock kids out that they would. It's very difficult to quantify.

He went on to describe the common disagreement between teachers and employers in their expectations of pupils which creates problems for a scheme such as Compact:

A problem last year was the tremendous mismatch between what a Compact graduate was in our eyes and what one was in the employer's eyes. They expected this wonderful being to turn up for the interview who would be totally skilled in all aspects of the job, social skills, interview technique, etc. What they got was the usual 16-year-old, lacking in confidence, lacking assertiveness, lacking skills to speak out, which is never going to be any different no matter how much work I do on interview skills, interview techniques. It will always be thus ... some will be good, some will not be so good. We're not suddenly going to turn out these wonderful people. There's a terrible mismatch in expectations, which always brings resentment.

He saw the problem of motivating pupils in both the first and subsequent cohort as a major worry:

There was a definite upsurge of interest at first but whether it motivated kids or not? It's difficult. I don't think it did, because it could only motivate if you get the results ... if, for instance, at the end of it all everybody had got a job as promised, then it feeds back in. I go to my next Year 9s and say, 'Hey – you remember last Year 11' ... you've got a motivator for the next cohort ... Unfortunately it didn't deliver, so the motivator just went away.

The job guarantee
Teacher 3:

Out of this school, of 35 students last year who were seriously looking for jobs through Compact, there were 12 who got jobs ... and who knows if they would have got them anyway? They're not 12 *new* jobs ... and they were good kids anyway.

He recounted several anecdotes to reinforce his points. In one case a female student had got a full-time job in a local fashion-wear factory as a machinist. This was regarded as a Compact placement but it turned out the school had well-established links with the firm to the point where jobs had been offered directly to the school in the past without being advertised. Teacher 3 found it a little ironic that this would be put down as a Compact placement when the school had been directly providing workers for the firm for several years. His general feeling was that:

> Compact have promised the children something which they cannot deliver: a job guarantee. And they were foolish, in my opinion, ever to do so. There's no way you can guarantee a job. It was a non-starter in a recession, in an area of bad unemployment.

He, once again, mentioned the lack of impact on motivation:

> Compact is there to help motivate students but it will not if it does not get the graduates jobs. The motivation for the other Compact students *would* have come if Year 11 had got jobs. What incentive is there now for Years 9 and 10? How can I say to my students, 'Do this, do that, work hard and you will get a job at the end of it'?

Clearly, for Teacher 3, the implicit promise in schooling had not been restored by an initiative such as Compact.

Teacher 3 saw some of the difficulties as resulting from the way the Compact initiative had been run in this authority. With just three schools initially there had been problems; with all the schools joining in there would be others, leading to Compact being a 'baseline qualification':

> When there's only three schools they are very, very wary of appointing somebody just from a Compact school. Why should they take somebody from here when they can get somebody better from elsewhere? They weren't going to risk a training programme that's going to cost several thousand pounds on one person. So when you look at the reason why somebody didn't get a job, it says, 'Lost out to a non-Compact graduate'. So it goes to a non-compact school. So in the end, what happens, every school goes in – that's the ultimate aim. Once every school's gone in it's defeating itself, isn't it? All it becomes then is a base qualification. If you *haven't* got a Compact goal, you're on your own and you go and get whatever you can. If you've got the Compact goals that's the baseline for the semi-skilled jobs. It's an indication to employers that there is something there that achieved the minimum, if you like.

The Compact goals thus provided the 'base level of education' which would be the minimum requirement for all children leaving school in two years' time when all schools in the region should be involved in Compact. Heaven help those who don't achieve the minimum level.

In conclusion
Teacher 3 was extremely open and honest in discussion, often

expanding at length upon the points summarized above. He had genuine feeling and concern for his students and on more than one occasion his frustration showed. The disappointment of his pupils in not being able to secure employment seemed to colour his judgement of other aspects of Compact that had benefited the school in general.

He felt that mistakes had been made and lessons learnt. For example:

> One mistake we made here was that we didn't have a Compact coordinator. The head kept that. A lot of us got involved – I probably got involved more than anybody but nobody's given any time for it. That was a big bone of contention. He's tried to delegate it out to a lot of different people, which has been a bit messy, to be honest ....

In the short term, the school would continue with Compact but use very different tactics, especially in liaising with parents:

> The initial outburst of parental interest won't be sustainable because we haven't delivered. Interestingly, this year's launch was a different launch ... it was very much more honest. There's no job guarantee any more. That's the way we should have launched it two years ago.

But in the long term:

> I think it'll just die a slow death. I think it'll be self-defeating in the end, it'll just disappear.

Concluding remarks

Certain points emerge from these cases which may well apply in other settings and indeed to other initiatives in linking education to employment. First, the difficulty – raised particularly in School B – of applying standards consistently and fairly across a range of institutions in an initiative such as Compact. Second, the problem (discussed in earlier chapters) of distinguishing between one initiative and another in a time of burgeoning innovation, or perhaps imposition, in schools – this makes the business of evaluating and assessing the impact of a particular programme especially difficult for teachers and outside evaluators. Third, the extent to which initiatives are often overtaken or undermined by events – either demographic, political or economic. Fourth, the mismatch between the expectations of employers and those of teachers in the personal qualities of a 16-year-old – this is illustrated vividly by the quote from Teacher 3. These are all general points which had practical meaning for the teachers in these settings. There may be others but the purpose of this section is more to present three cases than to provide lengthy discussion.

The future of Compact is uncertain – the report of its death (Dean and Nash, 1992) may be greatly exaggerated but the deeply felt comments recorded above indicate that the initiative as first conceived has already been re-moulded, if not killed off. The possibility of Compact restoring the implicit promise in schooling (Watts, 1983) of 'work hard at school to get a job after it' no longer seems a realistic one.

References

Davenport, E (1989) 'From Boston to Britain: the development work of Compact', *Local Work*, Monthly Bulletin of the Centre for Local Economic Strategies, April, 7, 1–6.

Dean, C and Nash, I (1992) 'Compacts collapse', *Times Educational Supplement*, 31 January.

Department of Education and Science (1989) *London Education Business Partnerships, The London Compact: East London phase*, Inner London Education Authority and the London Enterprise Agency, Report by HM Inspectors, London: DES.

Farley, S (1988) 'The social compact', *Times Educational Supplement*, 2 September, 20.

ILEA (1988) *The London Compact – Interim Evaluation: The views of school co-ordinators*, London: ILEA; Research and Statistics Branch.

Martineau, R (1988) 'How we got going with Compact', *CBI News*, 27 May, 12–13.

Nash, I (1987) 'Employers team up with schools to set pupil goals', *Times Educational Supplement*, 27 March, 14.

Watts, A G (1983) *Education, Unemployment and the Future of Work*, Milton Keynes: Open University Press.

Wookey, J (1986) 'American accent on beating the dole', *Times Educational Supplement*, 12 December, 9.

Wright, B (1988) 'The Compact route from Boston to London', *Transition*, May, 17–19.

SECTION 3

New Technology and the Vocational Imperative

This section considers the impact of new technology, and in particular information technology (IT), on the debate over education for employment. One of the driving forces behind recent vocational initiatives has been the conviction that students must be prepared for the 'computer-oriented' society which awaits them – in short, that education and training must prepare the workforce for a technological future. Chapter 6 explores that belief. First it considers the important landmarks in the development of IT education and training since 1981, and identifies the main pressures which have helped to push IT into the student curriculum. It then goes on to examine the connection between IT in education and IT in employment, arguing that there are clear strata within industry which mark out and often limit entry into employment opportunities. In addition, the numerical importance of IT-related work and thus the vocational significance of IT education and training may well have been overestimated.

Consequently, an overemphasis on the vocational aspects of IT education at too early a stage may actually be counter-productive for both students and the economy; this is identified as premature vocationalism. Similarly, a narrow, specific-skills approach to technology is unlikely to be of economic value in the future. Instead, a broader framework for IT education is put forward which can be justified on both educational and economic grounds.

This framework is discussed further in Chapter 7 where one particular answer to the vocational and technological imperative is considered: the City Technology College (CTC) programme. This programme was introduced as a response to the perceived link between 'vocationally relevant' technological education and the predicted needs of the economy in the future. Its aim, according to DES documents, was to provide a 'surer preparation for working life'. By presenting and discussing observations of two CTCs in action, Chapter 7 considers the value of a curriculum enriched (for a minority) by adequate resourcing in information technology, and the lessons to be learnt for the majority.

References

DES (1986) *A New Choice of School: City Technology Colleges*, London: DES.

6 The Technological Bandwagon: New Technology and the Drive for 'Relevance'

J J Wellington

The IT imperative

One of the key features of the vocationalism of the 1980s has been the emphasis on technology, and in particular information technology. This was especially evident in the launch of initiatives such as TVEI, YTS and the purpose of CTCs, and the rhetoric surrounding them. The purpose of the discussion below is to trace the growth of IT in education, to consider the relationship of that growth to the labour market in IT, and thus to examine the vocational significance of IT as an aspect of the work-related curriculum. The chapter concludes by offering a rationale and a structure for IT as a central element of the curriculum in the future. But first, what are the sources of the technological drive which was so apparent in education in the 1980s and is still ever-present in the 1990s?

Dale (1985) argued that the emphasis on IT in the TVEI initiative was strong for three reasons: first, the implicit belief that future employment prospects would be most propitious in IT-based industry and commerce; second, that even those not employed in IT work will still be 'affected' by it; and third, that education itself would use IT more and more. Certainly, the latter belief has proved to be true. It is the first belief which will be examined more closely here. In the same book, Finn describes the publicity justifying YTS as associating the programme with 'the new technologies at the forefront of employment creation'. As this chapter argues, the belief that IT is a creator of employment is far from proven.

The drive to introduce computers into schools actually preceded both these initiatives and began in 1981. Kenneth Baker, the Minister for Information Technology in 1981, launched the Micros in Schools scheme by claiming that the 'kids of today' should be equipped with 'skills' for the information age analogous to the skills that had gained their ancestors employment:

> I want to try and ensure that the kids of today are trained with the skills that gave their fathers and grandfathers jobs ... And that is the reason why we've pushed ahead with computers in schools. I want youngsters, boys and girls leaving school at sixteen, to actually be able to operate a computer.

The effects of Baker's push will be examined in the next section. Another programme launched a year later in 30 inner city areas set up the Information Technology Centres and was accompanied by a similar rationale from Baker:

> IT centres are an important initiative which will help to meet the needs of young people to gain relevant, transferable skills and provide the trained workforce which industry will increasingly need (*Employment Gazette*, January 1982, p.3).

In the same message, the purposes of the ITECs were also said to be to 'provide young people with the new skills necessary for Britain to take a leading part in the technological revolution'. Two features are prominent here: first, the belief in the notion of new, transferable skills which are deemed to be essential for the technological era. This is linked with the notion of reduced skill half-life and the need for transferability discussed in Chapter 4. Second, that the UK must compete and play a leading part in the technological revolution. This seems to underpin the belief that new technical and vocational education will help to overcome competitive disadvantages in relation to technologically more advanced nations, which may have prepared their labour forces more adequately to adapt to new technology and thus to produce goods of a higher and more saleable quality.

Thus the IT imperative seems to have come from a number of directions. Cerych (1985) suggested that the pressure to introduce IT into education is unique in coming from three directions; he refers to these as 'pedagogical', 'sociological' and 'economic'.

First, IT has entered education as a new pedagogic tool, fundamentally different from the tools of the past because it is *interactive.* Second, the introduction of IT into education has been accompanied by 'sociological pressure', from parents, local authorities, successive governments, European and international organizations. Finally, there has been a huge economic pressure behind the introduction of new information technology into education because IT is not just an educational tool as were, for example, the programmed learning machines of an earlier decade. IT is now pervasive in all economic sectors. The pressure has come from statements on the 'needs of industry', skill shortage, and on the 'growing demand for IT skills'. This latter pressure, an 'economic' one, has been particularly potent in the secondary and tertiary sectors where the *vocational significance* of IT has been stressed so strongly.

Another drive behind the demand for an increased emphasis on IT as a feature of vocationalism and the work-related curriculum has been the growth in the volume and popularity of literature predicting the onset of the 'post-industrial society' and the 'information era'. The literature began with authors like Bell (1974) and Touraine (1970) and became more popular with the paperback prophets such as Toffler (1970) and Naisbitt (1984) with his forecast of megatrends. This in turn led to a series of critical comment on the technological determinism in some of this material by writers such as Weizebaum (1984), Turkle (1984) and Gershuny (1978), who attacked particularly the idea of a service, post-industrial economy.

These, then, have been some of the major sources of the drive to include IT as a key element of education and training at all levels. They have come from a variety of areas: from politicians, from educators and trainers, from authors and other commentators on the advent of the so-called information era. In addition, of course, came the reality of the permeation of IT and its applications into society, which cannot be denied. The result has been a rapid growth of IT as an element and a driving force in both education and training.

The development of IT in education and training: a brief overview

The scale of investment into IT during the 1980s in the UK was on a level which no other aspect of educational technology has ever equalled or is ever likely to match. As this section will show, a total of £62.5 million was committed centrally to IT from 1981 to 1988.

In 1981, no less than £16 million was provided by the Department of Trade and Industry (DTI) to subsidize the purchase of British-made microcomputers in schools. This sum was exceeded by the Department of Education and Science (DES)-supported initiative to promote micro-electronics teaching and the use of computers in school education; £23 million launched the Microelectronics Education Programme (MEP) which ran until 1986.

Other sources of support have risen like springs to provide tributaries to the main flow of funds into school computing. The DTI belatedly subsidized educational software to the tune of £3.5 million, having been told repeatedly that, crudely speaking, a computer without software is like a car without petrol. The 1986 modem scheme attracted another £1m of DTI money to support the communications facet of IT, hitherto neglected, although the issue of who pays the telephone bill was left untouched. In the same year, the Microelectronics Support Unit (MeSU) was set up with £3 million to carry on the good work of the MEP.

Meanwhile, the Technical and Vocational Education Initiative provided manna from heaven to computer enthusiasts whose aim was to fill the school with microcomputers and associated peripherals. Though TVEI was in no way meant as a source of financial support for microcomputing, in many schools it was seen that way and, by 1986, some 'TVEI schools' had as many as 50 or 60 micros. A survey in that year showed that 'TVEI schools' had, on average, almost twice as many computers as 'non-TVEI schools' (Wellington, 1989). Finally, in 1988 the DES invested £19 million in educational support grants for IT, £8.5 million on hardware. These events, along with others discussed later, are summarized in Table 6.1.

What was the effect of this unprecedented central funding on the curricula of Britain's schools in the 1980s?

Prior to the DTI Micros in Schools scheme, computer studies as a secondary subject was on the fringe of the curriculum, and as an examination subject its entry figures were at a similar level to Spanish, geology and music. By 1984 examination entries had virtually tripled to place the subject firmly in the mainstream of the secondary curriculum (Wellington, 1984).

This strategy for introducing computer education into the secondary school curriculum was, however, already beginning to be questioned. First, computer studies was rapidly becoming the 'domain of the boys' with the boy:girl ratio of 2.4:1 at the 1984 O-level entry, a male bias exceeded only by physics with a male

Table 6.1 *The IT decade?: landmarks in IT education, 1980–90*

Date	Title	Description
1981–4	Micros in School Programme	£16m subsidy from DTI for purchase of microcomputers in schools
1980–6	Microelectronics Education Programme (MEP)	DES-supported initiative (£23m) to promote microelectronics teaching and use of computers in school education
1981	Information Technology Centres (ITeCs)	Government initiative to train young people in IT skills; 175 ITeCs now operating with approximately 6,000 trainees
1982	Information Technology Year (IT 82)	Government programme to increase national awareness of IT
1982	YTS	Youth Training Scheme, incorporating 'computer literacy'
1982	IT initiative launched for higher education	Designed to increase number of places in higher education and post-graduate courses related to IT, 1983–6
1982	'New Blood' Initiative	Money provided for higher education to recruit lecturers/researchers in IT (70 posts)
1983	TVEI	Technical and Vocational Education Initiative, allowing additional purchase of IT resources
1984	Information Technology in Further Education	Government grant designed to provide vocational students with an education taking account of the industrial and commercial applications of IT
1985	Engineering and Technology Initiative	£43m funding to increase the number of places in engineering and technology in higher education by around 5,000 by 1990
1985	IT Skills Agency (IT SA)	Agency set up by industry to monitor skill shortages in IT and encourage collaboration of industry, government and education
1985–6	DTI software subsidy	£3.5m provided by DTI to subsidize purchase of educational software in schools
1986	Modem Scheme	DTI subsidy of £1m to enable schools to purchase a modem for their micro, allowing links between computer systems
1986–7	Microelectronics Support Unit (MESU)	Set up with £3m funding for 1986/7 to carry on the work of the MEP
1986	TVEI Extension announced	White Paper, *Working Together – Education and Training*, announced national extension of TVEI programme, with average annual expenditure of £90m over next 10 years
1987	DES support for IT in schools and further education	Kenneth Baker announced Educational Support Grants (ESG) of £19m for the expansion of IT in the schools and £4.8m for IT in non-advanced FTE
1988	Information Technology in Schools Initiative (ITIS)	A separate ESG category for the ITIS included in the programme to promote IT in schools until 1994
1989	IT as a 'cross-curricular skill'	IT becomes an element of the National Curriculum as a cross-curricular skill
1990	IT as part of Technology	'IT capability' becomes one Attainment Target in the statutory order for Technology

dominance of 2.7:1. Second, questions were raised about the content of computer studies courses. The course content often involved topics such as the history of computing, the representation of numbers and characters in binary notation, programming in BASIC, and the study of Logic, which the subject's critics considered neither educationally worthwhile nor vocationally relevant. Finally, the subject at school level received criticism from both the influential Alvey Report, and from universities and polytechnics. The latter group failed to favour that area at school level, preferring traditional O- and A-levels. The Alvey Committee (1982; p.62) went further, suggesting that school computer education of the wrong kind, and the use of home micros, might actually do harm and, by implication, prejudice a student's chances of entering higher education:

> It is no good just providing schools with microcomputers. This will merely produce a generation of poor BASIC programmers. Universities are in fact having to give remedial education to entrants with A level computer science. Uncorrected, the explosion in home computing with its 1950s and '60s programming style will make this problem even worse.

Alongside the almost exponential growth of computer studies there lay an initiative which, in some sense, fought against that growth. The MEP ran from 1980 to 1986. One of its major aims was to encourage the use of computers as aids to teaching and learning *across* the school curriculum. At secondary level, the first main deviation from computer studies as an examination subject was to provide 'computer appreciation' courses for all pupils, often at second or third year level. However, a further stage, valued so highly by MEP, was confronted by obstacles both physical and mental. This is the stage of introducing computers across the curriculum into separate subjects, eg, computer assisted learning (CAL) across the secondary curriculum. The physical obstacle had been the creation of 'computer rooms' having anything between 10 and 20 computers and often part of the domain of the computer studies and maths teachers. Therein also lay the 'mental' obstacle. Computers had become widely seen, with some notable exceptions, as the province of the maths/computer studies boffins, kept under lock and key in a computer room which often must be booked well in advance, and in many cases contains micros linked or networked together. This prevented their 'physical diffusion' into the fabric of the school and their 'mental diffusion' into the curriculum planning and classroom practice of teachers.

Fortunately, the permeation of IT across the curriculum is now well established in virtually every secondary school, in principle if not in practice. The rise of computer studies has now reversed to a decline. This has been reinforced by the designation of IT as a cross-curricular skill by the National Curriculum Council. The 'horizontal' approach to IT in the curriculum is thus established, although a 'vertical' component has been retained by the inclusion of 'IT capability' as one of the Attainment Targets (ATs) in the Technology National Curriculum.

The evolution of IT in education from the 1980s to the 1990s is summarized in Table 6.2, which shows the shift from vertical to horizontal. This model will be referred to later, in considering IT as an element of the work-related curriculum.

At other levels, in other sectors, parallel (though often discounted) initiatives had been occurring in IT. Computer literacy, or IT literacy, was given a key position in YTS with its identification as one of the 'core skills' in the YTS programme. All YTS trainees were therefore expected to receive some grounding in computer literacy, although the interpretation of that term appeared to vary widely (Bailey, 1986). In addition, a number of young people are engaged in training at Information Technology Centres (ITeCs) around the country. The first ITeC was launched in Notting Dale, West London, in 1979. When Kenneth Baker, then

Table 6.2 *From vertical to horizontal: the evolution of IT education in secondary schools*

Stage 1	Computer studies as an examination subject: rapid rise in entries. 'Vertical' approach to IT education
Stage 2	Computer awareness across the board, to all ability ranges and both sexes, eg, to the whole first year, with an element of in-service education for staff as well as pupils
Stage 3	Introduction of computers across the curriculum in separate subjects to enhance learning in those areas, partly as a result of the 'diffusion' process in stage 2, ie, CAL across the curriculum
Stage 4	Increasing pressure on computer studies as a separate subject, and on the computer room as a resource for the whole school
Stage 5	Integration of IT and IT resources into the whole curriculum and classroom practice. Largely 'horizontal' approach to IT education.

Minister for Information Technology, visited the Centre in 1981, he was impressed enough to propose a national string of such centres from Scotland to Northumberland, to West Wales and Devon. Over a decade later there are around 150 ITeCs with up to 50 trainees in each, co-ordinated by a National Association of ITeCs (NAITeC).

A wide range of courses relating to IT developed and are currently offered in further education. As stated above, YT courses involve computer literacy as part of a common core, and these courses are widely provided by colleges of further education. In addition, further education provides courses leading to BTEC (Business and Technology Education Council), City & Guilds and RSA (Royal Society of Arts) qualifications, many of which are wholly or partly involved with information technology. Other important qualifications are Higher and Ordinary National Diploma Courses.

In higher education, a government initiative in 1982 increased the number of places on first-degree, higher diploma and certificate courses relating to information technology. The initiative also led to new one-year post-graduate conversion courses for 'good' graduates in non-IT subjects to become IT specialists in a relatively short time; the numbers of students graduating from these courses have now increased to over 800 per year. According to the Institute of Manpower Studies (IMS) reports, the graduate conversion courses have been well received by employers (Connor, 1985).

From the summary of the main landmarks relating to the growth of information technology in education and training provided in Table 6.1, it is clear that a number of significant initiatives have been centrally launched and funded since 1980. What is not clear, however, is that any links or coordination exist *between* the various schemes and initiatives. Certainly there is no guiding pattern or coherent picture of IT education from school level through to further and higher education.

For example, two adverse effects may have resulted from the growth of computing and IT courses in schools since 1981. First, the perceived nature of those courses and the resulting dominance by males may well have been a contributory cause to the declining number of women going on to computing courses in higher education and in turn the acute shortage of women in IT employment at graduate level and above. This issue was explored fully in work by Aylett (1986), Dain (1988) and others. Second, affecting both sexes of the population, a shortfall in the supply of science and technology graduates to employers may have been exacerbated by the growth of computer studies in schools. Teacher shortages in maths and physics must have contributed to this shortage during the decade. Evidence exists from several inquiries (for example, Straker, 1987; Wellington, 1989) that computer studies teachers were largely drawn from maths and the physical sciences. They were certainly not trained in their own right (Wellington 1984). Thus it can be postulated with the benefit of hindsight that the growth of school computing courses in the 1980s has contributed to teacher shortages in the foundation subjects for future science, technology and engineering graduates, in turn exacerbating the key shortages in parts of the IT industry.

Education and training in IT

Human resources are the key to the advanced information technology programme. Information technology is knowledge intensive and depends upon skilled manpower (Alvey Committee, 1982, para 7.1).

The notion that the IT industry is 'knowledge-intensive' is now a common one. But what does it mean? What are its implications for the education and training systems which have the job of producing the 'skilled manpower' required?

At one level, there is little evidence to show that *school* courses in IT are, or ever have been, a specified requirement of employers (Wellington, 1989). Inquiries since 1982 (summarized in Wellington, 1989) indicate that the key personnel shortages in IT are at graduate level and above.

The IMS examination (1986) of 'information technology manpower' (sic) predicted that IT skill shortages would remain a problem 'at least until 1990'. From their evidence, Connor and Pearson (1986) of the IMS estimated that demand for graduates for IT work would increase by 50 per cent by that time (although this has not been realized). The education system faces a huge challenge and certain fundamental problems (examined later) if the demands of a knowledge-intensive industry are to be met.

Strata in IT employment

The evidence cited above suggests that employment in relation to information technology is divided into strata or 'segments' (Brown and Ashton, 1987). Dore (1987) talked of a 'growingly institutionalised stratification in the youth employment market'. He suggested five levels:

> At the top are those in further and higher education with little fear of unemployment if they are not too selective about the jobs which they will take. One step down are those in apprenticeships and traineeships with a promotion future. Then come those who have some other regular job, even dead-end. Then come those on employer-based Youth Training Scheme (YTS) schemes or enrolled in YTS ITeC Centres. And finally come those who are on other YTS schemes – community projects and the like. It is a 'recognised hierarchy', and a unidimensional one, in the sense that there is a general agreement that anyone in a lower niche would probably acknowledge his preference for being in a higher one – if he could have succeeded in the competition to enter it. That perception colours both self-perceptions and employers' perceptions of employee desirability (p.217).

Up-skilling, de-skilling or polarization?

A parallel and closely connected debate concerns the issue of de-skilling, up-skilling and skill polarization as a result of new technology, including IT. There is a vast literature, which can only be touched upon here, on the issue of skill requirements and technological change. A starting-point lies in Braverman's thesis (1974) on the degradation of work in the twentieth century. Braverman argued that technological developments in this century are gradually bringing about de-skilling across the whole occupational structure. The trend is most marked at lowest levels ('the proletariat') and this brings about a polarization of skills by creating a small number of highly skilled intellectual and technical jobs. Ultimately even these latter jobs, he argued, may become de-skilled over time – perhaps Braverman was unwittingly anticipating expert systems and artificial intelligence now so prominent in IT research and development.

Braverman's thesis has been attacked by Attewell (1987) who, in his review of the de-skilling controversy, concludes that:

> Contra Braverman, de-skilling has not been the master trend of occupational change in the twentieth century, nor has it proven to be the fate of the proletariat as a whole (p.341).

From the manufacturing perspective, Zicklin (1987), in a more detailed empirical study of numerical control machining (NC) in the USA, suggests that there is no simple answer to whether machinists have been de-skilled; he concludes that:

> while Braverman deserves much praise for alerting us to the radical potential

of microelectronics to transform work, his assertion that the skilled machinist has been 'rendered as obsolete as the glassblower' ... seems more the simplification of ideological thinking than the fruit of careful research (p.463).

A useful framework for viewing new industrial structures and employment change in the future was suggested by Rothwell and Zegveld (1985). They showed how employment has evolved in advanced industrial societies from largely unskilled and labour-intensive to a more value-added, knowledge-intensive structure and argue that this shift has occurred in Britain and other nations as a result of evolving technology. The Japanese evolution has greatly influenced their education system, an influence analysed by Rothwell and Zegveld (ibid. pp.149–52). In particular, Japan made a massive investment in engineering education which created four times as many engineers per head of the population as in the UK.

A detailed analysis, based on more recent data is given by Gallie (1991). His main conclusions from a lengthy study are as follows: the use of advanced technology is generally associated with a rise in skill levels; men have 'benefited' to a much greater extent than women from the process of up-skilling; technological change is closely associated with the *polarization* of skills. He argues further that:

> The already major skills differentials between the intermediary and the non-skilled manual class appear to have been accentuated in the 1980s. Those that already had relatively higher levels of skill experienced an increase in their skill levels, while those with low levels of skill saw their skills stagnate (p349).

One final suggestion came from Sinfield (1981) in a discussion of unemployment ten years earlier. He suggested that one of the trends at the time, linked with growing unemployment, was that the 'frontiers of unemployability' are pushed forward. The *threshold of unemployability* may well be raised by technological change and the polarization of skills. This is a frightening prospect for both the education system and society as a whole.

Whilst the debate on the Braverman thesis will continue, it is clear that evolving patterns of work under the influence of technological change have far-reaching implications for education and training policy decisions. Far more research is needed from an educational perspective into this debate, perhaps along the detailed lines followed by Fitzgerald (1985). If there is any truth in the thesis that a highly skilled, technical élite of diminishing size will be required for future work, in contrast to an increasingly de-skilled 'proletariat' at the other end of the labour market, then how should education respond? The next section highlights some of the dangers and dilemmas faced by education in attempting to respond to the 'vocational imperative' associated with new technology.

Dilemmas

The general dilemma for IT as an element of vocational education is simply that vocationalism at one level may be counter-vocational when judged in the context of education for employment at all levels. This general dilemma is analysed below in terms of three sets of ideas: segmentation of the curriculum through initiatives such as TVEI and the CTCs; pipelines in education and training; and premature versus deferred vocationalism.

The segmented curriculum

First, one of the dangers of vocational education at secondary level is that it could result in a divided or segmented curriculum at too early an age. This was seen as one of the dangers of TVEI. If TVEI pupils are to be set aside within a school to follow a 'technical and vocational' curriculum they are being segmented from an academic curriculum, which may lead to higher education. With certain translations of TVEI into school practice, it may become 'the exclusive area for the less able pupil' (Blackman, 1987). Chitty (1986), for example, argued that, 'by its implicit operation TVEI will result in the re-emergence of the old hard-line tripartite system' (p.82) dating back to 1867 (Williams, 1961, p.159).

In previous labour markets such curriculum divisions, although arguably non-egalitarian, may not have mattered greatly since school-leavers were entering employment at a variety of levels from a range of educational backgrounds. But entry into IT employment is closely related to levels of education achievement (Wellington, 1989). TVEI pupils, as initially conceived, are unlikely to meet the pressing needs of employers in IT at key levels.

As yet, no evidence exists that TVEI courses in IT are a better preparation for employment, or are more demanded by employers, than other curricula (see Sims, 1989, for a study of employer relations to TVEI). Therefore, if they take pupils away from another course of education which is ultimately of more value to employers, then the TVEI could in fact prove to have been counter-vocational.

Similarly, the role of initiatives such as the City Technology Colleges needs to be examined. By providing an education with a scientific/technological bias, are CTCs segmenting the curriculum on the grounds of providing 'vocational relevance' for which there is little evidence? This issue will be explored in Chapter 7.

Pipelines in education and training

The notion of segmentation is related to the second instance of the general dilemma in vocational education. A simple but useful notion in considering education for employment is that of 'pipelines'. Pipelines into employment occur at several different levels from school-leavers at age 16 or above through YTS, to diploma, degree and postgraduate level. In certain areas of employment, such as biotechnology, the pipeline into employment is almost entirely at postgraduate level (Pearson, 1987). In other more traditional areas of employment such as manufacturing industry, entry has been through a variety of pipelines at different levels. The dilemma for vocational education is that a pipeline branching off from the mainstream at one level will reduce the flow at a later level – the analogy with fluid flow in a system of pipes or movement of electrical charges in branching circuits is an easy picture and a straightforward one. If initiatives are taken to create new pipelines into employment at certain levels, what side-effects will they have on the flow (pipeline) at later levels? The side-effects of central funding of education through specific grants have not been examined, or even perhaps anticipated. To pursue the fluid analogy, the creation of new pipelines has not been considered in the overall context of flow into employment generally.

For example, one pipeline which may have had serious side-effects is the Youth Training Scheme (including, especially in this context, the ITeC programme). It may be no coincidence that as YTS expanded in 1982–3, the number of pupils taking A-levels began to fall dramatically (Table 6.3). To attribute causality to the relationship may be unfounded, but there is surely a connection here. This was discussed by an all-party Commons Select Committee on Education in July 1986 (*TES*, 1986).

Premature and deferred vocationalism

Divisions and segmentation at the ages of 14 and 16 are important

Table 6.3 *Young people on A-level courses and YTS (as a percentage of 16-year-old population) from 1980–85*

	A-level pupils (%)	YTS/YOP (%)
1979/80	19.4	5.1
1980/81	19.6	9.6
1981/82	20.5	13.0
1982/83	20.3	18.2
1983/84	19.6	23.8
1984/85	19.2	25.8

Source: (*TES*, 1986)

factors in taking a holistic view of education for employment. Choices made at these ages are related to class, gender, parental pressure, financial situation, ethnic background and a host of interrelated factors (Banks *et al.*, 1991; Bates *et al.*, 1984; Brown and Ashton, 1987; Gray *et al.*, 1983; Grant, 1987). Within this, two notions worthy of consideration in this context are 'deferred vocationalism' (discussed earlier) and 'premature vocationalism'.

Evidence has suggested that many of the pressures to relate education to employment in information technology have led to premature vocationalism. Indeed the whole 'hi-tech bandwagon' (Norton-Grubb, 1984) created strong pressures for premature pipelines to employment which ironically are increasingly inappropriate in the knowledge-intensive IT industry (Alvey Committee, 1982) of the future. In Norton-Grubb's (1984) analysis of the American situation he points to several tendencies in education and training caused by premature vocationalism:

> One tendency is toward exaggeration, over-stating how many high-tech jobs will be available and over-promising what vocational education can do to solve the country's problems. Such over-promising can lead all too easily to preparing too many students for too few jobs, or to training students too elaborately for jobs that really need little more preparation than brief on-the-job training (p.450).

The tendency to overstate the numerical importance of high-tech jobs was prevalent in the launch of the 'Micros in Schools' scheme in the rhetoric behind TVEI and YTS, the stated objectives of the ITeC programme, and the launch of the CTCs. Similarly, Scheffler

(1991), from an American perspective, talks critically of the conviction that:

> ...training in computers would provide marketable skills to children growing up in an increasingly computerized world. The computer's role is that of a vocational educator, preparing the masses of our youth for jobs in the future (p.84).

The numerical importance and vocational significance of IT education has been considerably over-estimated:

> In the job market students will face when they leave school, the choice high tech careers will require many years of more professional and specialised education. Even so, those careers will be for the high-achieving few. For the many, the five most available jobs in the information economy will be janitors, nurses' aides, sales clerks, cashiers and waiters (Levin and Rumberger, 1983).

If indeed the requirement for IT personnel will increasingly be at a high level, the initiatives may prove to be 'counter-vocational' and self-defeating.

> ...training future skilled workers is likely to require higher educational levels than traditional craft apprenticeships. The key personnel in future growth industries and services will not offer craft-like skills. They will be designing and adapting new technologies for old and new products and markets. They will work in laboratories, drawing rooms, committees and task-forces with keyboards and print-outs rather than in traditional occupational committees. Training initiatives that endeavour to attract 16 year olds from full-time education could still prove self-defeating (Roberts, 1984, p.104).
> ...politics that continue to vocationalise public education at the expense of developing young people's literacy, work attitudes and abilities to compute and think will be a particular hardship for low-income students who are over-represented in vocational programs (Wilms, 1988, p.54).

Wilms' study of 172 firms in Los Angeles contradicts the 'conventional wisdom in the USA' that technology, job skills and vocational education are interrelated, a belief considered in Chapter 7 in the context of CTCs.

Another outcome of premature vocationalism and over-emphasis on the vocational significance of IT is the tendency towards a narrow skills-based approach to IT training, particularly where this occurs at the expense of basic abilities. A narrow skills-based approach to IT education will be counter-vocational in the 'information era'. Norton-Grubb (1984) supports this view in concluding his analysis of the American situation:

> ...in the high-tech area, the tendency towards specific skills is inappropriate because many students lack the general skills in science and maths that are prerequisites for further learning, and because the pace of change in high tech quickly makes specific skills obsolete (pp.410-11).

The notion of 'IT skills' and a framework for a future approach to IT as part of the work-related curriculum are discussed in Chapter 7.

Perhaps the only way to reconcile, or at least postpone, the premature vocationalism at 16 and the deferred vocationalism which still belongs to the 'middle classes' is to create a unified system of education and training for 16–19-year-olds which, however arranged, would be one way of helping the dilemmas for IT in vocational education. Those dilemmas involve the segmentation of the curriculum, the creation of financial support of the pipelines into employment with subsequent side-effects, and the conflict between premature and deferred vocationalism.

In essence, they arise because the short-term appeal of vocationalism is hard to resist in a time of high unemployment; however, its long-term consequences for the future of new technology industry may be disastrous. An over-emphasis on the vocational in the school curriculum and a desire to satisfy the immediate 'needs of industry' in school and youth training may in the long run prove to be counter-vocational, particularly if the crucial skill shortages continue to exist at the higher levels.

Education for employment in the 'information age'

The Crowther Report of 1959 spoke of the 'task of education in the technological age' as being a double one:

> On the one hand, there is a duty to set up young people on the road to acquiring the bewildering variety of qualifications they will need to earn their living. On the other hand, running through and across these vocational purposes, there is also a duty to remember those other objectives of any education, which have little or nothing to do with vocation, but are concerned with the development of human personality and with teaching the individual to see himself in due proportion to the world in which he has been set (p.53).

In the 30-odd years which have passed since Crowther's report, the West has moved some way towards the post-industrial society (Bell, 1974). Bell envisaged that the production of goods would require a decreasing labour force, while growth in employment would be mainly in the 'service areas'. At the same time, the 'post-industrial state' would be increasingly technocratic, with skills and education replacing birth and property as the basis of political power. Evidence considered earlier supports at least part of Bell's thesis, particularly his view of a 'technocracy' gaining importance in the information era.

Bell's predictions, made midway between Crowther and the present time, are being realized but change is still rapid and continuing. The adage that 'Constant change is here to stay' holds good. This remains the most important message for education in the technological age. Education must prepare people for change. Whiston *et al.*, (1980) made this point in collating available evidence on technological change and its influence on education:

> One of the problems with any study of the consequences of technical change for the training and educational requirements of jobs is that such studies have to operate to some extent in a static framework. It is quite conceivable that much employment in jobs requiring very high levels of education is related not to the particular state of technology at the time, but to its rate of change. Many highly trained and educated people may be needed to change the design of products, processes and organisations in an environment of rapid technological change. This applies not least to education itself, in which the teachers require constant re-education in order to equip themselves and their pupils for work and leisure in a changing world.

The rapidity of change makes any statement of specific skill requirements, and a narrow skills-based approach to IT education or training, totally obsolete:

> The rate of change of technology means that training should be based not on the understanding of a specific technology but on the ability to assimilate and gain an understanding of new technology as it appears (quoted in Wellington, 1989).

This discussion provides important pointers to the central question: what should be the aims of education in a technological age? Certainly they should include the ability to assimilate new knowledge and 'new technology as it appears'. This encompasses Taylor's (1985) notion of trainability. Writing in Worswick (1985), Taylor argues that even at graduate level employers are more concerned with 'trainability' than with specific skills and that:

> Ill-considered vocational specificity in schooling can produce training that reduces rather than enhances employability (Taylor, 1985, p.107).

Taylor's notion of 'trainability' as an aim of education is related to Dore's (1987) term, 'native abilities':

> The increasing sophistication of our technology (and I include our systems for gathering, sorting and evaluating information and processing it into decisions) makes native abilities – learning capacities, trainability – more important (p.213).

Dore's sentence in parentheses clearly refers to IT. His argument supports my contention that in a context of rapidly evolving information technology a narrow skills-based approach to IT education and training is of no long-term value.

The needs of employers are increasingly stated in such terms as motivation, willingness, awareness, ability to learn, communication, confidence and cooperative working – in short, a broad-based education involving literacy and numeracy with a growing emphasis on personal qualities. This is a position supported by an analysis of education and new technology by Jamieson and Tasker (1988):

> Ironically new technology places a premium on the fundamental skills of numeracy and literacy, and on the insights into the human condition provided by the humanities and social sciences.

Interestingly, this is remarkably similar to a point made eight years earlier by the Central Policy Review Staff (1980):

> ...we think there is some truth in the view that the qualities now emphasised in educational theory, such as resourcefulness, an enquiring mind, and enthusiasm are at least as appropriate for the jobs that will be available over the next twenty years as the rather dour and old fashioned views of obedience and discipline which were emphasised by some employers.

Evidence from the USA for an increasing convergence between the goals of vocational preparation and of personal development was presented by Chickering (1986) in summarizing the work of Klemp. Klemp and his research team identified successful individuals working in a variety of settings: civil service, small businesses, military, counselling, sales and so on. They examined the qualities which made them successful in their own role. Klemp consistently found three general abilities or characteristics. General cognitive abilities or skills were the first common factor: the ability to acquire and use knowledge. Second, they noticed that interpersonal skills contributed in all cases to success at work: communication, fluency, empathy and responsiveness. The third critical factor was motivation; without this characteristic, cognitive and interpersonal abilities would lack effectiveness.

Klemp's study may not apply to all the jobs which young people will acquire in a technological age – this might be to expect too much of future employment – but as educational goals, they relate closely to the goals of liberal education and the education of the individual. If vocational and technological education are correctly conceived, then their aims should coincide with those of a so-called liberal education:

> The antithesis between a technical and a liberal education is fallacious. There can be no adequate technical education which is not liberal, and no liberal education which is not technical; that is no education which does not impart both technique and intellectual vision. (A N Whitehead speaking in 1929, quoted by Marchello, 1987).

My final conclusion here is that IT should be used to enhance the worthwhile claims of education which will remain unchanged in a technological age:

> No matter how society changes, we must continue to train young people to speak and write clearly, to manipulate mathematical and logical concepts, to be familiar with history, literature and cultures, and to have an understanding of the world. The basic definition of an educated person will remain relatively stable (Marchello, 1987, p.565).

Jamieson and Tasker (1988) suggest in a similar vein that the most important task for education in the 21st century is to find 'a way of integrating the values and outlook of the humanities with the logic and language of the new technologies'.

In a context of continuing change the aims central to a broad-based education must remain constant. They must not be diverted by premature vocationalism, or by divisive curricula. They will be enhanced by the diffusion of information technology throughout education at all levels, by greater attention to equal opportunities and by a coherent, unified pattern of provision for the 16–19 age-group. Only along these lines will industry in the future be supplied with the personnel it needs at all levels.

References

Aleksander, I (1986) 'Information technology and the management of change', *Journal of Information Technology*, **1**, 1.

Alvey Committee (1982) *A Programme for Advanced Information Technology*, London: HMSO.

Attewell, P (1987) 'The deskilling and controversy,' *Work and Occupations*, **14**, 3, 323–46.

Aylett, R (1986) *Women and Computing in Sheffield City Polytechnic*, unpublished paper, Sheffield City Polytechnic.

Bailey, P (1986) *Computer Literacy: Notions, Courses and Perceptions*, unpublished M Ed Thesis, University of Sheffield.

Bates, I *et al* (1984) *Schooling for the Dole?: The New Vocationalism*, London: Macmillan.

Bell, D (1974) *The Coming of Post-Industrial Society*, London: Heinemann.

Blackman, S (1987) 'The labour market in school', in Brown, P and Ashton, D (eds), *Education, Unemployment and Labour Markets*.

Braverman, H (1974) *The Degradation of Work in the Twentieth Century*, New York: Monthly Review Press.

Brown, P and Ashton, D (1987) *Education, Unemployment and Labour Markets*, Lewes: Falmer Press.

Central Policy Review Staff (1980) *Education, Training and Industrial Performance*, London: HMSO.

Cerych, L (1985) 'Problems arising from the use of new technologies in education', *European Journal of Education*, **20**, 2–3.

Chickering, A (1986) 'The modern American college: integrating liberal education, work and development', in Burstyn, J (ed.), *Preparation for Life?*, Lewes: Falmer Press.

Chitty, C (1986) 'TVEI: the MSC's Trojan horse', in Benn, C and Fairley, J (eds), *Challenging the MSC*, London: Pluto Press.

Connor, H (1985) *The Destinations of 1984 IT Post-Graduate Students*, Brighton: IMS.

Connor, H and Pearson, R (1986) *Information Technology Manpower into the 1990s*, Brighton: IMS.

Crowther Report (1959) *15–18: A Report of the Central Advisory Council for Education*, London: HMSO.

CSE Microelectronics Group (1980) *Microelectronics: Capitalist Technology and the Working Class*, London: Conference of Socialist Economists.

Dain, J (1988) *Getting Women into Computing*, Research Report No.116, Department of Computer Science, University of Warwick.

Dale, R (ed.) (1985) *Education, Training and Employment: Towards A New Vocationalism?*, The Open University: Pergamon Press.

Department of Education and Science (1985) *Information Technology Initiative in the Public Sector of Higher Education*, Report by HMI.

Department of Trade and Industry (1985) *First Report: The Human Factor – the Supply Side Problem*, IT Skills Shortages Committee.

Department of Trade and Industry (1985) *Second Report: Changing Technology – Changing Skills: Shortages at Technician Level*, IT Skills Shortages Committee.

Department of Trade and Industry (1985) *Final Report: Signposts for the Future*, IT Skills Shortages Committee.

Dore, R (1987) 'Citizenship and employment in an age of high technology', *British Journal of Industrial Relations*, **25**, 2, 201–26.

Forrester, T (1985) *The Information Technology Revolution – The Complete Guide*, Oxford: Basil Blackwell.

Gallie, D (1991) 'Patterns of skill change: upskilling, deskilling, or the polarisation of skills?', *Work, Employment and Society*, **5**, 3, 319–51.

Gershuny, J I (1978) *After Industrial Society: The Emerging Self-Service Economy*, London: Macmillan.

Gershuny, J I and Miles, I D (1983) *The New Service Economy: The Transformation of Employment in Industrial Societies*, London: Francis Pinter.

Glyn-Jones, A (1984) *Job Skills in the Computer Age*, Devon County Council and The University of Exeter.

Grant, P (1987) *Youth, Employment and Technological Change*, Aldershot: Gower.

Gray, J, McPherson, A F and Raffe, D (1983) *Reconstructions of Secondary Education*, London: Routledge and Kegan Paul.

Harris, D (ed.) (1988) *Education for the New Technologies: World Yearbook of Education*, London: Routledge and Kegan Paul.

HMI (1992), *The Impact of the Information Technology in Schools Initiative 1988–1990*, Stanmore: DES.

Huxley A (1938) *Ends and Means*, London: Chatto and Windus.

Institute of Manpower Studies (1986) *Graduate Supply and Availability to 1987 and Beyond*, Brighton: Institute of Manpower Studies.

Jamieson, I and Tasker, M (1988) 'Schooling and new technology: rhetoric and reality', in Harris, D. (ed.), *Education for the New Technologies: World Yearbook of Education*, London: Routledge and Kegan Paul.

Jenkins, C and Sherman, B (1979) *The Collapse of Work*, London: Eyre Methuen Ltd.

Jones, K. (1980) *Microelectronics and Society*, Open University Press.

Levin, H and Rumberger, W (1983) 'The Educational Implications of High Technology', report of the Institute for Research on Educational Finance and Governance, Stanford University, February, p.5.

Manpower Services Commission (1985) *The Impact of New Technology on Skills in Manufacturing and Services*, Sheffield: MSC.

Marchello, J (1987) Education for a Technological Age, *Futures*, 555–65, October.

Naisbitt, J (1984) *Megatrends*, London: Futura.

Northcott, J (1986) *Microelectronics in Industry: Promise and Performance*, London: Policy Study Institute.

Norton-Grubb, W (1984) 'The bandwagon once more: vocational preparation for high-tech occupations', *Harvard Educational Review*, **54**, 4, November.

Pearson, R (1987) 'Key skills for biotechnology', in *Skill Needs for Technological Innovation*, Sheffield: MSC.

Roberts, K (1984) *School Leavers and Their Prospects – Youth and the Labour Market in the 1980s*, Milton Keynes: Open University Press.

Roszak, T (1986) *The Cult of Information: The Folklore of Computers and the True Art of Thinking*, Cambridge: Lutterworth Press.

Rothwell, R and Zegveld, W (1985) *Re-industrialisation and Technology*, London: Longman.

Scheffler, I (1991) *In Praise of the Cognitive Emotions*, London: Routledge.

Sendov, B (1986) 'The second wave: problems of computer education', in Ennals, R, Gwyn, R and Zdravchev, L (eds), *Information, Technology and Education*, Chichester: Ellis Horwood.

Sims, D (1989) *Leaving TVEI and Starting Work*, Sheffield: Training Agency.

Sinfield, A (1981) *What Unemployment Means*, Oxford: Martin Robertson.

Stonier, T (1983) *The Wealth of Information*, London: Methuen.

Straker, N (1987) 'Mathematics teacher shortages in secondary schools', *Research Papers in Education*, **2**, 2, 126–52.

Taylor, W H (1985) Productivity and Educational Values, in Worswick, G D N (ed.), *Education and Economic Performance*, Aldershot: Gower.

TES (1986) 'Government should monitor initiatives say committee', July 4.

Toffler, A (1970) *Future Shock*, London: Pan Books.

Touraine, A (1970) *The Post-Industrial Society*, New York: Random House.

Turkle, S (1984) *The Second Self: Computers and the Human Spirit*, London: Granada.

Weizenbaum, J (1984) *Computer Power and Human Reason*, Harmondsworth: Penguin Books.

Wellington, J J (1985a) *Children, Computers and the Curriculum*, London: Harper and Row.

Wellington, J J (1985b) 'Computers across the curriculum – the needs in teacher training', *Journal of Further and Higher Education*, **8**, 3, 46–53.

Wellington, J J (1989) *Education for Employment – the Place of Information Technology*, Windsor: NFER-Nelson.

Wellington, J J (1990) 'The impact of IT on the school curriculum', *Journal of Curriculum Studies*, **22**, 1, 57–76.

Whiston, T, Senker, P and Macdonald, P (1980) *An Annotated Bibliography on Technological Change and Educational Development*, Paris: Unesco.

Wilms, W (1988) 'Training for technology: a questionable investment', *International Journal of Educational Development*, **8**, 1, 43–54.

Worswick, G D N (ed.) (1985) *Education and Economic Performance*, Aldershot: Gower.

Zuboff, S (1988) *In the Age of the Smart Machine*, Oxford: Heinemann.

Zicklin, G (1987) 'Numerical control machining and the issue of deskilling', *Work and Occupations*, **14**, 3, 452–66.

7 Responding to the Technological Imperative: Two Examples of the CTC Programme in Practice

J J Wellington

This case-study will consider the notion of City Technology Colleges (CTCs) as a response to the perceived link between 'vocationally relevant' technological education and the needs of the economy in the future. It will consider the stated aims of the programme in centrally produced documents; the perceptions of the programme evident in other documents such as brochures and prospectuses; and finally, evidence from direct observation and discussion in two CTCs. The study will present in particular a framework for IT education based on the discussion in the previous chapter and link it with this study of the CTC programme in its approach to IT. The general aim of this case-study is thus to consider the role and philosophy of the CTCs and to pose questions of the programme in the context of IT.

Background and introduction

The CTC programme was announced by Kenneth Baker (then Secretary of State for Education) at the 1986 Conservative Party conference. The origins of the idea have been widely discussed (Edwards *et al.*, 1991; McCulloch, 1989; Walford and Miller, 1991), with explanations varying from the need for the energizing effects of greater diversity and competition (Edwards *et al.*, 1991), to the need for a concerted effort to promote secondary technical education after a century of failure (McCulloch, 1989) to the replication of the idea of 'magnet schools', emanating from the cities of the USA. Indeed, the DES document announcing the programme described them as 'beacons of excellence' (DES, 1986). One of its themes involved the idea of extending the 'range of choice for families in urban areas' by providing 'schools which measure up to their ambitions'. The same document talked of the CTCs providing an education with a 'strong technological element' thereby 'offering ... a surer preparation for adult and working life'.

Responses to the idea varied from 'a fundamental attack on comprehensive education', to the 'centrepiece of a new deal for the users of education', to 'a spearhead of Tory hopes of resurrecting a semi-independent sector outside of the control of LEAs' (Edwards *et al.*, 1991). The Conservative Party conference at which the announcement was made received the idea uncritically and enthusiastically however, and plans were set in motion for 20 colleges. It appears, with hindsight, that the start-up costs of the CTCs were greatly underestimated. The original promise of twenty looked unlikely early in 1992, by which time Kenneth Clarke (the then new Education Secretary) was promising additional cash to 'revive the flagging CTC programme' (*TES*, 1992). This report talked of the failure of the programme to attract substantial funding from private industry which had been the original aim. Nevertheless, by 1992 there were 15 colleges 'open or preparing to open', according to the CTC trust brochure.

The aims and philosophy of the CTCs: prospectuses and brochures

The brochure of the CTC trust, entitled 'A Good Education with Vocational Relevance', describes three benefits of the programme as 'imaginative use of IT across the curriculum', 'close links with industry, including early use of work experience' and 'experience of the world of work at an early age' (foreword by Kenneth Clarke). The technological/vocational imperative is not long in surfacing. On page 4, the chairman of the trust, Sir Cyril Taylor, talks of 'the urgent need for more schools teaching the technology skills required by British employers'. One is reminded here of the discussions in previous chapters in this book on first, the problematic notion of the needs of employers; second, the difficulty which employers have in identifying 'technology skills' of a specific kind and therefore the need to enter the problematic area of generic or transferable skills; and third, the employers reported by the Central Policy Review Staff in 1980 who actually preferred O-level physics to technology as a qualification, although they felt that the technology syllabus was more 'relevant'. Taylor goes on to quote Charles Handy's estimate that by the end of the century 'knowledge jobs' will account for 70 per cent of all jobs, requiring 'a skilled workforce to use their brains rather than their hands'. This estimate is not discussed further; presumably, readers are left to distil their own message from it. The complex issues linked to the notion of knowledge-intensive jobs (Alvey Committee, 1982), the level of education required to fill them and the problem of counter-vocationalism discussed in the previous chapter are left untouched.

Taylor instead goes on to outline the CTC curriculum which presumably follows (in his mind) as a result of his points about technology skills and the growth of knowledge jobs:

> ...50% of a CTC timetable from ages 11-14 is taken up by Maths, Science and Technology – a proportion which rises to 60% for ages 14-16 and sometimes to 100% for the over-16s.

Again, the reader is referred to Chapter 6 for a discussion of an appropriate curriculum for the information age with a rather different make-up – a broad-based and balanced curriculum.

The brochure goes on to discuss aspects of the CTCs' 'vocational relevance': 'they are sponsored by industry and maintain close links with local employers'; 'they seek to develop the qualities of enterprise, self-reliance and responsibility which young people need for adult life and work'. These qualities were discussed in an earlier chapter on the needs of employers.

Individual prospectuses

> Modern technology, active learning techniques and traditional teaching will provide our children with the skills which the world of industry and commerce is desperately seeking (taken from the prospectus of a CTC in an industrial town in the North of England).

The prospectuses of the individual CTCs make interesting reading and are well worth examining in the context of many of the discussions in this book, such as the 'needs of employers', the technological drive and the growth of IT education. The two case-study CTCs observed for this chapter both produced glossy, well-presented and readable brochures of their own.

In the first prospectus the opening paragraph came from the chairman of the major sponsor who talked of eagerly taking up the opportunity 'to interface truly in a major educational project' which appeared to be a 'unique plan to bridge the gap between the learning and work experience'. This foreword was followed by a piece from the Secretary of State at the time, John MacGregor, who described CTCs as, 'pioneering new teaching methods, new ways of managing schools and new approaches to science and technology'. The prospectus went on to present the curriculum of the college with some excellent photographic material. As for technology, the aim is to 'incorporate technology into all parts of the curriculum' and to 'produce young adults who are technologically competent and highly adaptable'.

The second CTC begins its prospectus with a foreword from the principal, who talks of 'rapidly developing times' and the need for a joint effort between parents, staff and industry to:

> tackle and respond quickly to the changing stresses and demands which life in a high technology society will place on us in years to come.

Whilst there are shades of technological determinism here (in the language used), the mood of the remainder of the prospectus is highly positive. It goes on to outline the difference between a CTC and other schools, including the:

> strong links with industry and business from year 1 onwards, providing invaluable experience of the world of work using the very latest computers, technical equipment and other vital tools.

Many schools and local authorities would disagree with the suggestion that 'strong links' are a distinguishing feature of a CTC but perhaps this can be forgiven. One of the aims of the college is later said to be to encourage 'an understanding of wealth creation, and a positive attitude towards industry and business'. The prospectus goes on to discuss the curriculum in more detail and the various 'Faculties' (take note) including the Centre for Industrial Studies and Library and Information Services. The work of the latter particularly will be commented on.

The mission statement of the same college talks in a similar vein of the unique opportunity of the CTC movement to 'explore fresh professional approaches ... as we move towards ... the post-information revolution era'. It also talks of preparation 'relevant to the needs of the next century as we perceive them to be from the viewpoint of the closing decade of this century'. This can be achieved by making 'particularly strong links with industry and commerce to ensure the vocational relevance of students'. As for technology and IT, the statement claims that 'we work in a technology-rich environment with a technology-rich curriculum', and later:

> The consequences of technological developments in equipment in general and in IT in particular will be effective across all areas of college work. Technology, its process and effect ... will pervade the entire curriculum as it does everyday life.

This is an interesting paragraph with tinges of technological determinism and an obscure use of the word 'effective' in the first sentence.

These are just some of the statements and aspirations printed in the various documents put out by the CTC trust and two of the CTCs. They do make interesting reading although, as with any documents of this kind, it may be unfair to attempt to read too much into them – they have many purposes, the least of which may be to describe.

Observations and interviews in two CTCs

CTC 1

The first CTC is located in an inner-city area of redbrick terraced houses and is easily identified by the three large satellite dishes outside its main entrance. Student intake is from the local area, with the average IQ quoted as being 'just over 90'. Pupils are selected by a 'written test' and interview, a potentially time-consuming process with over 400 applications for 168 Year 7 places in September 1992. Of these, perhaps 30 to 40 pupils will have an IQ of less than 80, and the present roll has 45 per cent of pupils on free dinners and 35 per cent from 'ethnic minorities' (cf. Walford and Miller, 1991, p.51). There are 45 teachers and 40 support staff – a very interesting ratio when compared with the relatively low numbers of support staff in other secondary schools. This was the staffing level for approximately 500 pupils from Years 7, 8 and 9 with roughly 50 students post-16. Whilst this level of staff would appear to be extremely generous it was made clear that the number of non-teaching staff would not go up significantly as the roll grew to its eventual 1100. Walford and Miller (1991) discuss the issue of staffing and class size in some detail in their study of Kingshurst CTC. My own impression here was that staffing is generous at present, although the class sizes in the lessons I observed would not be smaller than other inner-city schools. The main difference appears to be in the number of support staff and the way they were deployed, for example in managing the IT network.

IT is coordinated in the college through 'Library and Information Services'. The college has a network of around 100 Apricot computers at any one time, a machine with which they hope to go 'multi-media'. They also have a network of 24 RM Nimbus 186 machines with a 286 machine as server; however, this network is currently 'mothballed' and the college is hoping to sell them. This has obviously been a technological cul-de-sac for the CTC. The Apricots, however, seem to be well and widely used. There appears to be very little IT teaching as such, although the Year 7 pupils have an IT induction course and the IT facilities seem to be well and truly used across the curriculum. The college has a policy of a maximum of 12 Apricots in any one room, so that classes of say 24 will be seen split into two – one group with a teacher, the other with a member of the support staff.

The network system appeared to be easy to use with a log-in and a password giving access to the college menu. This included an impressive library system for the management of the library resources (incidentally, the college had no restrictions at all on the borrowing of books). Many items were available to pupils and teachers through the menu and network. These included PC GLOBE, an excellent program giving clear and well-displayed data for use in perhaps geography, science, general studies and other parts of the curriculum; many cross-curricular applications under the WINDOWS operating system; and a range of CD-ROMs such as the Hutchinson Encyclopedia, Guinness Disk of Records and Compton's Multimedia Encyclopaedia. The college was also about to install a CD-ROM with a ten-user licence for A-level mathematics.

It seemed, then, that the emphasis is clearly on cross-curricular work with non-subject-specific software. I observed one lesson, for example, where Year 8 pupils used the EXCEL spreadsheet (running under WINDOWS) to handle and display data, including simple calculations. Some had already used the same spreadsheet in a totally different context. The lessons involving IT were, it is worth noting, following the National Curriculum quite closely and deliberately.

The college was making its extensive IT facilities available to 'community users' of many kinds, including ex-pupils, pensioners and others in the locality. The impressive library was also openly available to the community.

The overall impression was one of general familiarity and ease from the staff and pupils with the IT facilities. The computers were there to be used and not admired, and access did not seem to be any problem with the current ratio of five students to each computer.

As for 'vocational relevance', the college did have its Centre for Industrial Studies but this was not in action at that time. The college was rethinking part of its 14–19 curriculum through the Technological Baccalaureate which would allow students to examine several occupational areas in some detail. It was also developing a Diploma of Vocational Education course and was involving industrialists in planning new courses such as Electronic Media Systems.

CTC 2

The second CTC is located one mile from its city centre, next to a dual carriageway in an area with a mixture of half-built new housing estates and old terraced streets. The college building was perhaps even more impressive than CTC 1, with a huge entrance hall and landings or galleries running off it. The whole building, like the first, was designed, decorated and equipped to a very high standard. Student intake was representative of the whole range and the pupils were from the inner-city area. A total of 430 students in Years 7, 8 and 9 had been selected through an NFER non-verbal reasoning test and group interviews in threes or fours. Again, demand for places had been high with 400 applicants for the present Year 7 group of 150.

For sheer numbers, the IT facilities were nothing short of impressive. The college was served by a NOVEL network and a total of 135 workstations. This was managed by the Department of Information Resources with a head recruited from a local school with considerable IT experience. The actual machines were more of a mixture than in the first CTC with an interesting blend of PCs, ten BBCs, several Archimedes and some Apples, one of which was used to do some very interesting embroidery. Again, the emphasis was clearly on IT across the curriculum with a library system, a Bulletin Board, and items available on the network such as a range of CD-ROMs including the Bible, various Encyclopaedias, Electromagnetism, the Guinness Book of Records again and a

World Atlas. For word-processing the college had WORKS, PAGEMAKER and other programs, and software such as PC-GLOBE, EXCEL and FUN WITH TEXT. Many applications were running under WINDOWS.

Again, in this case-study example, IT was being used across the curriculum to good effect with access available when and where pupils required it, perhaps not surprising with a computer:pupil ratio better than 3:1, although this would rise as more pupils came to the college.

General observations and conclusions

Leaving aside the political context, both CTCs were fascinating places to visit. One gains the impression that the staff and students somehow feel that they are special in some way – and indeed they are. Just to walk into the buildings as they are now, with their attractive decor, carpeted floors, extensive IT facilities and well-designed galleries, rooms and corridors is enough to give the impression of a privileged environment. These CTCs are indeed doing some impressive things and trying some interesting approaches. These include the Tec. Bac., the deployment of a large ratio of non-teaching staff (especially in CTC 1) and an approach to the National Curriculum which will not be constrained by rigid assessment requirements at Key Stage 4. The students have an obvious sense of enjoyment in their activity (including the extended school day), they exude self-esteem and a sense of being 'valued'.

The technological bias found in the brochures and prospectuses was not at all apparent in visiting the colleges. The 'strong technological element' spoken of in the DES document is not immediately obvious to the visitor, except through the wider availability of, and access to, IT facilities.

These case-studies have offered some brief comments on two CTCS based on observation and discussion. The aim of the remainder of this chapter is to consider those observations, and the stated aims of the CTC programme, as part of the wider context.

Issues for the CTCs

Feeling special

The visitor to a CTC has an intuition that the pupils and the staff feel 'special' in some way; indeed, this may even rub off on the visitor. This can be a very energizing and enabling feeling for those studying and working in a CTC. Within that context, neglecting the outside world, it can be very empowering. But does it have side-effects? There is a great danger that the special status and feeling of the CTC may have negative effects on other schools and children in the area. Walford and Miller (1991) talk of the side-effects of selection. Although CTCs do not cream-off the higher ability pupils, some children mistakenly confused selection with 'selection by ability' (p.119). Those who are not selected, and their parents, experience disappointment and even anger. They often do not understand the reason for not being accepted; this may well result in negative feelings, reduced self-esteem and lack of motivation. This seems to be an issue which has not been fully explored and yet is a vital one for considering the wider effects of programmes such as the CTC, especially when four times as many pupils are rejected as are accepted and the grounds for selection and rejection may not be as clear as they were, say, with the 11-plus examination.

Vocational relevance

The CTC trust document talks of a good education with 'vocational relevance'. Observation suggests that perhaps this is not as prominent in the CTC as might be expected, and is probably no more a feature of the curriculum than in many comprehensive schools.

Several commentators on the CTC programme have criticized the crude notion of vocational relevance and the idea of a technologically-oriented curriculum preparing students for the demands of a modern industrial society (Edwards *et al.*, 1991). McCulloch (1989) talks of the promotion of the CTCs implying a 'simple and unproblematic relationship between "practical" education and the needs and demands of the "world of work"'. By considering the history of technical education, he argues that this connection is far from the truth, and historically employers have not supported direct links with schools (for example, the secondary technical schools) which aimed to produce leavers appealing directly to industry and commerce. There may not be as close a comparison between those examples from the past – the 'prep schools of industry' (McCulloch, 1989, p.36) – and the CTCs as he suggests, but it can certainly be said that industry did not provide the level of sympathy and support for the programme that was expected.

The notion of narrow vocational relevance was also questioned when the concept of CTCs was first launched. The *Times Educational Supplement* in May 1987 wrote of the danger of a new promise to employers and the 'limited view of the skills they need at any time from school leavers' taken by commerce and industry. The article concluded:

> It has to be the job of real schools – even CTCs – to prepare students for something beyond immediate demands and horizons foreshortened in job terms (Nash, 1987).

Interestingly, this accords with a study of pupils' attitudes to schooling carried out earlier in that decade (Grant, 1987) which found that schools where pupils follow a vocational curriculum are not always seen by their pupils as more satisfactory in preparing them for work. Indeed, the detailed study of choice at Kingshurst CTC carried out by Walford (1991a) showed that, in brief, pupils chose the CTC because they saw it as providing a 'better education' – the technological emphasis of the curriculum was *not* one of the major reasons why children wanted a place.

IT policy

The IT policy of CTCs has not been studied in detail. From very limited observation in the two case-study colleges, it is clear that, despite some of the narrow and technologically deterministic statements in the documents cited above, they have adopted a very *healthy* attitude to the use of IT in education. Indeed, similar approaches (though with less resourcing) can be found in many comprehensive schools which have adopted an open, cross-curricular attitude to IT in the curriculum, particularly where IT use is seen as an important component of a good, general education.

Following on from discussions in the previous chapter it can be suggested that approaches to IT as an element of the vocational curriculum form a spectrum (see Figure 7.1).

One approach, which seemed prominent in the early days of IT in education, concentrated on specific skills and was often bound up with the notion of 'computer literacy'; the emphasis was on the development of IT skills and the drive to make people computer literate. This approach is no longer tenable for a number of reasons: employers do not specify their requirements in terms of particular IT skills (Wellington, 1989); the pace of change of technology makes a narrow, skills-based approach inappropriate;

Figure 7.1 *IT as part of a vocational curriculum: a spectrum of approaches*

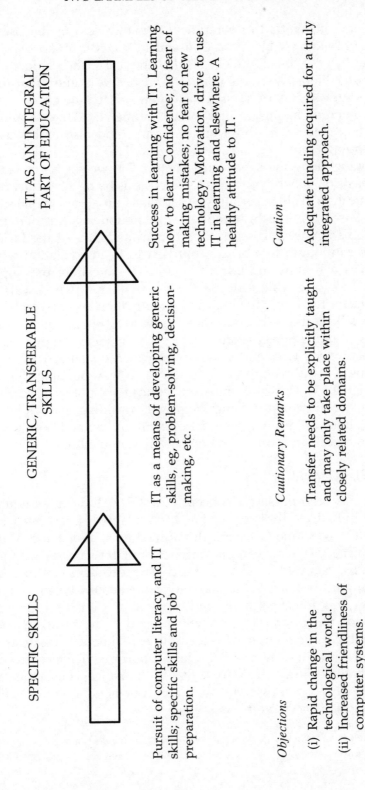

SPECIFIC SKILLS

GENERIC, TRANSFERABLE SKILLS

IT AS AN INTEGRAL PART OF EDUCATION

Pursuit of computer literacy and IT skills; specific skills and job preparation.

IT as a means of developing generic skills, eg, problem-solving, decision-making, etc.

Success in learning with IT. Learning how to learn. Confidence; no fear of making mistakes; no fear of new technology. Motivation, drive to use IT in learning and elsewhere. A healthy attitude to IT.

Objections

(i) Rapid change in the technological world.
(ii) Increased friendliness of computer systems.
(iii) IT skills not specified by employers.

Cautionary Remarks

Transfer needs to be explicitly taught and may only take place within closely related domains.

Caution

Adequate funding required for a truly integrated approach.

each new generation of computers demands less of the user in terms of IT knowledge *per se*. Consequently, commentators such as Roszak (1986) have attacked what he calls the 'chimera of computer literacy'. In a similar vein, it can be argued that there is no such category of 'IT skills' as a new or separate group which have emerged alongside literacy and numeracy. They should be seen as a sub-set of those broader aims, and also as a way of developing them.

Moving along the spectrum in Figure 7.1, we see an increased emphasis on generic or transferable skills as being a product of IT in education. This is certainly an advance on a narrow, specific-skills-based approach, although the notion of transfer is a problematic one, as discussed earlier in the book. At the far end of the continuum is a broad approach to IT in education which involves a healthy attitude to IT and IT education: developing confidence, removing fear, making IT an integral part of learning and the curriculum, thus improving motivation and drive and the much talked about 'learning how to learn'. This is the approach observed in the two case-study CTCs and in some comprehensive schools, which is so encouraging but which does need adequate funding. IT, in this approach, is seen as a way of enhancing the traditional, worthwhile aims of education, not a means of displacing them or replacing them with a shifting, narrow brand of 'IT skills'. Ironically, the ideal curriculum for the information/ technological age is not a technologically-oriented one.

The CTC concept

There has been no single concept of a 'CTC'. Indeed, as with so many initiatives, the concept has been adapted, interpreted and distorted over time (a point fully argued by Walford and Miller, 1991). The CTCs have been variously put forward as magnets, flagships, catalysts for change, beacons of excellence, a means of breaking the mould of secondary education, a new type of school, and an area for experiment and innovation. Can the individual CTCs and the programme as a whole be any of these things? There is a problem in seeing them as areas for experiment or catalysts for change in that the level of financial support they have received is on a totally different scale from that of the typical comprehensive school. This point was made quite vehemently by the *Times Educational Supplement* in 1988:

> Just what sort of a public education initiative is it which puts up £9 million from public funds for a private school? And just what sort of priorities are

being pursued when one private school gets £9.05 million, while the county of Nottinghamshire's entire capital allocation is less than £2.5 million? (*TES*, 1988)

The same point was vividly illustrated by Chitty (1988) who commented that the government,

> will spend £33 million on three CTCs in 1989 – some £3 million more than has been set aside for the introduction of the National Curriculum into all 30,000 schools in the country.

How can lessons be learnt and transferred from one domain to another when the circumstances and support are so vastly different? In addition, the relationships between the local authority and schools on the one hand and the CTC on the other, are not good to say the least. The necessary contact, communication and sharing which might allow catalysis and learning to take place are clearly lacking in my observations – a point, incidentally, which saddened the CTC staff I spoke too.

This lack of contact and sharing also undermines the concept of the CTC as a beacon of excellence or a flagship. Teachers will not see them as either of these things if there is just no basis for realistic comparison. Similarly, the concept of the CTCs as 'magnets' has little grounding in reality. Walford (1991b) suggests from his analysis of the magnetism notion that they may act more as a source of resentment than a 'competitive spur'. From his detailed study of one CTC, he concludes that, 'there is a fundamental conflict between its role as a magnet school and its private status' (p.174).

The main lesson which can be learned from observing CTCs in action comes from the sheer excitement of seeing just what can be achieved with inner-city children from a range of abilities given an adequate level of resourcing and a sense of being valued in both staff and students. The alleged technological bias and vocational relevance of the curriculum are of no apparence or importance. What really matters is the excitement, the special feeling, the self-esteem, the easy access to information and the technology for handling it, and the ethos of activity and learning that can be generated by putting students and teachers in an attractive, modern, well-resourced environment. This is the lesson which can be learned for comprehensive education. If all comprehensive schools were designed, modernized and equipped to this level, we could then truly have secondary education for the information age.

References

Chitty, C (1989) 'City Technology Colleges: a strategy for elitism', *Forum*, **30**, 37–40.

DES (1986) *A New Choice of School: City Technology Colleges*, London: DES.

Edwards, T, Gerwirtz, S and Whitty, G (1991) 'From assisted places to City Technology Colleges', in Walford, G (ed.) *Private Schooling: Tradition, Change and Diversity*, London: Paul Chapman.

McCulloch, G (1989) 'City Technology Colleges: an old choice of school?', *British Journal of Educational Studies*, **XXXVII**, 1.

Nash, I (1987) 'Trust may force sale of sites for CTCs', *Times Educational Supplement*, 22 May.

TES (1988) 'Editorial', 27 May.

TES (1992) 'Clarke promises cash cure for CTCs', *Times Educational Supplement*, 27 March, 1.

Walford, G (1991a) 'Choice of school at the first CTC', *Educational Studies*, **17**, 65–75.

Walford, G (1991b) 'City Technology Colleges: a private magnetism?', in Walford, G (1991a), op cit.

Walford, G and Miller, H (1991) *City Technology College*, Buckingham: Open University Press.

SECTION 4

Student Identity and the Work-related Curriculum: Vocational Initiatives Make Way for a New Era

The aim of this section is to consider the vocational imperative from the perspectives of the student and of his or her curriculum.

Millman begins the section by examining the position of the student from one perspective – that of gender. She discusses the issue of gender inequalities at the interface between education and work, and goes on to present the policies and practices of one region in attempting to tackle those inequalities. A framework is put forward as a means of placing gender equality at the centre of curriculum planning rather than its periphery. By considering three selected cases, the practical value of this framework is examined.

Millman weighs up the relative impacts of TVEI and the 1988 ERA in creating a context for addressing gender in the work-related curriculum. She suggests that TVEI did succeed in increasing the emphasis on monitoring and analysis of gender differences in pupil performance in secondary schools; however, the implementation of the 1988 Act – in particular through Local Management of Schools and the National Curriculum – has not always aided that emphasis. The renewed dominance of the subject curriculum, the complex organizational structure of many secondary schools, and the reduced capacity of local education authorities to support gender policies, present a considerable challenge to teachers in the future.

MacLure and Stronach follow the theme of the National Curriculum by considering the 'pupil identities' which emerge from their own reading of NCC documents; these identities largely involve the relationship of pupils to their future role as citizens and workers. They identify and discuss implicit views of students such as 'consumer', 'producer' and 'middle manager', and go on to discuss the pupil attributes and virtues that seem to be embedded in National Curriculum texts. Among the many important messages in this chapter is their illumination of the way in which some of the 'contradictory accretion' of vocational initiatives from 1976 to 1990 have become embedded in the National Curriculum.

Jamieson examines further the position in the new curriculum of work-related teaching and learning. He outlines the four central concerns which shape the work-related curriculum: concerns about the economy; school-to-work transition; curriculum relevance; and the need for educated citizens. Despite these four clear concerns, we still lack a coherent conception of the work-related curriculum. Its implementation in practice, Jamieson argues, is affected by a number of complex factors. In addition, its status in the National Curriculum, the guidance offered by NCC documents and its interpretation by teachers, are problematic. Jamieson concludes by raising questions about the future of work-related teaching and learning in the context of recent educational change. He talks of the 'new unleashed forces of the market' which now dictate changes in schooling and education and which may well remove work-related activities in the curriculum. It seems an interesting irony that the very market forces and pleas for economic relevance and efficiency which gave rise to vocationalism may now contribute to its downfall.

8 Gender Equality in the Work-related Curriculum: Policies and Practices in One Region

Val Millman

Introduction

The interface between education and the workplace has always been the point at which gender inequalities have been most sharply revealed. The divergence of young women and young men into different areas of the adult workforce and their subsequently differentiated career paths and earning power have for many decades raised questions about the nature of the education that has preceded or predetermined these routes (Weiner, 1989). In the early 1990s, as girls begin to 'overtake' boys in overall school examination performance at age 16 (see Table 8.1), questions need to be addressed towards women's continued under-representation in many areas of public and working life (see Table 8.2).

In Britain and elsewhere, such questions have been repeatedly asked by a variety of organizations during the past decade; on occasions, funding has been specifically directed towards seeking answers. Indeed, one of the first national projects in Britain to explore gender equality in schooling, undertaken by the Schools Council in 1981–3, was a response to a draft resolution from the EEC in 1979,

concerning measures to be taken in the field of education to improve the preparation of girls for working life and to promote equality of opportunity for girls and boys in society (Millman and Weiner, 1985, p.12).

Table 8.1 *16-year-old pupils in England 1989–90. Results graded from A–C at GCSE for selected subjects (DES, 1991)*

	Boys	*Girls*	*Total*
Any subject (000s)	**177.5**	**197.7**	**375.2**
Any subject (%)	60	69	64
English	40	57	48
Mathematics	36	33	35
Single/dual award sciences	13	13	13
Technology	18	5	12
Physics	19	9	14
Chemistry	14	12	13
Biological sciences	11	17	14
Other sciences	1	1	1
Geography	20	17	19
History	15	18	17
Creative arts	16	27	21
French	16	25	20
German	6	10	8
Spanish	1	2	1
Other modern languages	1	1	1
Religious education	4	9	7
Computer studies	6	5	5
Business studies	5	11	8
Home economics	1	16	8
Classical studies	2	3	2

This chapter will first consider briefly the way in which gender equality issues and strategies have developed in the school curriculum over the past ten years, in particular through the impact of the Technical and Vocational Education Initiative (TVEI) and the 1988 Education Reform Act, both of which have shaped the context for gender equality and the work-related curriculum in the early 1990s. Second, the chapter will suggest a framework for placing gender equality at the centre of curriculum planning and evaluation. It will then go on to consider how aspects of this

Table 8.2 *Occupational employment by sex (United Kingdom)*

Occupation	1971			1981			1990			2000		
	M %	F %	Total 000's	M %	F %	Total 000's	M %	F %	Total 000's	M %	F %	Total 000's
Managers and Administrators	79.1	20.9	2,661	76.3	23.7	3,043	72.2	27.8	3,675	69.0	31.0	4,139
Professional Occupations	68.1	31.9	1,546	63.4	36.6	2,041	61.9	38.1	2,633	60.3	39.7	3,192
Associate Professionals and Technical	59.5	40.5	1,514	54.7	45.3	1,818	52.4	47.6	2,151	50.2	49.8	2,487
Clerical and Secretarial	33.6	66.4	3,982	27.6	72.4	4,031	23.5	76.5	4,437	20.8	79.2	4,435
Craft and Related	87.3	12.7	4,673	89.5	10.5	4,053	90.0	10.0	4,048	91.8	8.2	3,789
Personal and Protective Service	38.0	62.0	1,423	35.1	64.9	1,618	32.5	67.5	1,873	33.1	66.9	2,067
Sales Occupations	46.6	53.4	1,605	40.0	60.0	1,672	33.9	66.1	2,074	32.5	67.5	2,141
Plant and Machine Operatives	75.1	24.9	3,548	77.3	22.7	2,884	76.6	23.4	2,563	79.4	20.6	2,198
Other Occupations	59.7	40.3	3,213	50.3	49.7	2,850	44.2	55.8	2,703	39.5	60.5	2,521
All Occupations	63.5	36.5	24,165	59.4	40.6	24,010	55.7	44.3	26,157	54.0	46.00	26,969

Source: Institute for Employment Research, Review of the Economy and Employment Occupational Assessment 1991, University of Warwick, Coventry, 1991.

framework relate to initiatives taking place in Coventry by describing three selected cases:

1. work experience placements on employers' premises for teachers;
2. course development within education-industry partnership centres;
3. school-based curriculum initiatives drawing on outside resources.

Unfortunately it is not possible within the ambit of this chapter to explore how perspectives such as 'race', 'class' and 'disability' impinge on that of gender equality in the context of the work-related curriculum either in theory or in the context of the three cases of initiatives that are presented. The fact is, these other perspectives do significantly impinge. Therefore, although it is likely that the gender equality issues identified in this chapter apply to all young people, it is also likely that they apply differentially and unequally across the experiences of different ethnic groups, different economic groups and across varying degrees of ability and disability. Much work in this area remains to be done.

Gender issues in education: the background and context for the 1990s

The impact of the TVEI project

Throughout the past decade, developments on gender equality in education have been stimulated and shaped by a variety of influences and 'interest groups'. Between them they have kept gender issues on the agenda (Weiner, 1989) through a period of unprecedented change which has substantially re-ordered the pieces in the educational jigsaw of earlier years. Increased concern for issues of equality and justice in the early 1980s and the practical response to this concern by a number of local education authorities combined, sometimes uncomfortably, in the mid- and late 1980s with an anticipation of skill shortages in the labour market. The latter brought with it an emphasis on the need for equal opportunities to be a key feature of government education and training initiatives. The TVEI project, which was launched in pilot authorities in 1983, was a significant example of this. Its first criterion was that:

Equal opportunities should be available to young people of both sexes and they should normally be educated together on courses within each project. Care should be taken to avoid stereotyping (MSC, 1984).

TVEI's contractual arrangements with LEAs and its identification of equal opportunities as its first criterion resulted in a sharp rise in the profile of gender equality on the agendas of many education authorities which had previously not addressed the issues. However, there was an initial failure to draw on what had been learnt from earlier development work on gender equality in pioneering authorities and schools (Herbert, 1985); little account was taken, for example, of differences between anti-sexist and equal opportunities frameworks and strategies (Millman and Weiner, 1987; Weiner, 1986). Many of those who had management responsibility for equal opportunities in early TVEI projects felt under pressure to 'deliver' equality as quickly and visibly as possible. This often resulted in superficial definitions of 'the problem' and superficial, sometimes counter-productive, solutions.

However, TVEI succeeded in bringing into project secondary schools an increased emphasis on the monitoring and analysis of gender differences in pupil performance. Early analysis of TVEI project take-up, subject take-up and outcome data revealed many girls and boys moving from a sex-stereotyped curriculum at 14-plus to sex-stereotyped education, training and career destinations at post-16, despite the project's stated commitment to equal opportunities (Millman, 1985). At first, over-simplistic solutions were derived from this analysis, for example focusing on girls' unwillingness to choose newly-developing technology courses. Strategies for change concentrated on trying to persuade girls to take 'non-traditional' courses either through 'counselling' or through making such courses compulsory for all. Neither strategy resulted in the scale of changed performance that many people had hoped for and it was only later acknowledged that more deep-seated changes needed to take place in curriculum content and pedagogy.

By the late 1980s many TVEI projects had recognized that the locus for change had to be more broadly defined and schools were developing a variety of strategies for moving towards gender equality. This included positive action strategies that were located in both the planned and hidden curriculum of the school (Bridgwood and Betteridge, 1989; MSC, 1987; Skinner and Jones, 1987). At national level the TVEI project recognized that performance indicators relating to gender equality needed to be identified *within* each area of priority identified by local projects as well as at times being a discrete focus for action (Training Agency, 1991).

The effect of the 1988 Education Act

By 1990 the majority of local education authorities had developed equal opportunities policies. In different areas, however, there were considerable variations in the priority and resources given to policy implementation; schools and colleges were therefore at a variety of stages in the development of their own policies and action plans. The introduction of the Local Management of Schools has recently reduced the capacity of local education authorities to influence and support school practice on equal opportunities except through those advice and support services which schools continue to use. Schools have therefore moved into local management equipped to varying degrees to integrate gender equality perspectives in their responses to the 1988 Education Reform Act and in particular in their plans for implementing the National Curriculum.

The Education Reform Act has provided schools with a context for both the work-related curriculum and equality of opportunity which is riven with contradictions. Much has been made of the National Curriculum being an 'entitlement' curriculum; time will tell the extent to which its particular definition of entitlement brings about equality for all groups of pupils. The Act's emphasis on monitoring of performance and reporting to parents has stimulated analyses of test and examination data which will be one means of testing reality against rhetoric over a significant period of time. The National Curriculum Council (NCC) has published guidance for schools, repeatedly underlining the importance of equal opportunities 'permeating' the whole curriculum. The Council's Guidance on Economic and Industrial Understanding and on Careers Education makes practical suggestions to teachers on how this dimension can be applied to curriculum planning and delivery. Unfortunately, however, the notion of permeation stops with the non-statutory guidance; the statutory orders make little overt reference to gender equality.

The context for the 1990s

The 1990s agenda for gender equality in the school curriculum therefore sees contradictions emerging which are reminiscent of the TVEI experience in the 1980s, albeit within radically changed educational structures (Burchell and Millman, 1989). For a variety of reasons, the emphasis on the work-related curriculum has increased at the same time as has the need to address factors other than level of examination performance which lead to differentiated outcomes for young women and men in the workplace. The rhetoric of equal opportunities is now a familiar part of educational and employment agendas.

Although resources directed at equality issues *per se* have diminished dramatically in recent years within the education service there are many secondary school teachers who have not only demonstrated their adeptness at working through the earlier contradictions of the TVEI project, but who also now have heightened awareness of gender issues and considerable experience of gender equality strategies. In the 1990s these teachers will be strongly placed to continue to identify equality perspectives in work-related curriculum initiatives. Much has been learnt from the variety of gender equality initiatives that teachers developed in the 1980s that is applicable to educational change and development today.

However, the wider arena for stimulating, implementing and monitoring changed practice on gender equality has substantially changed. This arena, together with the roles and responsibilities of its key players, will need to be closely examined to guard against the re-invention of wheels that took place in the early days of the TVEI project. Resourcing of the work-related curriculum is increasingly dependent on a variety of sources together representing a diversity of policies on equal opportunities. There is thus a danger of separately-funded 'one-off' curriculum initiatives, which carry confusing and inconsistent messages to pupils; or short-term initiatives increasingly constrained by the uncertainties of annual budgetary reviews, which are unlikely to achieve the aim of embedding gender equality into on-going educational practice.

The more widely schools choose to cast their nets for resources and services to contribute to the work-related curriculum, the more explicit they will need to be to outside organizations about their equal opportunities policies, the more they will also have to guard against the temptation to make unacceptable compromises. They will need to make clear their expectations that pupils' curriculum experiences will be consistent with equal opportunities policies, whatever the mode and locus of curriculum delivery. Furthermore, they will need to ensure that their female and male pupils are aware of their entitlement to equality of opportunity and are well-equipped to recognize for themselves where their experiences fall short.

So far, the 1990s have seen a significant increase in numbers of organizations who recognize the economic, social and moral imperatives behind equal opportunities policies. It is therefore likely that the work-related curriculum will be increasingly shaped by organizations who are familiar with the rhetoric of equality of opportunity but whose practices remain diverse. Equality for female and male pupils will depend, above all, on the extent to which both schools and employers are prepared to put gender equality at the centre of their own development plans as organizations and communities.

A framework for planning and evaluation

In working with partner organizations on work-related curriculum planning, development and delivery, whether taking place within or beyond the school, schools will therefore need to do what they can to achieve maximum coherence. While recognizing that day-to-day school life makes complete coherence an impossible goal, schools will nevertheless need to aim at ensuring the following:

- that aspects of the work-related curriculum are planned and delivered within a well-co-ordinated whole-curriculum framework so that, for example, pupils can see the relationship between the responsibilities of the workplace and the responsibilities of the home;
- that female and male pupils have equal access to all aspects of the work-related curriculum and that its content and organization recognize the different experiences, perspectives and aspirations they may bring with them, while at the same time aiming to extend these beyond stereotyped boundaries;
- that strategies designed to raise pupil awareness of gender equality issues relate directly and practically to pupils' lives, and do not suffer from 'overkill'.
- that the deployment of staff in the planning and delivery of the work-related curriculum reflects the aims of the school's equal opportunities policy, and that opportunities are taken to involve other women and men in presenting a wide range of role models;
- that gender equality perspectives are consistently represented

within cross-curricular areas such as the work-related curriculum as well as within the core and foundation subjects;

- that there are explicit equal opportunities (gender) objectives within any set of objectives established for work-related programmes;
- that pupils' assessment objectives and modes of assessment recognize the range of preferred approaches and styles of both female and male pupils;
- that structures established for managing and reviewing work-related curriculum initiatives include mechanisms for integrating equality perspectives in their planning and delivery, by including the school equal opportunities coordinator for example;
- that materials acquired and developed for use in the work-related curriculum are consistent with the school's equal opportunities policy on gender equality;
- that all involved in the planning and delivery of the work-related curriculum, both within and outside the school, are aware of the equal opportunities policies of the organizations involved and clear about the gender equality objectives to which the programme is committed;
- that all the parties involved – pupils, teachers, employers, LEA advice and support services, community organizations – have a clearly defined role in monitoring the gender equality dimension of the work-related curriculum and are equipped to carry out this role.

Equal opportunities in practice

Coventry: policy and practice

Coventry is a compact cosmopolitan city of over 300,000 people situated in the West Midlands. Having suffered devastating war damage, the city took great pride in its successful post-war reconstruction and economic boom, which was largely as a result of its expanding manufacturing industries. Since that time the city has weathered periods of recession and high unemployment; most recently it has witnessed the beginnings of a contraction of its manufacturing base and the relocation of new businesses to the city. Despite increasing diversification, the latest recession has had a significant impact on the training and job opportunities open to young people at 16-plus.

Coventry's Education Service has a tradition of responsiveness to changing trends in the local employment situation. Its Careers Service is decentralized, with careers officers being placed in each secondary school, which facilitates close links between educational and employment initiatives. Secondary school work-experience placement programmes are centrally co-ordinated through the Careers Service; in recent years all pupils have continued to have two-week work placements in Years 10 and 11 and increasing access to a variety of post-16 work-experience opportunities. The Careers Service has a well-developed equal opportunities policy and its representatives have been well-placed to bring gender equality issues to the forefront of initiatives such as COMPACT, the city-wide work experience programme, the central INSET programme and the Education-Business Partnership.

The Education-Business Partnership consists of local authority education department, Training and Enterprise Council and employer representatives. The purpose of the Partnership is to give greater coherence to the resourcing, planning and evaluation of local education-industry initiatives. One of Coventry's major initiatives has been the funding and establishment of five Partnership centres, each based in accommodation dedicated by a local employer to the support of the work-related curriculum of both primary and secondary schools and to programmes aimed at adult returners to education. The Partnership centres are staffed by employees of the 'host' employer and employees of the city education department. Pupils attending programmes at the centres are accompanied for some of the time by their teachers. One of the Partnership's strategic initiatives for 1991–3 was to promote modules of activity aimed at positively promoting interest in occupational areas traditionally associated with a single gender.

Since Coventry City Council published its new equal opportunities policy in 1990, the education department has identified its own equal opportunities action plan for those initiatives and services for which it is responsible; schools which have adopted City Council policy have been invited to do the same. Both equal opportunities and the work-related curriculum initiatives have therefore enjoyed a heightened profile in recent years in Coventry, although, as elsewhere, this has been 'in competition' with the statutory requirements of the National Curriculum and a diminishing level of overall resource within the education department and in many schools. The fact that the cases reported below are only a handful of the range of initiatives on gender equality and the work-related curriculum undertaken by teachers is testament to their commitment, resilience, expertise and that of their partners in the process.

The following cases of initiatives undertaken in Coventry aim to illustrate ways in which gender equality can be a significant dimension of the work-related curriculum in schools and colleges. The cases selected are from those aimed at 14–19-year-old students which have taken place since the introduction of the Education Reform Act in 1988. As they are those with which the author has had particular contact in her role as education adviser for equal opportunities, these brief accounts are likely to be described from an advisory service perspective rather than that of a school or a college. The three cases selected are:

1. Work-experience placements on employers' premises for teachers.
2. Course development within Education-Business Partnership centres.
3. School-based curriculum initiatives drawing on resources from outside the school.

These aim to illustrate the diversity of contexts within which aspects of the work-related curriculum operate and the complex requirement this therefore places on a range of individuals and organizations to ensure that equal opportunities policies are consistently and coherently implemented.

Each account will describe the aims of the initiative and its context, followed by a brief analysis of the extent to which the approach adopted towards gender equality was successful. This analysis will make general reference to the planning and evaluation framework outlined earlier.

Case 1: Work experience on employers' premises for teachers

The brief of the TVEI project's Equal Opportunities Curriculum Group for 1990/91 was 'Gender Equality and the Work-Related Curriculum' (Coventry City Council, 1993). The group consisted of five teachers seconded for a morning a week from comprehensive and special schools and from one of the further education colleges. One of the group's major tasks was to add to the guidance already offered to schools on the preparation of pupils for work experience by focusing particularly on gender equality issues.

In addition to the group's researches into existing approaches to this aspect of work-experience programmes in schools and colleges, two of the teachers decided that their own experience of placements with employers might usefully inform the guidance that they developed.

The two teachers discussed their proposal with colleagues in their schools, both in relation to arrangements for their release from teaching and to how their secondment experience might feed into school-based developments on their return. Both teachers had responsibility for coordinating gender equality initiatives in their schools. They subsequently negotiated five-day placements at two Coventry banks through Coventry's teacher placement service.

The aim of their placements was:

> to develop an understanding of equal opportunities (gender) issues young people will face in their working lives so that we can prepare them more thoroughly and further develop the work-related curriculum (Coventry City Council, 1993).

Prior to their placements the teachers agreed the following objectives with staff at each of the banks, a number of which were met through interviewing employees on the basis of a prepared questionnaire:

- to examine the career paths followed by women and men entering the profession at different entry points;
- to look at the skills, qualifications, training and qualities needed to progress up the career ladder;
- to look at the equal opportunities policies of the two banks and how the policies are managed and implemented;
- to look at jobs done in banking and note the balance of male and female employees;
- to interview a number of employees at different stages of career development in order to develop 'snapshots' of career profiles that can be used in school;
- to shadow a senior employee;
- to look at training provided in banking;
- to look at the use of appraisal in career development.

There are now increasing examples of equality of opportunity becoming either the major focus of teacher placements, as in the above example, or being identified within the objectives of placements which have other areas of focus. The TVEI group suggested that the following information would be an appropriate backcloth for teachers on all placements:

- *Policy:* is there an equal opportunites policy? If so, what mention is there of gender equality?
- *Balance:* to what extent are numbers of women and men equal?
- *Typical jobs:* is there a division in the sorts of jobs done by men and women?
- *Seniority:* are there approximately equal numbers of women and men in senior positions?
- *Environment:* is the atmosphere likely to be equally attractive to both sexes?
- *Flexibility:* are there arrangements for flexi-working, job-sharing or other arrangements which might help parents manage their dual roles more effectively?
- *Young employees:* are any steps being taken to recruit on the basis of equality of opportunity?

Towards the end of their placements, the teachers discussed their observations with staff at the banks; this gave them the opportunity to voice their concerns as well as to identify what thinking they would be taking back with them to schools. On the basis of this discussion, they wrote reports which they later presented to colleagues within the TVEI Curriculum Group, other teachers who had recently returned from placements and colleagues within their own schools. One of the teachers wrote:

I spoke to 'career-minded' young men and women. Most of the women at or near management level felt that their opportunities were much better as a new generation of managers moved to the top although one or two commented that being single or childless was an advantage. The bank had yet to come to terms with women at management levels combining children and a career as there are not yet many examples. One manager assumed (wrongly) that a female manager would not be interested in her career after having children. However, at this level I met several women who had made rapid progress in their career and only one who had dropped out of the Management Development Programme. This person did feel that men who started with her had received more encouragement.

At clerical level the differences were more apparent. Most of the men ... claimed to be career minded and to want promotion. Many of the women were less clear about their futures and were likely to settle for a senior clerical post. Yet I observed some highly efficient and competent young women who were clearly capable of management but had not, perhaps, made the right decisions early enough or perhaps had not been encouraged early enough (Coventry City Council, 1993).

The teachers' experiences of their placements in banks highlighted the importance of providing as part of the work-related curriculum an opportunity for pupils to think about their long-term career plans and their 'choice' of 'lifestyles'; it also highlighted the importance of building close links between this and the personal and social education programme with an emphasis on self-assessment skills, personal review and development targets.

At a whole-school level, the teachers' placement experience had furnished them with new ideas relating to appraisal and mechanisms for implementing the gender dimension of equal opportunities policies, especially in relation to personnel practices; for example: schemes to attract women returners, preparation for maternity leave, flexible employment practices, child-care arrangements and career development programmes aimed at equality of opportunity.

On return from their placements and after discussions with a variety of colleagues, the members of the TVEI Equal Opportunities Curriculum Group compiled a set of teacher and pupil materials aimed at securing equality of opportunity for female and male pupils on work experience placements. These materials were designed to complement equal opportunities procedures already in place, in the work of the Careers Service for example, and to support teachers and pupils in moving towards gender equality at each of the following stages of the process:

- the initial identification of placements;
- the preparation for pupil choice of placement;
- the process of choosing a placement;
- the preparation for the placement;
- the monitoring and support during the placement; and
- the review and follow-up of the placement experience.

The TVEI group's experience confirmed the view that there was much to be learned from teacher placements in industry that could help secure gender equality in work experience for pupils. In addition, the experience provided an opportunity for a two-way exchange of equality perspectives and strategies between schools and employers supported by LEA structures responsible for coordinating and monitoring the process as a whole. It appears that many schools are under-utilizing the opportunities provided by parallel processes and learning experiences involved in the work-experience placements of both teachers and pupils. In both these processes the daily pressures of school timetables often lead to short-cuts being taken at the crucial preparatory and review stages of the process. These stages are clearly important in assuring a high-quality learning experience; without a focus on gender equality at these stages it is likely that female and male pupils will continue to make stereotypical choices and have unequal experiences within the workplace.

Case 2: Course development within Education-Business Partnership centres.

Coventry Education-Business Partnership's mission statement for 1991–3 included 'making the best use of available talent through ensuring equality of opportunity for all, focusing particularly on "disadvantaged" groups.' Its strategic objectives included equality objectives for the five developing Partnership centres in Coventry.

In 1991, staff from the BTEC National Business and Finance Team at Tile Hill College of Further Education, led by a lecturer with particular responsibilities for gender equality in the college, approached the head of the Rover Group Partnership Centre with a proposal for a two-week flexible learning project for BTEC Diploma students on design, costing and marketing (Tile Hill College, Coventry, 1991). One of the key project aims was to allow students to see the best of industrial practice in terms of equality of opportunity. The college chose the Rover Centre because of the Rover Group's commitment to equal opportunities policies.

Prior to this proposal, the BTEC National Business and Finance course tutors had been concerned that students of both sexes, despite their equal numbers on their courses, continued to hold stereotypical career aspirations; for example, male students wanting to move into finance and accounts and female students wanting to move into reception, clerical and secretarial posts. The tutors had therefore decided to conduct a survey of 120 full-time Diploma students and 90 part-time Certificate students to explore female and male views of gender equality in the workplace.

The survey gathered interesting information on gender differences in career ambitions and perceived barriers in the workplace. It was significant in shaping the flexible learning project's aims and approaches and its findings were used as a basis for discussion with students prior to their period at the Rover Group Partnership Centre.

Although large numbers of students thought that many employers were now changing their recruitment and employment practices in line with equal opportunities policies, many thought that males and females are still perceived differently by employers. Interestingly, day-release (part-time) female students identified and stated examples of problems far more frequently than full-time female students, who generally denied there was a problem. Both female and male students thought pay, training and promotion prospects would be important factors in their future career choices; female students also particularly identified respect from male colleagues, flexible working hours, job satisfaction and positive relationships with staff.

The project developed by the college and the Partnership Centre focused on the design of a product chosen from a pre-selected list and prepared for a commercial launch. The project specified that the 'scenarios' listed should be 'gender-friendly'; they included: teenage bedroom furniture, display and signposting in college, the 'male' handbag, garden furniture, the young person's bag, classroom furniture, the shopping-bag problem and a toddler's walking toy. The product was ultimately presented to a team of buyers from the EEC, role-played by college lecturers and Rover staff; attempts were made, not always successfully, to achieve a sex balance in the staffing of the project and to ensure that staff roles were not stereotyped.

The project was supported by course materials which guided staff and students through it as fully as possible. The students, who were working in balanced mixed-sex groups of about ten, were undergoing continuous assessment against the following criteria: working with others, oral communication, identifying and tackling problems, numeracy, and design and visual discrimination.

At the end of the project, students were asked to evaluate their experience including gender equality aspects of the project. Although it was not possible to assess from their comments the extent to which the experience had influenced their views of employment as reflected in the earlier survey, it appeared that female and male students had generally experienced equal participation in all aspects of the project. Staff evaluation, which included evidence from group observations and transcripts of group discussions, confirmed that females and males had generally taken equal turns in group roles of leadership and support and also in non-stereotypical aspects of assignment tasks.

Since the end of the project, the course materials have been disseminated, accompanied by in-service training opportunities, to other schools and colleges in Coventry and the experience has therefore been made available to other 16–19-year-old students.

Case 3: School-based curriculum initiatives drawing on outside resources

In recent years many schools have piloted gender equality initiatives connected to the work-related curriculum. Some of these, such as Year 9 'What's my line?' conferences, have aimed to generally challenge sex-stereotyped attitudes of both girls and boys; others have targeted only one of these groups (most often girls) with more specific aims.

Many of the initiatives targeted at girls have aimed at increasing female pupils' participation and success in scientific and technological subject areas and careers. Such initiatives are often jointly planned by individual schools or clusters of schools and local authority support services, higher education institutions, local employers and community groups. Although the scale of such initiatives varies, the complexities of planning, implementation and evaluation are often similar. The two examples described briefly below both draw significantly on resources from outside the school and underline the importance of the planning points listed earlier (pages 162–3) if gender equality perspectives are to be coherently addressed within jointly-planned initiatives.

The WISE bus

A number of Coventry's comprehensive and special schools have incorporated the 'Women into Science and Engineering' bus into their work-related curriculum programme. The bus, which was part of a project originally sponsored in 1984 by the Equal Opportunities Commission and the Engineering Council, consisted of a mobile classroom equipped with a variety of technological activities, work stations, kits and careers materials targeted at girls in Year 9 upwards. The bus was usually based on the school site for a week. The school timetabled groups of girls to use the bus for 1-hour periods, usually accompanied by a (where possible, female) science or technology teacher and a technician. Some schools extended the use of the bus for hands-on experience by female staff or by community groups.

Some schools have used the bus as a focus for more ambitious cross-curricular equality programmes involving all departments in activities related to gender equality and the work-related curriculum. These have included day-time and evening events, such as a Women and Technology conference; many of these have also been targeted at parents, governors and employers. Although most of these have been considered successful at 'raising awareness' within the school, numbers attending from outside the school have not usually been high.

However, the major outcome of such initiatives has been an immediate increase in self-esteem and enthusiasm for related technological activities among the girls and women who have been the focus of such initiatives and towards whom resources have been exclusively addressed. 'I'm glad this bus is for women only because if boys were here they'd think they knew everything and they'd boss us about'. This was the sort of remark made in mixed schools even where girls had access to similar activities in their classrooms. Boys often did not feel the same enthusiasm for their exclusion from the week's activities; they usually undertook parallel programmes which had 'gender awareness' as their focus!

The Women's Training Roadshow

The Women's Training Roadshow was a city-wide initiative in which Year 10–13 students from all Coventry's secondary and special schools were invited to participate. The roadshow was part of a national 'Industry Matters' initiative, spearheaded by the government. The roadshow aimed to show women and girls that through appropriate training they can take advantage of the wide range of jobs open to them.

The three-day event, which was the focus of school curriculum activities, was located in the Coventry Polytechnic buildings in the city centre. It was planned by a steering group consisting of representatives from Industry Matters, the education department, local schools, employers and community groups, who brought with them a considerable diversity of experiences, expectations and perspectives on gender equality. The local Careers Service took responsibility for day-to-day coordination of the event.

Female pupils from groups of schools, accompanied by their teachers, were booked in for half-day programmes which consisted of workshops, exhibitions, seminars, a theatre performance and take-away materials about training opportunities and careers. (Schools showed such a high level of interest in the event that numbers attending from each school had to be limited.) There were also open evenings for parents and other adults, but these were not well attended.

The organizational issues were complex, both centrally and within schools, and this resulted at times in pupils experiencing inconsistent 'messages' about gender equality. As with the WISE bus, schools had found it difficult to prepare for an event of which they had no direct experience and which they had not helped to plan. Timetabling and staffing arrangements for the half-day were complicated by the fact that in mixed schools a curriculum had to be prepared for the remaining 50 per cent of pupils – boys – from each class. The event itself aimed to target the needs and interests of a wide-ranging audience within a very limited budget. Those who staffed the roadshow's activities included adults from the City Council, the Polytechnic, community groups and employers, who had volunteered to run workshops and to staff stalls. These adults often did not represent 'role models' to whom the range of young people were able to relate and, despite their briefing, some had not understood what was expected of them or did not have experience that enabled them to target their materials and their activities sufficiently to their pupil audience.

Summary and conclusions

It is clearly the case that the more complex the initiative, the more difficult it is to ensure coherence in approach, quality and therefore outcome for pupils. This is particularly the case when a large-scale initiative combines two areas of focus – gender equality and the work-related curriculum, both of which are relative newcomers to the school curriculum. Much of the success of such initiatives depends on the smooth working of established machinery both within schools and between the range of organizations involved. Education-industry relationships and structures are still evolving as are cross-curricular structures in most secondary schools, which still appear sometimes at odds with established practices and procedures.

It is important that those responsible for instigating cross-curricular gender equality initiatives recognize their complexity from the outset; it is vital that the good intentions behind them can be translated into achievable objectives and that lessons learnt from one development are applied to the next. There is much evidence of successful practice in this dimension of the work-related curriculum despite the pressures under which schools are currently working; experience shows that this can most easily be achieved where all partners in the process share a commitment to gender equality, a willingness to learn and responsibility for involving themselves in ensuring successful outcomes.

In this chapter I have used three cases of educational initiatives in Coventry to demonstrate ways in which gender equality objectives can be built into the work-related curriculum in schools and colleges. The introduction of the National Curriculum has set a curriculum context for schools which makes it essential from the outset to build equality objectives into the planning, delivery and evaluation of the work-related curriculum. A framework has been suggested for planning and evaluation which schools could also use as a basis for discussion with partner organizations who make either one-off or regular contributions to the work-related curriculum. Parallel frameworks need to be developed by schools to address other dimensions of their equal opportunities policies such as 'race' and 'disability'. Alternatively, an overarching equal opportunities framework could be developed within which examples of objectives relating to each of these dimensions are identified.

The nature of change in secondary and further education in recent years has appeared to challenge many of the principles and working practices on which gender equality strategies were founded in the early and mid-1980s. The TVEI experience has demonstrated, however, ways in which many of these principles and practices have been sustained and developed by teachers and have become an accepted agenda for action in project schools. More recently, following the introduction of the 1988 Education Reform Act, there is evidence that many of the cross-curricular approaches pioneered in equal opportunities development work in the 1980s are recommended as the best professional practice by bodies such as the National Curriculum Council. The NCC's guidance to schools on cross-curricular themes, skills and dimensions replicates the emphasis of 1980's equal opportunities strategies on whole-school policies and planning and the management structures necessary to the delivery of cross-curricular elements.

However, there is little doubt that the subject-centred structure of the National Curriculum, the organizational infra-structure of most secondary schools, the reduced capacity of LEAs to direct funding towards gender equality and the uncertainties of LMS provide a formidable challenge to teachers who wish to ensure that all their pupils receive their entitlement to equal opportunities. However, in theory, it is hard to see how the gender dimension of the work-related curriculum could afford to be ignored at a time when so much public debate centres on women's vital economic role, when a new Sex Equality Unit is established in the Department of Employment and when the government makes much of its support for the Opportunity 2000 campaign. In practice, the achievement of gender equality for young people will doubtless continue to be highly dependent on the energy, ingenuity and professionalism of teachers who make it their business to put equality for all their pupils at the centre of their day-to-day practice.

Acknowledgements

I would like to thank colleagues in Coventry's schools and colleges whose professional expertise and experience I have drawn on in this chapter; in particular the following members of the TVEI Equal Opportunities Curriculum Group: Julia Bond, Ann Duggan, Anna Kennedy, Miriam Mole, Rona Taylor and Ann Yeomans.

I would also like to thank Adrian Booth, Graham Hall, Gaby Weiner and Jerry Wellington for their helpful comments.

References

Bridgewood, A and Betteridge, J (1989) *Equal Opportunities for Girls and Boys within TVEI*, Windsor: NFER/Training Agency.

Burchall, H and Millman, V (1989) *Changing Perspectives on Gender*, Milton Keynes: Open University.

Coventry City Council (1993) *Gender Equality in the Work-related Curriculum*, Coventry: author.

DES (1991) 'School educational survey 1989/90', *DES Bulletin*, 22/91, December.

Herbert, C (1985) *TVEI: Equal Opportunities*, Centre for Applied Research in Education, University of East Anglia.

Millman, V (1985) 'The new vocationalism in secondary schools; its influence on girls', in Whyte, J. *et al.* (eds) *Girl-Friendly Schooling*, London: Methuen.

Millman, V and Weiner, G (1985) *Sex Differentiation in Schooling; is there really a problem?*, final report of the former Schools Council project on Reducing Sex Differentiation in Schools, London: Longman.

Millman, V and Weiner, G (1987) 'Engendering equal opportunities; the case of TVEI', in Gleeson, D (ed.) *TVEI and Secondary Education*, Milton Keynes: Open University Press.

MSC (1984) *TVEI: Annual Review*, Sheffield: MSC.

MSC (1987) *TVEI Developments 2: Equal Opportunities*, Sheffield: MSC.

Skinner, J and Jones, P (1987) *Promoting Equal Opportunities within TVEI*, Sheffield: MSC.

Tile Hill College, Coventry (1991) *A Design Project with the Rover Partnership Centre*, Coventry: author.

Training Agency (1987) *TVEI Evaluation Working Papers 1: Equal Opportunities for Girls and Boys*, Sheffield: Training Agency.

Training Agency (1990) *TVEI Programme Performance Indicators*, Sheffield: Training Agency.

Weiner, G (1989) 'Feminism, equal opportunities and vocationalism: the changing context', in Burchall, H and Millman, V, op cit.

9 Great Accidents in History: Vocationalist Innovations, the National Curriculum and Pupil Identity

Maggie MacLure and Ian Stronach

The purpose of this chapter is to look at some of the recurrent and non-recurrent features of educational discourse in the UK in order to examine the ways in which they relate to the construction of pupil 'identities'. The analysis will examine vocationalist innovations of the last decade or so, and connect these to the National Curriculum reforms which are currently being formulated and introduced in England and Wales. It will be argued that, on the one hand, nothing seems to have changed over the past 15 years or so: the construction of the educational 'problem' and the idealization of the 'solution' is highly ritualized, predictable and stable over time. On the other hand, there is an increasingly eclectic and contradictory accretion of initiatives. These proliferating attempts at solutions are, we suggest, comprehensively embedded in the National Curriculum and we try to give the National Curriculum a post-modern reading, seeing it as a set of discrepant prescriptions about what pupils are and should be, and an agglomeration that is designed to end educational history in one final-until-the-next-time resolution.

The first task of the chapter, then, is to sketch out the recurrent constructions of the educational 'problem' and its 'solution', indicating their ritualistic and recurrent nature at the level of general political debate. We then turn to an explanation of the non-recurrent accretion of different initiatives that developed in the UK between 1970 and 1990, and which became embedded in the National Curriculum[1].

Constructing the ideal problem

In previous analyses, it was argued that the British state tended to deploy vocationalist diagnoses and prescriptions as a kind of 'magic artillery' (to redeploy Levy-Bruhl's phrase) against economic decline (Stronach, 1990). The intense personification and individualization of the problem, as well as the 'cosmic' nature of the envisaged solution, suggested that these could be read as contemporary rituals. The recurrent narratives of recovery were most clearly told in advertisements:

Introducing the successor to YTS, New Youth Training (summer 1990):

There's only one thing stopping Susan Clarke getting a better job. Susan Clarke ... take a look at yourself. Are you the person that you want to be? If not, this is your opportunity to do something about it and change the course of your life.... It's called New Youth Training. But before you jump to any conclusions, we should point out straight away that it's not the same as YTS.... There's only one person that can stop you getting a better job now, and that's you.

We can see the copywriter struggling with history in this advertisement ('... before you jump to ...'), trying to construct the amnesia that will separate NYT from YTS, and produce a credible brand image ('new', 'different'). For whom? We suggest that these are ritual images which address an adult as well as a youthful 'congregation' (Rappaport, 1968): they seek to offer reassuring 'responses' to 'problems' in a broad political arena. They are a kind of moral theatre, in which redemptive plays can be staged and re-staged, and in which notions of personal agency and responsibility can substitute for structural change.

Constructing the ideal solution

Ritual explanation proceeds from the personal to the cosmic (Turner, 1981), employing polar opposites and synecdoche in order to 'explain' why minor physical actions can have profound personal consequences. These archetypes create positive and negative poles around which blame and redemption can be wrapped, and are evidenced in vocationalist profiles, where personification creates polarities (weak/strong, competitive/non-competitive, motivated/unmotivated) which become embedded in curriculum rationales and 'profiling' assessment procedures. A common polarity is between the real and the ideal, and creates an archetype of the citizen/worker. In most of these procedures the pupil/trainee is required to confess rather than just accept his or her evaluation. There are signing rituals (appraiser and appraisee must both sign the document in order that the learner can 'own' the verdict).

The covert matching of real self against ideal can be more subtle than ticks, boxes and grades. In this example, the appraisee offers the following confession:

> I am usually a quiet person, both at home and at school, but if I say something which I think is right I will argue my point. I am quite active when the weather is nice to be out in, in the way of sports. I am careful both in what I do and what I say so that I do not upset anybody. I try not to take large unnecessary risks which put either me or anybody else into danger. I am not a good leader and I do not really like being a leader in social circles, but I think many people follow (or try to follow) my example in academic circles such as maths. I try to be cooperative to everybody if they ask me to do something which I think is possible for me to do but I do not really like joining in really large groups. I always insist on finishing everything it is possible for me to do. I attach quite a lot of importance to appearance and try always to be clean and neat, though not always fashionable. I always try to be reliable and never late unless I can't help it. I always keep my word, especially where I am asked to keep a promise (Broadfoot, 1986, p.10).

The narrative obscures *a priori* categories such as quietness, activity, risk-taking, leadership, example to others, cooperativeness, reliability, etc. It is a piece of directed writing written as 'spontaneous' narrative. It is, therefore, a kind of forced confession, in which the learner is channelled towards a particular and ideal version of the self. Its claims to 'holism', of course, are bogus, as are its student-centred pretensions (Stronach, 1989). But the student is left in no doubt as to the qualities and ideals to which she must aspire, and against which she must judge herself.

To conclude, these idealizations of 'problem' and 'solution', of 'real' and 'ideal', employ a subtle or unsubtle play of opposites, and presume that minor physical actions may stand for great change. They contain both an incorporating pedagogy ('ownership', 'self-assessment', 'negotiation', signing rituals) and an alienating structure (imposed categories, covert norming, compulsory 'negotiation'). They project responsibility on to the individual, illustrating the subtle alienations of self-assessment, as well as a seductive fantasy for the construction of 'identity'.

Meta-narrative and developing the plot

We might regard these broad polarized stories as a kind of meta-narrative, within which a series of reports, projects, initiatives, curriculum proposals, assessment procedures and evaluations elaborate a more precise discourse and practice. There are several features of this process of elaboration that seem to be relevant to a post-modern reading of contemporary curricula. In particular, we should note that not all aspects of educational change are recurrent. This is partly because there has been a fragmentation of meaning in the discourse of educational policy, such that the basic vocabulary of education and vocationalism has become increasingly polyvalent, and the generation of initiatives increasingly frenetic. As we suggest below, there are both economic and organizational reasons for this proliferation.

The dispersion of meaning

This is a process whereby the meaning of innovations (such as 'work experience', 'profiling' or 'enterprise') shifts and fragments as the economic and social context changes. It can be illustrated by a brief retrospective of the role of work experience in vocationalist discourse. Work experience set off in the 1970s as a minor element of education for the 'less able' 15-year-old, premissed on a simple 'bridge' theory of the transition from school to work. But it also created an enduring ambivalence:

> By shifting social learning to a more central position, work experience opened up both progressive and conservative possibilities: on the one hand, open schools and experiential learning; on the other, the subordination of educational goals to employer needs (Stronach, 1984).

This ambivalence was further exacerbated by mass youth unemployment in the late 1970s and early 1980s. By 1980 the 'problem' was having to be redefined, and different identities created. Suddenly, 'work' itself – hitherto an unproblematic reality, if insufficiently experienced by the young – was open to expanded definition, even achieving a definition as the antithesis of employment:

... appropriately prepare young people for economic survival – for work rather than employment (Stern and Hilendorf, 1981).

Work is all sorts of things: a livelihood, a source of job satisfaction, a way of passing the time, the interface for a variety of relationships (Gibson, 1983).

Thus work experience developed a whole series of personal and cultural justifications. The economic logic of the situation prompted new definitions of 'work', new notions of 'preparation', and softer pedagogic approaches: personal development, self-assessment, negotiation, individual learning agendas, ownership.

Much the same process took place within profiling/Records of Achievement developments, and within the evolution of mini-companies/mini-cooperatives/mini-enterprises. What is significant in these variations on the vocationalist theme is that meaning fragments in the face of economic contradiction, and that the rather singular version of work experience, or profiling, or mini-company, in terms of definition, rationale, clientele, and presumed efficacy, splits into a series of versions which covers the whole spectrum of ideological possibility.

The contest for meaning

If meaning tended to fragment from the late 1970s onwards, it was also a site of contest, in a quite literal sense, as curriulum developers felt increasingly compelled to fit their ideas to the funding priorities of the government. This period of curriculum and assessment development in the UK was characterized by what came to be called 'categorical funding'. Throughout the 1980s the government provided broad parameters for initiatives and sub-contracted development to local education authorities. These competitive bids ensured that these authorities defined the 'problem' and proposed 'solutions' that were in keeping with government ideology; but it did not prevent subsequent redefinition and subversion. As a result of this 'domestication', vocationalist schemes came to include the most instrumental of ideas with notions of Freirean emancipation, and offered identities based on everything from employer needs to self-actualization. Small wonder, then, that commentators on TVEI, for example, should note that 'there appears to be no clear-cut understanding among teachers of what "technical and vocational education" means in its present guise' (Ball, 1990; Sikes and Taylor, 1987, p.60).

Thus 'projects' tended to attract a whole range of political interventions and, once again, meanings proliferated. Over the piece, each initiative – whether it concerned experiential learning, assessment, or pedagogy – came to span most of the field of ideological possibility concerning the identity of the young.

Finally, it should be noted that a growing plurality of meaning was also prompted by competition between two national ministries jostling for control of the secondary curriculum: Education and Employment. As their 1986 joint Report (DES/ DE, 1986) suggests: all qualifications would 'need to be practical and relevant to employment' (Department of Employment), within an education system designed to enable 'people to progress to the limit of their creativity and potential' (Department of Education and Science).

Thus, to summarize the position in terms of the production of educational innovation, we envisage a rather simple and ritualistic meta-narrative, allocating blame and prescription in a broad political theatre, and reassuring the 'public' that problems were being addressed and (this time) that solutions would work. This meta-narrative triggered financial investment by the state in educational and training 'revolutions' such as YOP, YTS and TVEI, as well as a host of smaller initiatives. Increasingly, these solutions were marketed as well as implemented, through advertising, media events (such as Education Secretary Baker's launch of CPVE balloons on the banks of the Thames), and through increasingly glossy journals and materials. To note the growing importance of this symbolic marketing of vocationalist solutions is to acknowledge how important it had become to sell policy rather than simply to produce it. In this sense, vocationalism had become a theatre of signs, rather than a means of altering the factors of production.

Nevertheless, the vocationalist theatre put on a series of plays which were loosely scripted (on account of economic change, and also the pattern of categorical funding), and which were open to a certain amount of improvisation. The result was that the basic vocabulary of education and vocationalism became increasingly polyvalent. Concepts like 'work', 'basic skills', 'self-assessment' and 'enterprise' came to have many possible readings, and so too did the processual vocabulary of 'negotiation', 'ownership' and so on.

What is very different about the current context is the range and extent of *structural* change. In 1976 the great debates were about progressive methods versus traditional teaching (variously represented by Tynedale, Neville Bennett and Callaghan's Ruskin speech) and about the interface between education and industry. But *The Times'* editorial was surely right to ridicule the difference between Education Secretary Mulley's heavy rhetoric and his rather light policy touch in proposing to bridge academic and vocational learning via ten small pilot projects – 'ten pilot mice' as the *TES* (26 March 1976) put it. Pilot mice were the accepted technique for educational development. In 1990 the same kind of educational discourse is wrapped around a wide range of structural changes. There are billion-pound vocational initiatives. There are schools opting out of local authority control. There is devolved financial management of schools, with attendant consequences for the future of whole sections of local authority provision, edging LEAs, advisors, and Teachers' Centres nervously into a newly created market for their management and support skills. In addition, such novelties as vouchers, school marketing, Records of Achievement, school fund-raising strategies, extended governors' powers, teacher appraisal, magnet schools, City Technology Colleges, etc. jostle for attention.

Thus the development of innovation in UK education before the advent of the National Curriculum became a bizarre mixture of cottage industry and ministerial initiatives, many of them reinventing developments in other places and other times, some centralizing, some devolving, several of them apparently contradictory. It was against this pattern of recurrence and profusion that the National Curriculum emerged.

Getting to grips with the National Curriculum: readings and responses

Our concern in this section is to interpret the 'sacred texts' of the National Curriculum. First, we intend to look at the way in which implementation of the initiative has involved the act of 'reading' in a very particular way. Then we explore some of the identities they promote for pupils, before turning to a consideration of how these readings and identities connect to the processes of recurrent and non-recurrent change that we identified earlier.

As others have noted (eg, Ball and Bowe, 1992), in one sense, implementation of the National Curriculum is essentially a matter of 'reading' – of exegesis. In order to 'deliver' the new system, teachers are instructed to read the new 'sacred' texts, examine their hearts and their practice, and adjust the latter, if not the former, accordingly. An advisory teacher for English, whose job is to support teachers in the classroom, describes the kind of close reading that has been undertaken:

> We read (and re-read and re-read) 'English 5–16'. We found ourselves able to quote 'chapter and verse' or to turn instantly to any particular reference needed to back up an argument. The Adviser began telling groups of teachers that we reminded him of fundamentalist Christians: 'For it sayeth in Cox [ie the report of the Working Party on the English Curriculum] Chapter 15, verse 20 that language shall not be linear in development, rather that it shall be recursive... (Bain *et al.*, 1991).

One additionally interesting aspect of the implementation strategy is that it has, of necessity, generated a *mass* reading strategy. Because of the extent of the 'reforms', the speed of their introduction, the top-down style of development and dissemination, and the strategy of drip-feeding the statutory orders for the various subjects in serial chunks, everyone with a professional interest in the matter finds themselves reading the same glossy curriculum documents at the same time (and waiting to get hold of the next ones to emerge). This means that huge sections of the teaching profession and the satellite occupations which encircle it – academics, teacher educators, textbook publishers, journalists and officials of the local education authorities – are engaged in a common interpretive task at roughly the same time. This may seem to be a trivial fact, but it is unique in the English and Welsh education systems, and it has created an interesting situation. One of the outcomes is that it foregrounds the act of interpretation. Because all of those with a stake in the system have been forced to contemplate what the new curriculum means *for them* – ie, in terms of its anticipated impact upon their values and practices – the innovation has acted as a focus for the concerted airing of educational preoccupations and assumptions. It has acted as a kind of 'breach', in Garfinkel's (1967) terms, of the educational culture, and has therefore exposed the norms and assumptions that sustain that culture, but which usually remain tacit and taken for granted. This period of explicit mass critique will not last for long: once the innovation has become familiar, if not domesticated, the educational ideas will return to the background of public discussion.

What are the deeper implications of this mass reading strategy? One might anticipate that it will ultimately lead to the development of a common and consensual discourse about education. In one sense, this is already happening. The lexicon of the new system, with its Key Stages, Attainment Targets, Standard Assessment Tasks, etc. is already firmly embedded in the discourse of teachers, publishers and other commentators. The advisory teacher quoted above describes how the language has spread:

> The other strange thing was that, however hard we tried, we were unable to stop ourselves speaking in acronyms. We constructed whole sentences of them, 'You will know that these chapters outline the PoS and the related SoAs for each PC's KAL component, which has implications in terms of SATs, of course'.[2]

The educational publishers have rapidly issued schemes written in the language of the new framework, or else provided interpretive guides which help teachers 'translate' their existing publications into the new system. More than this, the new schemes are packaged in the same format: 'the pack comes bound and four-hole drilled (like NCC materials)' (Newcastle University publication advertisement, *TES*, November 1990). In addition, the new lingua franca seems to undermine the separate subject cultures of the secondary curriculum, with their different views of the child, of 'development' and of 'progression'. Finally, without pre-empting the analysis that we present below, we can note that pupils have already begun to be invested with a particular new identity: the 'Key Stage Pupil.'

Does this wild-fire spread of the new technical vocabulary indicate an emerging consensus about *meaning and values*? (Or indeed an organized resistance?) It is too soon to say; but we want to argue here that it would be premature to conclude that the new system will act as a funnel or filter, rendering uniform a set of curriculum beliefs and practices that were previously diverse and plural. One of the reasons for this, we argue below, is that the texts which enshrine the new curriculum are themselves multivalent, and that they are therefore available for multiple interpretation. While all texts have this open-endedness to some extent, we want to contemplate the possibility that the National Curriculum documents have some (though not all) of the features which have been said to be characteristic of *post-modern* texts, and to explore the implications of that possibility.

What kinds of reading, then, have been made of the National Curriculum texts? And what kinds of pupil identities can be read into, or out of, them? We start by offering some of our own readings, and then turn to a discussion of readings that have been offered by other commentators.

If previous initiatives have tended to construct particular identities for pupils according to their symbolic roles as the champions of economic recovery, what we find in the NC texts is a proliferation of identities, roles and characters. Certainly, young people continue to be constructed as the prospective heroes and heroines of the meta-narrative of economic recovery, and in precisely the same language as before: 'With increasing economic competitiveness, both in the European Community and world-wide, the nation's prosperity depends more than ever on the knowledge, understanding and skills of young people' (NCC, 1990f). But there is a much greater diversity of specific, yet fragmented identities.

Some of these identities are *aspirational*: they mimic valued adult identities, in ways that we describe below in shorthand-form as 'middle manager', 'consumer', 'democrat', 'producer', etc. Others are *learner* identities: they construct pupils in terms of personal attributes and predispositions to learn in particular ways. For instance, we identify below the 'self-actualizing individual' and the 'proto-person'.

These identities are not new; nor are the pedagogies that are associated with them. What does seem to be new is their casual and fragmentary juxtaposition, sometimes within a single sentence, as in one of our examples below. Where previously each identity would have characterized a discrete moral, educational or ideological position, with its own recruits and opponents, they now jostle one another on the page. One outcome of this state of affairs is a blurring of intellectual (and discursive) pasts and presents (Denzin, 1989). In one document we find, for instance, the recently fashionable discourse of individual potential and self-awareness. 'Careers education and guidance aims first of all to help pupils to develop self awareness.... The shrewd awareness of one's talents, strengths and weaknesses', immediately followed by a fragment curiously reminiscent of an improving text from the early years of this century: 'There can be nothing more important than inculcating in the young the values of "a healthy mind in a healthy body"'. Two pages later, the time-frame has seemingly moved forward a few decades to the world of outward-bounding 'youngsters':

> Outdoor education can make a significant contribution as a focus of cross-curricular work. Many youngsters leave home for the first time when going to an outdoor centre and the experience of living in a community with others, sharing objectives and testing themselves in new environments, can be rewarding.

Note, however, how these anachronistic youngsters are simultaneously placed in a more contemporary landscape of 'cross-curricular work' and 'objectives' (themselves, arguably, figures in different discourses). Elsewhere the 'healthy body' turns up in a very contemporary economic story:

> People's health is one of the most important products that any society can create and one of the most important resources required for the creation of any other kind of wealth (NCC, 1990d).

The slogan becomes 'a wealthy mind in a wealthy body' as the money lenders enter the temple.

In the next section we delineate some of the pupil identities that are, we would argue, discernible in the National Curriculum documents. We have given these identities labels – 'middle manager', 'democrat', etc. – but we would not wish to suggest that these refer to fully-rounded, 'realistic' character or occupational types. They are intended as shorthand references to constellations of pupil attributes and virtues that seem to us to be implied in the NC texts.

Pupil identities in the National Curriculum

Pupil as middle manager

One of the recurring aspirational identities in the NC texts is that of the pupil as prospective middle manager or service sector administrator, inhabiting a future world of databases, spreadsheets, advertising campaigns, market research questionnaires, reports, mini-companies, visual presentations, personal action plans, committee meetings and market surveys. This identity is particularly noticeable, perhaps not surprisingly, in the NCC document relating to Education for Economic and Industrial Understanding, and the statutory documents for Design and Technology, and Information Technology. But it also features quite prominently in the statutory orders for English, particularly in the examples which accompany the statements of attainment for Speaking and Listening. For instance the ability to 'express a point of view on complex subjects persuasively, cogently and clearly' is exemplified at Level 9 in the business-person's language of OHPs and 'presentations':

> Introduce a researched environmental topic for discussion, using slides, OHP transparencies, notes or diagrams in the presentation

and at Level 10 (the highest level) as:

> devise and mount an advertising campaign concerned with a matter of principle.

It is interesting to note that the business-like language is usually tied to morally acceptable activities, as here, where the topic in the first example is 'environmental', and the advertising campaign in the second concerns 'a matter of principle'.

In these examples the 'middle manager'-type attributes stand alone. More often in the English document, they intermingle with fragments of other identities. As examples of the ability to 'take an active part in group discussions', for instance, we find, at Level 6:

> Introduce a new, relevant idea to a group discussion about the planning of a visit, or the making of a database; show respect for the contributions of others

and at Level 7:

> Take part in a real or simulated committee discussion which requires an agreement; express views and cite evidence in group discussions of books or poems.

Here we have middle managerial roles such as planning, constructing databases and participating in committee meetings adjacent to fragments of the more familiar identities of the traditional English curriculum, ie, the book-reading, 'rational', cooperative individual (see further below). In the composite discourse of the NC, you can make a database and show respect in a single sentence.

Pupil as consumer

Throughout the key texts, pupils are also constructed as consumers. It is necessary for them to learn the *role*, and not just the activities associated with consumption – to know 'what it means to be a consumer'. Their first role-play in the English curriculum document (NCC, 1990b) is consumerist: 'Play the role of shopkeeper or customer in the class shop' (AT1, Level 1). The central ideas associated with the consumer identity are opportunity, (informed) decision-making and personal choice. 'Economic and industrial understanding', for instance, is framed within a consumerist ethic of choice:

> Throughout their lives pupils will face economic decisions. They will face choices about how they contribute to the economy through their work. They will decide how to organise their finances and which goods or services to spend their money on. They will form views on public issues, such as the environmental effects of economic development or the economic arguments involved in elections.

Pupils are constructed as consumers, then, not only of commodities, but also of ideas, opportunities and ideologies. The consumerist exercise of choice is framed within an education that will help them to 'form views', 'handle differences of economic interest in a group', 'communicate effectively and listen to the views of others on economic and industrial issues'. They are to be taught, it seems, to actively engage in their roles as consumers, but only to be the talk-show hosts of its critique.[3] Here as elsewhere, the brake upon critical thinking is the need for 'balance'.

Pupil as producer

The producer is most clearly articulated in the NC document on Economic and Industrial Understanding (NCC, 1990f). The intention is to prepare children for future roles, 'as producers, consumers and citizens in a democracy'. The producer is given a subtle priority when the text offers to be even-handed: economic education 'should be balanced, embracing, for example, the needs of producers as well as the rights of consumers', as if teachers were more likely to recall the latter than the former, and history had been a struggle between down-trodden producers and overbearing consumers.

The producer is enshrined in a multiple reference to 'enterprise'. First, 'enterprise' is expressed as an economic system concerned with wealth creation: 'how business enterprise creates wealth for individuals and the community'. Then 'enterprise' is made to refer to activities ('mini-enterprises') and skills ('plan a simple budget and understand that external influences have effects on business activity'). Finally, 'enterprise' turns up as a set of personal qualities 'such as the ability to tackle problems, take initiatives, persevere, be flexible, and work in teams'. In this way, the text is able to explain enterprise in terms of the 'enterprising person', and to spirit away less voluntaristic versions in the kind of 'rhetorical evocation' that Edelman noted (1977, p.16). Nor is the traffic one-way; the account offers both personal solutions to economic development, and economic solutions to personal development. In the latter case, economic language and practice invest the discourse of personal development:

> understand some of the costs and benefits in situations relevant to themselves;

> people's health is one of the most important products that any society can create;

> DANCE: working in groups, demonstrate mechanical processes involved in production.

The producer is also cast in multiple roles. There is the post-Fordist worker ('work in groups in collaborative tasks, taking turns and elaborating ideas') the leader (taking initiatives, setting up 'business plans') , and the middle manager, as outlined above. (Note, however, that the producer as wage slave is not offered as an aspirational identity). In all of these formulations, 'enterprise' is a consensual affair: positive, collaborative and successful. Indeed the text is careful to separate out the possibility of conflict from the definition of enterprise, when it refers to 'issues as *diverse* (emphasis added) as industrial relations and the nature of enterprise'. The producer creates and inhabits the harmonious and benign world of enterprise.

Pupil as democrat

Then there is a strand which constructs the pupil as the rational, moral individual, able to assemble evidence, weigh it, take others' contributions into account, and apply his or her cognitive skills to the formulation of solutions to problems and the making of just decisions.

The democratic persona is, of course, a familiar one in the liberal arts strand of British education. Not surprisingly, it is found throughout the English document (NCC, 1990b), but the democratic identity has its most explicit formulation in 'Education for Citizenship' (NCC, 1990e), which is defined as developing 'the knowledge, skills and attitudes necessary for exploring, making informed decisions about and exercising responsibilities and rights in a democratic society.'[4]

Pupil as cultural connoisseur and critic

Again, this identity is familiar within the English curriculum: this is the person who has his or her finger on the cultural pulse: who can 'read' the ideologies behind adverts; who understands the ways in which people use rhetoric to make their arguments; who is able to diagnose social injustice and prejudice; who engages with literary texts in an active and critical way. In English, for instance, pupils should be able to: 'e) demonstrate in discussion and in writing some understanding of attitudes in society towards language change and of ideas about appropriateness and correctness in language use'.

It is partly in the guise of 'cultural critic' that the NC documents address politically sensitive issues such as race, class and gender. Questions of inequality and exploitation are frequently characterized as cultural issues which students must understand.

Pupil as self-actualizing individual

This is both an aspirational and a learner identity. It is the identity which was most clearly signalled in TVEI, and to some extent overlaps with the middle manager identity, since it delineates some of the attributes that are held to be generic to the good manager, such as flexibility, initiative, leadership, etc. It also borrows the emancipatory rhetoric of holism, self-directed learning and personal growth which first appeared in the progressive humanities curricula of the late 1960s and 1970s, and reappeared more recently in Records of Achievement. The self-actualizing identity is particularly visible in the non-statutory guidance for Design and Technology (NCC, 1990a) which lists ten 'aspirational' qualities such as creativity, enterprise and perseverance.

Pupil as proto-person

In direct opposition to the self-actualizing identity, this is in fact a deficit identity – the 'empty vessel' notion of the child in its contemporary guise. It constructs 'the child' as a primitive or deficient adult, whose identity as a whole person is in suspension until she or he has completed the path to maturity, a path which is wholly determined by the teacher. The documents on classroom assessment (SEAC, nd), where it predominates, speak of 'behaviours' and 'performances'; of 'allocating children to tasks'. Children's learning – indeed the contents of their heads – are to be surveyed and controlled by the teachers who must be on their guard lest children 'run away with or prematurely complete the [assessment] activity'. It could be argued that the macro-structure of the new system as a whole – the machinery of attainment targets, key stages and levels – is predicated on a deficit identity of children as learners.

The reading that we have presented of the National Curriculum texts is one that sees it as a multivalent text, in which many voices speak, in a kind of clamorous patchwork. There are elements of the traditional subjects and fashionable cross-curricular sentiment; there are traces of 'progressive' curriculum development and 'back to basics' conservatism. There is multiculturalism and nationalism;[5] there is feminism, vocationalism and the reaffirmation of 'family values'. There are pupils who are self-directing, think for themselves, able to critique, cooperate and collaborate, but must be covertly surveyed, taught in discrete stages and held back from getting ahead of the teacher. How have other readers interpreted the texts?

Other readings

There is no doubt that the Education Reform Act antagonized the British educational and academic establishment. The British Educational Research Association launched special conferences and publications (eg, Simons, 1988; Torrance, 1988) to counter and try to influence the government's proposals. As we noted above, the Act was therefore a perfect 'breach', in Garfinkel's terms, of the educational culture, and steps had to be taken to restore equilibrium.

A familiar response, we suggest, has been to try to achieve singular readings of the National Curriculum, which eliminate ambiguity and look for interpretive closure. This kind of reading tends, as Jeffcutt notes, 'to either prioritise one element of a duality ... or to seek to resolve or harmonize oppositions' (1991, p.4). One set of responses reads the National Curriculum in terms of a dramatic encounter between good and evil (cf. Denzin, 1988). A typical reading of this kind finds state interventionism to be the enemy lurking behind or beneath the 'reforms'. The 'goodies' are located in some pre-existing philosophy or initiative. Such accounts are built round polarities: then/now, process/product, democratic/totalitarian, etc.

Broadfoot offered the most imaginative rebuttal of the proposals by contrasting the 'pumpkin' of the government's assessment proposals with the 'glass slipper' of the 'new' assessment paradigm represented by Records of Achievement. (Broadfoot, 1990, p.201). The ipsative, progressive, negotiated and positive assessment movement led by RoA – ie, Cinderella – had met Prince Charming, in the guise of TVEI, and had fallen for his student-centred ways and his 'relevance'. Then along came the Ugly Sisters of the National Curriculum.... In an earlier document, Broadfoot had seen the conflict, not in terms of folk or fairy tale, but as Greek tragedy, 'a story in which the classical principles of tragedy may be clearly traced – nobility and virtue flawed by some fatal weakness ultimately destroying itself' (Broadfoot, 1988, p.3). The nobility and virtue was embodied in 'the attempt to make assessment serve the needs of the learning process' (Broadfoot, 1988, p.13), with RoA as the most virtuous of all such endeavours.

Other commentators told the same kind of story, without the characters. Pring, for example, rejected 'false dualizing' yet contrasted the inventory of the 'new think' (process curricula, relevance, pre-vocationalism, personal development, practical knowledge) with the 'old think' of the National Curriculum (product oriented, traditional subjects and pedagogy) and lamented the end of the fairy tale – 'It's as though TVEI had never happened' (Pring, 1988). One of the outcomes of such singular readings of the National-Curriculum-as-enemy is that they tend to offer pre-lapsarian or golden age accounts of the very recent past, as in the two examples above. This can result in some surprising historical (re)classifications, as when Sutcliffe, fearing that the National Curriculum will do for schools what super-markets did for high street shopping, warns that 'there will be no return to the dear, dead old days of the corner shop comprehen-sive' (Sutcliffe, 1990). Ten years ago the comprehensive was the supermarket.

It can also result in apocalyptic visions of the future. Broadfoot fears that the marriage of Cinderella and Prince Charming may in fact spawn a monster:

> ... it could well be that with national testing and mandatory curriculum objectives fulfilling primarily the requirements for the regulation of content, competition and system control and RoA providing a complementary basis for individual control and a broader regulation of content, the two together may provide one of the most effective forms of surveillance ever devised in education (Broadfoot, 1990, p.214).

Elliott fears the emergence of hordes of pupil monsters:

> By neglecting the 'inner being' [of pupils] the proposed curriculum will unwittingly alienate young people from their own natural powers, which

193

will nevertheless manifest themselves on a massive scale in ever new and sophisticated forms of human destructiveness (1988, p.51).

Despite the apocalyptic, or at least pessimistic, vision of the near future which these stories unfold, they never close with the triumph of the forces of evil. They typically end with an exhortation to teachers and their allies to rally against the enemy:

> The outcome of current policy initiatives will largely depend on the extent to which [teachers] can defend the notion of partnership between teacher and pupil in assessment that has been at the heart of the records of achievement movement (Broadfoot, 1990, p.214).

> The task, especially for parents and teachers together, is to reconstruct the national curriculum in a form which reflects both authentic educational values and parental concerns (Elliott, 1988, p.62)

The tendency to interpret the texts in polar terms is not confined to these parables of dramatic struggle, where one of the poles exists in the present and the other in the past. It is also found in dichotomous readings which find both poles *within* the texts. Such readings recognize a conflict of meaning, but try to resolve it by privileging one of the discourses. Optimistic readings find good and bad elements coexisting in the texts, but (like the apocalyptic readings) are hopeful that, under the right conditions, the good will prevail. Thus Anderson (1988) weighs the evidence for and against gender equality in the texts and concludes that there is encouragement to those who are fighting for equality. Carr (1988) finds a basic opposition in the aims of the Act between education for social reproduction and education for democracy. He argues that the latter aim would be progressive if the conditions for genuine democracy existed in British society, though he concludes that those conditions do not prevail at present. The flaw is not, therefore, in the Act and the curriculum *per se*, but in the consumerist and individualized society which the government has promoted. In a more internal kind of resolution, some found the statutory orders for the core subjects alienating and prescriptive, but felt much better about the 'whole curriculum' documents published by the National Curriculum Council.

Inconclusions

> ... history consists of a swarm of narratives, narratives that are passed on, made up, listened to and acted out; the people does not exist as a subject; it is

a mass of thousands of little stories that are at once futile and serious, that are sometimes attracted together to form bigger stories, and which sometimes disintegrate into drifting elements (Lyotard, 1989, p.134).

We began this chapter by noting that educational innovations have tended to become increasingly symbolic acts addressing the hope of larger recoveries, in economic or technological terms. As a result, the sponsors of large-scale innovations construct their images of recovery and market their new identities – of pupil, teacher and school – for an essentially political audience. In that sense, the National Curriculum has no opinion but public opinion, and that 'openness' allows it to display such an eclectic approach. It is in this context that we should understand the contrast between these glossy surfaces and the shabby fabric of the schools themselves; the decline in real spending on schools, the increasing enrolments in the private sector – to which the 'National' Curriculum does not apply – and the diversion of state investment to innovation and public relations.

The constellation of innovations that constitute the National Curriculum reforms also express the development of internal markets within the state-sponsored education service. These markets, in so far as they are competitive, support the commodification of pupils (Records of Achievements), teachers (appraisal), schools (brochures, examination 'league tables', financial 'autonomy') and professional development (privatized in-service training). The purpose of this commodification is to construct the image of accountability through quantifying or publicly representing some token of 'excellence'. The circulation and trade in symbols (Baudrillard, 1975) takes place, therefore, both within the education system and between it and society. This does not mean that the National Curriculum reforms are *only* such an exchange; but the trade in symbols is an important determinant of the political 'reputation' of teachers, pupils and schools, as well as a determinant of the perceived 'success' of government policy.

As we have suggested, this symbolic discourse has something for almost everybody. It is the most of all possible worlds, and has an unusually piecemeal nature. On the basis of their empirical work, Ball and Bowe describe it as 'driven by serendipity, ad hocery [and] chaos' (1992). While all change is characterized by confusion and extemporization, there are important differences in the ways in which the central texts of this reform are created. Previously, curriculum change would have claimed its authority by reference to intellectual ancestors: it would be premissed on some canon of expert knowledge, some philosophy of education, some conceptualization of the child, or some theory of learning (as, for example, Scottish curricular reforms of the 1970s invoked the authority of Hirst or Phenix). There are no intellectual heroes in the National Curriculum, no Piagets, Bernsteins, Deweys or Bruners. The debates have been much more of a mix of educational belief, economic myth, populism and prejudice: skills for the future; history with Kings and Queens, dates versus empathy; spelling, punctuation, parsing and arithmetical tables. The distinction is not an absolute one, but the National Curriculum has been much more of a 'low culture' debate – and unapologetically so – than a 'high culture' one. In that respect, it might be held to exhibit a post-modern abandonment of the meta-narratives of the curriculum in favour of a large number of common senses.

The casual borrowing of authorities, references and discourses from across the time and space continuum is what gives the curriculum texts their quality of being, like Billy Pilgrim, unstuck in time. It is tempting to read them as a symptom of the post-modern malaise described by Jameson, who writes of the amnesia of a social system that has 'little by little begun to lose its capacity to retain its own past, has begun to live in a perpetual present and in a perpetual change' (1988, p.28). A less apocalyptical analogy would be to think of the National Curriculum as a product in the sense of a multiple road accident, in which can be found, jack-knifed and shunted together, an old furniture van full of subjects, the juggernauts of TVEI, assorted delivery vans marked 'RoA' or 'PSE', and school buses of mystified children.

Notes

1. This is a version of a paper presented to the Annual Meeting of the American Educational Research Association, Chicago, April 1991. We are grateful to Saville Kushner, Barry Macdonald and Nigel Norris for their comments on that earlier draft.
2. PoS: Programme of Study; SoA: Standard of Attainment; PC: Profile Component; KAL: Knowledge about Language; SAT: Standard Assessment Task.
3. The only clear exception to this learned dispassion seems to be the cross-curricular theme of 'Environmental Understanding', where 'sensitivity' is the appropriate response.
4. While the 'citizenship' document devotes a substantial amount of space to delineating the democratic identity, it is notable that its

specific suggestions tend to revolve around a rather special notion of democracy which is tied strongly to the notion of 'community'. Thus the group activities suggested for Key Stage 4 consist mainly of what could be called 'good works' in the locality, such as 'painting and decorating, carrying out environmental improvements, gardening, work experience with young children, the elderly, the handicapped, the disabled and the disadvantaged'. Interestingly, more global issues are described in the same language of community: at Key Stage 3, 'Awareness of national and international communities will develop'.

5. For example, the requirements of the English curriculum for all pupils to speak and write in Standard English, and to read literature mainly from the existing (white, mainland British) canon is, arguably, a nationalist strategy, though it is couched in the language of 'access' and 'entitlement' for all pupils to the discourses of power and employment. Similarly, the government instructed its History working party to 'increase the emphasis on British history'.

References

Anderson, B (1988) 'Equal opportunities and the National Curriculum', in Simons, H (ed.), op cit.

Bain, P, Fitzpatrick, M and Hubbard, S (1991) 'Cascading', *NATE News*, Spring.

Ball, S (1990) *Politics and Policy Making in Education*, London: Routledge.

Ball, S and Bowe, R (1992) 'Subject departments and the "Implementation" of the National Curriculum', *Journal of Curriculum Studies*, **24**, 2, 97–115.

Baudrillard, J (1975) *The Mirror of Production*, tr. M Poster, St Louis, MI: Telos Press.

Broadfoot, P (ed.) (1986) *Selection, Certification and Control. Social issues in Educational Assessment*, London: Falmer Press.

Broadfoot, P (1988) 'The national assessment framework and Records of Achievement', in Torrance, H (ed.), op cit.

Broadfoot, P (1990) 'Cinderella and the ugly sisters: an assessment policy pantomime in two acts,' *Curriculum Journal*, **1**, 2, 199–215.

Carr, W (1988) *Education for Democracy? A philosophical analysis of the National Curriculum*, University of Sheffield, mimeo.

Denzin, N (1988) '*Blue velvet*. Postmodern contradictions', *Theory, Culture and Society*, **5**, 2/3, 461–73.

Denzin, N (1989) *Interpretive Biography*, Qualitative Research Methods Series 17, Beverly Hills, CA: Sage.

DES/DE (1986) *Working Together: Education and training*, London: HMSO.

Eagleton, T (1983) *Literary Theory*, Minnesota, MN: University of Minnesota Press.

Edelman, M (1977) *Political Language: Words that succeed and policies that fail*, New York: Academic Press.

Elliott, J (1988) 'The State versus education: the challenge for teachers', in Simons, H (ed.), op cit.

Garfinkel, H (1967) *Studies in Ethnomethodology*, New Jersey: Prentice-Hall.

Geertz, C (1988) *Works and Lives: The Anthropologist as Author*, Cambridge: Polity Press.

Gibson, T (1983) 'Simulating production units in schools', in Watts, A G (ed.) *Work Experience and Schools*, London: Heinemann.

Iser, N (1974) *The Implied Reader*, Baltimore, MA: Johns Hopkins University Press.

Jameson, F (1988) 'Postmodernism and computer society', in Kaplan, E (ed.) *Postmodernism and its Discontents*, London: Verso.

Jeffcutt, P (1991) '*From interpretation to representation in organisational analysis: postmodernism, ethnography and organisational culture*', paper presented to the GAPP Conference on The Anthropology of Organisations, Swansea, Wales, January.

Lyotard, J F (1989) *The Lyotard Reader*, Benjamin, A (ed.), Oxford: Basil Blackwell.

Pring, R (1988) 'Education Act 1988: lessons not learnt from TVEI', in Simons, H (ed.), op cit.

Rappaport, R (1968) *Pigs for Ancestors: ritual in the ecology of New Guinean People*, New Haven, CN: Yale University Press.

Sikes, P and Taylor, M (1987) 'Some problems with defining, interpreting and communicating in vocational education', in Gleeson, D (ed.) *TVEI and Secondary Education: A Critical Appraisal*, Milton Keynes: Open University Press.

Simon, B (1988) 'The curriculum and the Reform Bill', in Simons, H (ed.), op cit.

Simons, H. (1988) (ed.) *The National Curriculum*, papers presented to a British Educational Research Association Conference, University of London Institute of Education, mimeo.

Stern, E and Hilendorf, L (1981) *Developing Learning at Work: Review for the MSC*, London: Tavistock, mimeo.

Stronach, I (1984) 'Work experience: the sacred anvil', in Varlaam, C (ed.) *Rethinking Transition: educational innovation and the transition to adult life*, London: Falmer Press.

Stronach, I (1990) 'The rituals of recovery: UK education and economic "revival" in the 70s and 80s', *Anthropology Today*, **6**, 6, 4–8.

Sutcliffe, J (1990) 'Brown ale and bridges, but no Brylcreem', TES, 12 January.

TES (1976) 'Ten pilot mice', 23 June.

Torrance, H (1988) *National Assessment and Testing: a research response*, papers presented to a conference of the British Educational Research Association, London Institute of Education, mimeo.

Turner, V (1981) *The Drums of Affliction: a study of religious process among the Ndembu of Zambia*, London: International African Institute/ Hutchinson.

National Curriculum documents

Department of Education and Science
DES (1989) *Science in the National Curriculum*, London: HMSO.
DES (1990a) *English in the National Curriculum (No 2)*, London: HMSO.
DES (1990b) *Geography: Proposals for Ages 5 to 16*, London: HMSO.
DES (1990c) *Technology in the National Curriculum*, London: HMSO.
DES (1990d) *History for Ages 5 to 16. Proposals to the Secretary of State for Education and Science*, London: HMSO.

National Curriculum Council
NCC (1990a) *Design & Technology Capability: Non-Statutory Guidance*, York: NCC.
NCC (1990b) *English: Non-Statutory Guidance*, York: NCC.
NCC (1990c) *The Whole Curriculum. Curriculum guidance 3*, York: NCC.
NCC (1990d) *Health Education. Curriculum guidance*, York: NCC.
NCC (1990e) *Education for Citizenship. Curriculum guidance 8*, York: NCC.
NCC (1990f) *Education for Economic & Industrial Understanding. Curriculum guidance 4*, York: NCC.
NCC (1990g) *Environmental Education. Curriculum guidance 7*, York: NCC.

Secondary Examinations Assessment Council (SEAC)
SEAC (not dated). *A Guide to Teacher Assessment. Pack C: A source book of teacher assessment*, London: SEAC.

10 The Rise and Fall of the Work-related Curriculum

Ian Jamieson

Introduction

The phrase 'the work-related curriculum' gained something of a currency in the UK at the end of the 1980s. The phrase marked a stage in one of the longest debates in education: a liberal education or a vocational education? Of course the dichotomy was never an absolute one either conceptually or empirically. If one of the features of a liberal education is a concern to equip people to make their own free, autonomous choices about the life they will lead (Bailey, 1984) then clearly this must entail some knowledge and understanding of the world of work and occupations, the traditional territory of vocational education. Empirically also it is a commonplace to remark that training for an occupation, the priesthood, constituted one of the first formal forms of education.

More recently, fundamental changes in the economic infra-structure and the structure of occupations have forced increasing parallels to be drawn between vocational education and liberal education or, to use more conventional terms, between education and training. In essence the argument is straightforward. It is claimed that we have seen the passing, at least in the advanced industrial world, of the sort of semi-permanent occupations which require an easily identified set of skills for which training could be designed and given. In the 'post-industrial' world, citizens and workers are required to master an ever-wider range of complex information. What is needed, it is claimed, is the ability independently to acquire new knowledge and skills, so that learning how to learn becomes increasingly important. People also need to understand the procedural nature of work, to improve their general problem-solving skills, and to be able to move flexibly from one task to another as the situation demands.

These changes have the effect of drawing the central concerns of liberal education and vocationalism closer together. Hodkinson (1991), for example, argues that the progressive educators and the new progressive trainers have much in common in their focus on the needs of students and pedagogy rather than subject content. Bridges (1992) has attempted to show how the major principles of the Enterprise in Higher Education initiative show remarkable similarity with the principles of liberal education. Jamieson (1985) has argued that the concerns of the schools-industry movement in the UK have at least as much to do with notions of pedagogic liberation as they have with succumbing to the dictates of an 'industrialized curriculum'.

Whatever the merits of these various assertions, it is clear that many of the old social, economic and educational certainties are under attack if they have not already disappeared. The resulting post-modern confusion is nowhere better seen than in the terminology in the field of the work-related curriculum, especially in the Technical and Vocational Education Initiative. Whatever its merits or effects it was neither technical nor vocational in its thrust. Part of the terminological confusion is a reflection of genuine uncertainties over what label to place on developments that do not fit into old schemata. For example, with the decline of old craft skills associated with metalwork and woodwork in schools, and the rise of a desire to induct all children into the world of designing and making, then clearly 'technological' is the correct term, not 'technical'. But part of the confusion also results from a political desire to avoid certain of the old labels because of their unhelpful, even pejorative, overtones. The word 'vocational' is a good example. Once it had lost its helpful associations with the professions or semi-professions (the idea of a 'calling'), it became clearly associated with the skills of low-level occupations and, more importantly, with non-academic children. As writers like Raffe (1985) have clearly shown, the status of courses and occupations owes a great deal to the qualities of the people entering them.

The term 'pre-vocational' which began to flourish in the 1980s tried to capture the fact that students were studying generic, underlying skills and knowledge and that they could safely undertake this study in educational establishments because it was not fully vocational. But it is in the use of the term 'work' that the dilemma of vocationalism is fully confronted. Work can be a legitimate object of study; academic subjects can legitimately consider their applications in the workplace; even an experience of work can be justified in academic terms. Work also has merits in that it is broader than the terms 'industry' or 'business' which both enjoy something of a currency but which have their problems. So the phrase 'work-related curriculum' can be seen as part of a strategy to widen the appeal of considering work and the workplace inside the curriculum of compulsory schooling. Even this phrase is not without its difficulties, however. Richardson (1992), in a report on recent developments in this field, writes:

> Deliberately the Report avoids the term 'work related curriculum' which has been widely used since the 1980s. This is because it can imply too instrumental an approach to curriculum design and can be lacking in appeal for two important groups of teachers: those whose approach remains strongly didactic, with a dominant emphasis on pupils' acquisition of knowledge through subjects; and those for whom such a concept suggests too prominent an emphasis on 'work' in an otherwise broad and balanced curriculum (p. 9).

In its place, Richardson proposes 'work-related teaching and learning' in schools.

The forces shaping the work-related curriculum

I have argued elsewhere (Jamieson, 1992) that there are four distinctive concerns which are shaping the work-related curriculum: about the economy; about the transition from school to work; about the relevance of the curriculum and student maturation; and finally, about the needs of an educated citizenry. In practice these concerns tend to merge together but they are logically distinct and one needs to understand them in order to make any sense of the concept of the work-related curriculum.

The perceived problems of the economy are central to the conception of the work-related curriculum. Although the decline of the British economy has been a feature for over 150 years, and there has nearly always been a tendency to link it with the performance of the education system (Reeder, 1979), it is only relatively recently that the connection has been so minutely scrutinized (McCullough, 1987). At the heart of this particular debate is the contention that what happens in the education system must have a connection with economic performance. The fundamental problem is that even if we wished to tie the goals of the education system tightly to the needs of the economy, it is not entirely clear what we would need to do. The debate revolves around three key propositions. First, there are claims about the general standards of education. It is variously asserted that educational standards are lower than those of competitor countries and that industry has to engage in remedial education, and therefore does not have the raw material to produce a high-skill workforce. Second, there are claims that the sheer quantity of education is deficient, and critics point to the low staying-on rates in the UK compared to many other countries. Finally, there are criticisms of the content of education, that not enough education is relevant to the needs of the economy.

All of these assertions are problematic in one way or another. Are educational standards in the schools too low? The basis for this assertion itself seems beset with difficulties. The international comparative studies, for example the 1988 international assessment of mathematics and science (ETS, 1988), shows Britain doing well in science but comparatively less well in mathematics. Is maths or science more fundamental from an economic point of view? Such a question takes the results at face value, ignoring the criticism that such tests demonstrate very little given the tremendous variation in syllabuses and goals between one country and another. A similar criticism can be made of the much-publicized work of Prais and his associates at the National Institute of Economic and Social Research (eg, Prais and Beadle, 1991; Steedman, 1992). Most of these studies ignore the fundamental question of how the possessors of certain levels of educational qualifications perform in the economy now, and how they might perform in the future. How certain individuals with qualifications perform must be a function of the nature of the job they are doing. Prais in particular appears to ignore the fact that much of Britain is still locked into a low-skill, low-value-added economy where the demand for high skills is still modest, *and* the fact that it is predicted that traditional engineering-type skills will not be required in the high technology future, which will demand generic polyvalent skills.

The debate about levels of attainment is further complicated by the fact that its terms of reference move between the needs of employers and the needs of the economy. This is an important distinction in the British context because one feature of the British problem is alleged to be that employers take a short-term view of education and training at the expense of the long-term needs of the economy. Certainly there is evidence to suggest that employers very often do not know very much about the skill demands of the jobs in their own companies (Townsend *et al.*, 1982), and do not demand sophisticated qualifications from their potential work-force (Moore, 1988).

It is possible to bring a similar set of arguments to bear on the assertion that the quantity of education is insufficient in the UK. The focus here is on the staying-on rate at school and college beyond 16. Although the participation rate for 16–18-year-olds in the UK is poor by OECD standards, if one adds Britain's part-time students into the picture the UK position looks much more respectable (Raffe, 1992). We seem to be obsessed with the participation rate and with getting youngsters through certain qualification hurdles; for example, the National Education and Training Targets want 80 per cent of young people to reach NVQ II or its academic equivalent by 1997, and by the year 2000 for 50 per cent of young people to reach NVQ III. But the real question is, to what end? Exactly how will the possession of this wide variety of qualifications, all allegedly at the same level, produce economic performance? At the very least that performance must depend on matching the competences of young people with the demands of certain jobs. The difficulty at the moment is that the youth labour market still produces relatively highly paid jobs for school leavers at age 16 and employers tend to reward experience over qualifications. Is it that employers do not know their own interests? If this is so, we have a case of market failure, ie, the market is not acting as an efficient allocative system. Furthermore, despite the existence of the alleged failure of the current education system, a significant number of British firms appear to perform well, indicating, perhaps, that our economic problem is as much to do with labour utilization and in-company training as it is with the education system *per se*.

The final economically-related assertion concerns the content of education. Do we know with confidence what an economically-relevant curriculum would look like in compulsory schooling and at what age it should start? It is perfectly possible to construct an argument which suggests that, because the economy is changing so quickly, the only sensible education is one that concentrates on absolute fundamentals which do not change, like mathematics, English and science. If we could also show that the study of subjects like history and geography developed a range of transferable skills like data processing, graphicacy, etc., and we added modern languages on the grounds that with the globalization of trade these will always be relevant, then we are back to the fundamentals of the traditional liberal education. It is perhaps interesting to note that these have not been the grounds on which the National Curriculum has been argued for in the UK.

The second strand feeding the work-related curriculum can be labelled the 'transition problem', ie, the worries that are associated with the transition from school to work by young people. The transition problem is predicated on the view that the culture of schooling is very different from the culture of the workplace, and that the culture of youth is markedly different from adult culture, such that when this 'double transition' is made, considerable difficulties are experienced. In fact there is remarkably little evidence that many young people find this transition difficult, simply because both hypotheses are suspect. As Willis (1977) has shown in his classic study of low-achieving boys, they made the transition with consummate ease, exchanging a set of school roles where they resisted the orders of their teachers for a set of blue-collar worker roles where their resistance was transferred to their new industrial managers. And the hedonistic youth culture found a ready echo in the culture of young working-class adults in the workplace where the new recruits swelled the ranks of a blue-collar culture that in many instances was resistant to the managers' 'right to manage'. So the transition problem belonged to management not to the school-leavers.

From around the mid-1970s, however, the transition from school to work was disrupted for many young people as full employment policies were jettisoned and youth unemployment rose. A succession of unsatisfactory training schemes (WEEP, YOP, YTS), whose objectives seemed as much concerned with 'ware-housing' young people and keeping the unemployment figure down as with genuine training, caused a different sort of transition problem.

Another strand contributing to the idea of the work-related curriculum is that of curriculum relevance and its associated belief that if the curriculum could be made more relevant to young people then they would work harder, achieve more and continue in education and training. Sometimes the argument seems almost tautological – evidence of relevance is seen in better results and higher-staying on rates. On the other hand it cannot be denied that compulsory education is seen as unrewarding by many 16-year-olds who feel that they have been classed as failures. It is also the case that the England and Wales Youth Cohort Study shows a significant improvement in attitudes to schooling coinciding with the introduction of GCSE with its more student-centred, active approach (Raffe, 1992).

The main problem with the relevance argument in the context of the work-related curriculum is a simple-minded connection between the adult world of work and the problems which young people perceive as 'real' and therefore relevant to them. There is no one-to-one connection. The other problem concerns pedagogy. One of the distinctive features of the work-related curriculum was intended to be its stress on the importance of experiences and experiential, or at least active, learning. There is again a belief that such modes of learning always generate more motivation than their more passive, didactic counterparts. But not all children have this mode as their preferred learning style, and not all learning tasks lend themselves to the experiential mode.

The fourth strand feeding the work-related curriculum is concerned with the concept of citizenship. The idea is straightforward: it rests on the assertion that the world of work dominates our lives, dominates our political debates and our media. In order to be an active citizen (as well as a discriminating consumer, say), we need an understanding of industrial and economic affairs. The paradox is that despite this fact, the traditional school curriculum has paid remarkably little attention to such matters. It is difficult not to concede the citizenship argument; the problem lies in determining what might constitute 'economic and industrial understanding' as the National Curriculum frames it, particularly the industrial understanding element, and who might teach it in both primary and secondary schools.

The work-related curriculum in practice

What does the confluence of different purposes for the work-related curriculum, described in the previous section, lead to in practice? It is difficult to describe the curriculum in any detail because we have few studies which take the necessary overall look. Instead, we have piecemeal evidence gained from evaluations linked to TVEI (eg, Dale *et al.*, 1990; Gleeson, 1987); specific reports on aspects of the curriculum from HMI (eg, work experience; mini-enterprise); and evaluations of aspects of the curriculum (eg, Jamieson and Harris, 1992; Harris and Jamieson, 1992). Despite these problems, the general characteristics of such a curriculum are clear enough:

- A set of attainment targets and programmes of study related to the core and foundation subjects of the National Curriculum which relate to the world of work.
- A framework for knowledge, understanding and skills provided by the two directly relevant cross-curricular themes: Economic and Industrial Understanding, and Careers Education and Guidance.
- Aspects of the personal and social education programme which set out to develop qualities and skills relevant to the world of work.
- A set of specific work-related activities like work experience, mini-enterprise and industry weeks which may or may not be integrated with the mainstream curriculum.

Clearly, how all this works out in practice will vary enormously from school to school. The major factors which influence implementation include the following: school policy and the interests of the heads of departments and their colleagues; the local industrial infrastructure and any influence or pressure which it might exert on the school; the view taken by teachers of the interests of pupils and their parents. In the past, clearly LEA policies and structures have been important, and in the present and future, governors, TECs and EBPs will assume greater influence.

The fact that there has been some government pressure for schools to draw closer to the world of work and that there is a cross-curricular theme called 'Economic and Industrial Understanding' has not automatically meant that schools have embraced any conception of the work-related curriculum. It is certainly possible in both primary and secondary schools to deliver most aspects of the National Curriculum without any systematic study or contact with the world of work. Only in the subject technology is the business context one of five compulsory contexts in which technology must be examined. Given the twin pressures of parental choice through open enrolment, and the government's desire to persuade schools to differentiate themselves one from another to give parents more choice, then a school could well decide to concentrate on a curriculum which made little contact with the working world. As Watts and Jamieson (1992) have argued, most of the recent pressures have been to move schools *away* from the work-related curriculum.

Although the overall school policy will set the framework for the curriculum, it is the academic departments which will ultimately determine what is delivered. One of the obvious difficulties is that no particular department is the natural 'home' of such activities and, perhaps more importantly, none of the traditionally big and powerful departments like mathematics, English or science. Mathematics and science have obvious relevance if one considers the arguments in general about the needs of the economy, and teachers of maths and science have certainly felt the need to make their subject seem more relevant to children. This has led to a large number of projects in these fields showing the application of these school subjects to the world of work. Research conducted at the University of Bath into mathematics materials showed very modest impact and take-up. I have no doubt that a parallel study in science would show similar results. How does one account for these findings? Several reasons suggest themselves: first, maths and science have traditionally had very crowded syllabuses; second, many of the work-related activities do not, in the eyes of the teachers, appear to develop understanding of the subject; third, the industrial applications contained in the materials may not have any *local* applications.

The other major subject, English, appears to provide more fertile ground for work-related activities; studies of work experience, for example, consistently show that English frequently provides the academic subject framework (HMI, 1990; Miller *et al.*, 1991). The major reason for this is the lack of strong content-framing to be found in English which means that the subject is able to make use of the sorts of experiences very often provided by the work-related curriculum, eg, work experience. Further, the content frame of English is such that recollection of (and reflection on) experience is a central activity. The 'problem' is that English teachers very often do not frame the activity from an informed stance.

Both geography and history can make important contributions to an understanding of some aspects of the world of work. Geography looks at the interplay of natural and human resources and at specific topics like the location of industry, whilst history pays certain attention to topics like the industrial revolution. In primary schools, the origin and growth of local industry, and where products come from, can also be covered.

It is in the new National Curriculum subject, technology, that the world of work, or at least the business context, is formally addressed. The subject is supposed to mirror the ways in which real products are planned, designed, made, tested and evaluated. The debate about technology is at the heart of the debate about the work-related curriculum. In the first place it tries to tackle the academic-vocational divide by making the traditional subject of CDT take on a broader, more holistic view of the whole process of designing and making. It recognizes, for example, that there are important elements of design, marketing and costing involved in the production of goods and services. In this sense the subject has been made more intellectually demanding because it requires a broader range of skills and understanding from pupils. It was this element in technology which it was hoped would appeal to a broader cross-section of children. It was also hoped that the subject could focus the attention of separate subject departments in the school, in particular CDT, home economics, business studies and whichever department had responsibility for information technology. In some schools the art department has also been involved. Third, it was hoped that the new subject could give a real focus for the world of work by attempting to mirror aspects of the real world of designing and making. This last point was reinforced by the belief that very many of the teachers of the individual constituent subjects would have had some form or other of industrial experience.

National Curriculum technology has rapidly slipped from being the shining new jewel in the National Curriculum crown to being a curriculum area singled out for urgent reform. The HMI Report (HMI, 1992), the Engineering Council (1992) and the NCC (1992) have all posted urgent notices for change. The problems which technology has run into are instructive for a more general consideration of the work-related curriculum. In an attempt to break down the academic-vocational divide, critics argue that they have diluted the practical, craft aspects of the subject, and made it intellectually too demanding for children who would have been happy with old-style CDT, but not made it intellectually demanding enough for academically-abler children. In particular, critics have focused on the apparent move from the hard edge of working on real materials like wood and metal to the straws and cardboard of many designs. *The Sunday Times'* comment on the HMI Report summed up the situation:

> The findings reinforce widespread criticism of the emphasis in school technology lessons on 'Blue Peter' activities involving cardboard, paper and egg boxes. Academics warned this weekend that it was putting Britain's industrial future at risk (31 May 1992).

There are several comments that one can make about this debate. First, that in fact it is very common for architects, designers and professional engineers to work with cardboard and similar substances to make models. In this sense the activity does resemble the world of work. Second, that the decline in emphasis in working in a craft-like way with metal and wood is surely a reflection of the fate of these skills in the national economy. Third, even at the top level on degree courses there is very little manipulation of raw materials in subjects like engineering where the emphasis is on academic subjects like science and mathematics. Eggleston (1992) even suggests that the real reason for the worry over technology is that by exposing children to the *whole* process of designing and making (not just the making), and thus giving all children access to the high-status areas of design, marketing, etc., then 'if the endeavour succeeds it may confuse the social order by producing too many chiefs and not enough Indians' (p. 4).

The other difficulty which the travails of the technology curriculum expose is the that of bringing together different subjects to focus on one diffuse area; in this case technology, but the arguments could apply equally well to the concept of work. The conception of National Curriculum technology ignored the difficulties in the micro-politics of schooling of bringing together teachers working in what they saw as discrete subject areas with their own traditions and ways of working. In particular, one might point to the home economics tradition, usually composed of female teachers used to working with girls, compared to CDT teachers, largely male and with a tradition of teaching boys.

The technology curriculum is a miniature case-study of the difficulties of handling the work-related curriculum in schools. The major problem is that there does not appear to be a clearly agreed curriculum framework for handling a complex area like 'work'. It is true that the NCC has given us the cross-curricular theme, Economic and Industrial Understanding. *Curriculum Guidance 4* (NCC, 1990) defines it as a mixture of knowledge, understanding and skills, plus direct experience of industry and the world of work, and experience of 'small-scale business and community enterprise projects'. Knowledge includes key economic concepts, the organization of industry and commerce, consumer decisions, economic systems in different countries, the role of technology in the workplace and the role of government and international organizations. Skills include analytical, personal and social skills, including the ability to collect and analyse economic and industrial data, economic problem-solving, the distinction between fact and value in economic situations, the ability to communicate effectively on economic and industrial issues, plus skills related to working life, eg, teamwork and leading. The attitudes include an interest in economic and industrial affairs, respect for evidence and rational argument, concern for the use of scarce resources, a sense of responsibility for the consequences of their own economic actions, respect for alternative economic viewpoints, sensitivity to the effects of economic choices on the environment and, finally, concern for human rights as these are affected by economic decisions (NCC, 1990, pp.3–5).

This guidance by the NCC is non-statutory so teachers are not obliged to follow it to the letter. There are several difficulties with it. In the first place it seems to lack internal coherence; there is no clear idea of what it is intending to achieve. In view of the various interest groups involved in its construction, the speed at which it was put together, and the various possible objectives of the theme (cf Jamieson, 1992), this is hardly surprising. The conventional wisdom is to argue that schools are faced with the task of *coordinating* EIU, of bringing together all the disparate subjects which can make a contribution to the pupils' understanding of the world of work. In fact the problem is far more fundamental. Schools need to formulate an adequate conception of the whole before they can tackle the job of coordinating the parts. In particular, they need to decide what the balance is to be between teaching *for* the world of work; *through* the world of work; or *about* the world of work.

A great deal of the cross-curricular theme, Economic and Industrial Understanding, is concerned with teaching *about* the world of work and yet it can be argued that schools are, in general, ill-equipped to make such a study. This assertion is based on the fact that few teachers are qualified in those academic subjects which have traditionally taken the world of work as their field of study: economics, sociology and psychology. I have argued elsewhere that the study of the world of work can be successfully hung on two key ideas:

> Whatever the nature of the economy, the industrial system and the particular enterprise, two questions always need to be faced. The first concerns the basic problem of choice. The second aspect is the fundamental problem of interpersonal relationships which always have to be managed (Jamieson, 1992, p.62).

From these two central issues flow a web of concepts and concerns which could successfully map out the study of the world of work.

One of the first things which such a mapping exercise should do is to get to grips with the varieties of work in our society. At the moment, the curriculum concerns of teachers seem almost wholly concerned with paid employment in the formal economy. If more notice were taken of young people's experiences then the inadequacy of this conception would soon be realized. Various studies have shown that something like 50 per cent of pupils in their last year of compulsory schooling have some form of paid employment (Mizen, 1992) and much of this is in the hidden economy. Nearly all older children have experience of work in the household and communal economies (Gershuny and Pahl, 1980). If these experiences were systematically combined with those of work experience and mini-enterprise, which the majority of children now experience, then the possibilities of a much richer curriculum of the world of work would be opened up. In particular there would be an opportunity for a move away from the study of the world of work which was locked inside a framework of concepts derived wholly from academic school subjects, eg, geography and economics. The experiences of young people could at least provide a starting point for a serious consideration of issues like why some goods cost more than others, why prices rise, why women tend to earn less than men, why industrial disputes occur, etc. A constructivist approach, which encouraged children to construct their own hypotheses, grounded in their own experiences and vicarious experience derived from the media, could then be tested out. Their hypotheses and evidence could be compared with the conventional explanations derived from the traditional disciplines. If this approach were taken seriously it would follow that the teachers' own experience of the world of work outside of teaching would be important. Many teachers in secondary schools already have substantial experience of industry (Jamieson *et al.*, 1985) and the Teachers into Industry Scheme, sponsored by the Department of Employment, is close to reaching its target of providing an industrial placement for 10 per cent of teachers per year. In 1992 it placed 33,348 teachers into industry (Newslink, 1992).

There are several issues concerned with the experiential model of learning which are worthy of consideration. The first is to recognize the strengths and limitations of the model. Its strengths are largely in the affective domain; it can show what it feels like to work under certain circumstances, to be in a non-school environment. It is likely to be quite good in developing certain skills that are thought to be required in the world of work. Its limitations are an obvious weakness in the cognitive domain and this is particularly serious if the participants, say in work experience, believe that after a one-week placement they 'know' about the world of work. All the evidence suggests that merely having the experience does not of itself lead to much under-standing of the world of work (HMI, 1990; Miller *et al.*, 1991). Another problem specific to work experience is that in the absence of any particular curricular intervention by teachers, young people are inclined to place a 'career choice' framework around such experiences. This need not be a problem if that is the intention of the exercise, although again all the evidence suggests that the experience needs to be supplemented if it is to perform this function. Experiences of work tend to be essentially local (despite the current popularity of 'European work experience'). Pupils are exposed to local versions of the world of work in a vivid way by work experiences, yet this experience is unlikely to provide them with a very accurate picture of the world of work on either a national or international scale. Education ultimately must be about going beyond the immediate experiences of the locality, although this is probably a good place to start.

The work-related curriculum is also faced with the fundamental problem of coherence, progression and continuity. Progression, the building up of knowledge in a logical and systematic way, faces two particular problems in this area of the curriculum. First, unlike many traditional school subject areas, many pupils derive a significant amount of their knowledge from *outside* of school, eg, from part-time work or from relatives. Even an activity like work experience takes place off school premises and largely out of sight of the teacher. Second, because it has not been a traditional area of systematic study, there are no generally accepted schemes for what experiences should take place when, and in what order certain concepts should be encountered.

The problems in schools are graphically illustrated by this quote from an HMI Inspector:

> Pupils have to sub-divide into groups of five or six to make paper darts: simple artifacts from A4 sheets. The aims were to learn to work effectively as a team and to develop understanding of production and profit and loss, since materials had to be bought and products sold at given prices. Two pupils acted as supplier and buyer respectively and the teacher orchestrated the activity into production time periods (Trainor, 1992, p.16).

The HMI then goes on to make this important point:

> Now there are two very interesting points about this description. So far, it is

not possible to tell whether that describes a class of 6, 7, 12, 15 or 17 year olds because that kind of activity is going on in key stages 1, 2, 3, 4 and at FE colleges and, as it stands, is a process-based activity which develops skills. What skill, precisely, is being developed? Are skills developed differently according to whether the activity is in key stage 1, 2, 3, 4 or beyond? I suggest that such an activity will achieve progression only if somebody has thought not only about skills-development but also whether there is a conceptual and knowledge base for such work which is being progressed across the years (Trainor, 1992, p.17).

Finally, we might ask how such a curriculum is to be kept up to date. There is, of course, the general problem of keeping the National Curriculum up to date now that the research and development function, which the old Schools Council and its successors had, appears to have been neglected by the National Curriculum Council. Furthermore, the channels for up-dating through the LEA advisory service also appear to be drying up. It is difficult to see Education-Business Partnerships, with their fundamental lack of curriculum know-how, filling these gaps. These bodies are essentially parts of the Training and Enterprise Councils which are dominated by local employers. It is difficult to resist the notion that the dominant view here will be what Dale and his colleagues (1990) call 'occupationalism', ie, a focus on promoting the acquisition and utility of locally needed skills set against a backdrop of knowledge and appreciation of local industries. There is a clear contrast here between the essential particularism of occupationalism (this job, this company, here and now) and the universalism of school academic subjects.

Conclusion

It is difficult not to conclude that the current conception of the work-related curriculum lacks coherence. The four streams that fed the concept have not developed into a clear flowing river in the context of statutory curriculum planning. If the fate of the work-related curriculum is to be left in the hands of a non-statutory cross-curricular theme, then it is difficult to see how it can be rescued. It may well collapse in compulsory schooling through the newly unleashed forces of the market, as Watts and Jamieson (1992) argue.

It is possible to construct a scenario which shifts the main burden of the work-related curriculum to post-16 education. There are already signs of policy shifts in this direction, with the introduction of BTEC First Diplomas in schools and, more significantly, the planning for General National Vocational Qualifications, which aim to combine a vocational orientation with academic study. There are also interesting proposals for ordinary and advanced diplomas which combine academic and vocational study. One can see all these developments as part of a long line of policies to bridge the academic-vocational divide. All such proposals have to solve certain fundamental problems of parity of prestige if they are to be successful. Solving these problems means being concerned about who takes these qualifications initially, ie, who finds them attractive: what skills, knowledge and attitudes students acquire whilst studying them; how the gatekeepers to higher education and élite jobs react to holders of the qualification. As Bourdon (1974) observed, in societies structured by class and other inequalities, the greater the variety of different routes through the education system, the greater the likelihood that the system will reproduce the existing pattern of differentiation.

References

Bailey, C H (1984) *Beyond the Present and Particular: a theory of liberal education*, London: Routledge & Kegan Paul.

Bourdon, R (1974) *Education, Opportunity and Social Inequality*, New York: Wiley.

Bridges, D (1992) 'Enterprise and liberal education', *Journal of Philosophy of Education*, **26**, 1, 91–8.

Dale, R *et al* (1990) *The TVEI story: policy, practice and preparation for the work force*, Milton Keynes: Open University Press.

Educational Testing Services (1988) *A World of Difference*, London: ETS.

Eggleston, J (1992) 'Editorial', *Design and Technology Teaching*, **24**, 3, 3–4.

Engineering Council (1992) *Technology in the National Curriculum – Getting it Right*, London: Engineering Council.

Gershuny, J I and Pahl, R E (1980) 'Britain in the decade of the three economies', *New Society*, 900, 3, January.

Gleeson, D (ed.) (1987) *TVEI and Secondary Education: a critical appraisal*, Milton Keynes: Open University Press.

Harris, A and Jamieson, I M (1992) 'Evaluating economic awareness, part 2: teaching and learning issues', *Economic Awareness*, **5**, 1.

HMI (1990) *Work Experience and Work Shadowing for 14–19 Students: some aspects of good practice, 1988/89*, London: DES.

HMI (1992) *Technology Key Stages 1, 2 and 3 – a Report by HM Inspectorate on the First Year 1990–91*, London: HMSO.

Hodkinson, P (1991) 'Liberal Education and the "New Vocationalism": a progression partnership', *Oxford Review of Education*, **17**, 1.

Jamieson, I M (1985) 'Corporate hegemony or pedagogic liberation? The schools-industry movement in England and Wales', in Dale, R (ed.) *Education Training and Employment*, Oxford: Pergamon Press.

Jamieson, I M (1992) 'School work and real work: economic and industrial understanding in the curriculum', *The Curriculum Journal*, **2**, 1, 55–68.

Jamieson, I M and Harris, A (1992) 'Evaluating economic awareness, part 1: management and organisation issues', *Economic Awareness*, **4**, 3.

Jamieson, I M, Haig, J and Megaw, J (1985) 'Teachers into Industry Schemes', in Jamieson, I M (ed.) *Industry in Education: developments and case studies*, Harlow: Longman.

McCullough, G (1987) 'History and policy: the politics of TVEI', in Gleeson, D (ed.) *TVEI and Secondary Education: a critical appraisal*, Milton Keynes: Open University Press.

Miller, A, Watts, A G and Jamieson, I M (1991) *Rethinking Work Experience*, London: Falmer Press.

Mizen, P (1992) 'The extent and significance of child working in Britain', *British Journal of Education and Work*, **5**, 1.

Moore, R (1988) 'Education, employment and recruitment', in Dale, R *et al* (eds) *Frameworks for Teaching*, London: Hodder & Stoughton.

National Curriculum Council (1990) *Curriculum Guidance 4: Education for Economic and Industrial Understanding*, York: NCC.

National Curriculum Council (1992) *National Curriculum Technology: The Case for Revising the Order*, York: NCC.

Newslink (1992) *The Teacher Placement Service Newsletter*, June, London: UBI.

Prais, S J and Beadle, E (1991) *Pre-vocational Schooling in Europe Today*, London: NIESR.

Raffe, D (1985) 'Education and training initiatives for 14–18s: content and context', in Watts, A G (ed.) *Education and Training 14–18*, Cambridge: CRAC/Hobsons.

Raffe, D (1992) *Participation of 16–18 year olds in Education and Training*, London: National Commission on Education.

Reeder, D (1979) 'A recurring debate: education and industry', in Bernbaum, G (ed.) *Schooling in Decline*, London: Macmillan.

Richardson, W (ed.) (1992) *Work Related Teaching and Learning in Schools*, Coventry: Centre for Education and Industry, University of Warwick.

Steedman, H (1992) *Mathematics in Vocational Youth Training for the Building Trade in Britain, France and Germany*, London: NIESR.

Townsend, C *et al.* (1982) *London into Work Development Project*, Brighton: University of Sussex, Institute of Manpower Studies.

Trainor, D (1992) 'Coherence, progression and continuity in "work-related" teaching and learning', in Richardson, W (ed.) *op cit*.

Watts, A G and Jamieson, I M (1992), 'Is there life beyond TVEI?', *Education*, May 22.

Willis, P (1977) *Learning to Labour: How Working Class Kids get Working Class Jobs*, Aldershot: Gower.

SECTION 5

The Education-work Relationship for the Future

This final section concludes the book by examining the future of the education-work relationship and, more generally, the role of education in future society.

Carr begins by clarifying the terms of the debate and showing the important role played by language in marking it out. He talks of the new educational discourse which has defined the terms in which discussion about the future of education can proceed. This discourse, he claims, needs to be challenged in order to re-think the connection between education and work. Carr goes on to describe two paradigms of education, each with a different purpose, a different pedagogy and a different discourse. In one, the function of education is primarily economic and vocational in transmitting 'technically exploitable knowledge'. In the second, the function of education is political and cultural. Reflection on the interaction and tension between these two paradigms can help to clarify the contemporary debate on the purpose of education. Carr also distinguishes 'work' from 'labour'. While work can develop human identity and allow self-expression, labour is devoid of any intrinsic value. In a society where work degenerates into labour, both vocational and general education will be devalued.

Carr's message is that the contemporary debate must be opened up by taking it beyond a particular view of society and a narrow mode of discourse on education.

Richardson's chapter examines the response which education should make to the changing nature of work. He suggests that there is no clear causal connection between technological change and workplace organization – in reality, the crucial decisions are made by managers. Similarly, the complexity of the connection between education and industry or the economy is greatly underestimated. He talks of a 'complex nexus of forces' influencing the education-employment relationship. An interesting problem identified is that most analysts are only familiar with one aspect of the connection, eg, the labour market; education policy; or curriculum change. Literature and expertise on the issue come from one perspective or the other but rarely offer an overview.

What is the relationship between curriculum change and change in workplace skills? This is one of Richardson's central questions. He suggests that the power of economic forces to influence curriculum change has often been overestimated, and goes on to argue that the curriculum can be a shaping critical force in itself, rather than being passive and responsive to the skill demands of employers. Thus Richardson's chapter returns us to many of the recurrent themes and arguments of the book which have attempted to examine the relationship between education and employment.

11   Education and the World of Work: Clarifying the Contemporary Debate

Wilfred Carr

The manufacturers and capitalists ... declare that ignorance makes bad workmen; that England will soon be unable to turn out cotton goods, or steam engines, cheaper than other people; and then, Ichabod! Ichabod! the glory will be departed from us. And a few voices are lifted up in favour of the doctrine that the masses should be educated because they are men and women with unlimited capacities of being, doing and suffering and that it is true now as ever it was that the people perish for lack of knowledge (Huxley, 1893).

Introduction

Throughout the history of state education in Britain, the question of how schools should prepare their pupils for the world of work has been the subject of a continuous political debate. It emerged in the mid-nineteenth century as a conflict between those who saw the need for secondary schools to respond to the new realities of an industrialized society and those who wished to continue with that form of liberal education which evaded the educational consequences of industrialization by pursuing knowledge for its own sake (Wiener, 1981). Similarly, at the time of the Education Act of 1870 it was commonly argued that the expansion of state-provided elementary education was vital to Britain's industrial and economic progress. As F W E Forster famously remarked: 'Upon the speedy provision of elementary education depends our industrial prosperity' (Forster, 1870).

During the 1920s, in the social upheavals created by World War I, debates about the role of secondary education again revolved around the question of its 'liberal' and 'vocational' function. One view, expressed largely by industrialists and employers, was that any expanded system of secondary education should be firmly based on scientific, technical and practical studies. This view was attacked in the *Atheneum* journal as 'the capitalist theory of education' – a 'theory' which simply revived the old Platonic dichotomy between a 'liberal' education for the aristocracy and an education governed by economic needs for the working class:

> Education must not be viewed in terms of vocational goals but in terms of the individual and the citizen. The worker is not merely a worker but a citizen with rights. Education should be enjoyed by every individual of every class (quoted in Kazamias, 1966, p.232).

This 'democratic' view of the role of secondary education had already received official approval from the Board of Education which, in 1918, acknowledged that the future development of a democratic society depended on expanding education provision so as to ensure 'the intelligent participation in public affairs by the rank and file of the population' (ibid, p.233). During the next 50 years this emphasis on equality of opportunity as the key to the development of a more democratic society became the cornerstone of British educational policy.

After the Education Act of 1944, the principle that the state has an obligation to provide future members of society with a general education that would prepare them for democratic life was officially pursued and enacted, and questions about the effectiveness of this kind of education in preparing pupils for the world of work were largely ignored. It is thus unsurprising that, during the post-war period, technical and scientific education remained underdeveloped and 'practical' and 'vocational' subjects continued to be low-status subjects marginalized from the mainstream of general education.

However, in the climate created by the economic crisis of the 1970s, the values and assumptions informing official educational policy began to be questioned, the tone of the educational debate was tranformed and the question of the relationship between education and work was once again put back onto the political agenda. A major impetus to this tranformation was given by James Callaghan's Ruskin speech of 1976, in which he gave notice that the democratic principles that had dominated educational policy would have to be tempered by the need for schools to become more responsive to the economic needs of society in general and the labour requirements of industry in particular. In his speech, Callaghan echoed many historical concerns: the dissatisfaction of employers with the educational standards of their recruits; criticism of ways in which schools foster an aversion to careers in industry; and the failure of the education system to be more directly responsive to national economic needs. After the Ruskin speech, the view that the *democratic* aim of promoting greater educational opportunities and the *economic* aim of producing the appropriate workforce for a modern industrial society could be effectively combined was officially abandoned. Subsequently the emphasis in educational policy was gradually switched from the democratic principles of equality and social justice to the vocational principle of preparation for 'the world of work'. The introduction of TVEI in the early 1980s was one of the major practical examples of this change and up to and beyond the Educational Reform Act of 1988, there has been a concerted political effort to redefine the role of schools in preparing pupils for the world of work (Jones, 1989).

The new educational discourse

Central to this political effort has been the reintroduction of a particular form of educational discourse – a distinctive way of talking about education which serves to define the 'problems' of education in a particular way and to support a particular stance towards their resolution. The central problems to which this discourse draws attention are those associated with economic failure and decline, problems for which the education system is, at least in part, to blame. Nowhere is this discourse – the discourse of the new vocationalism – more clearly evident than in the remarks of the chairman of the Institute of Directors, Parry Rogers, who was also chairman of BTEC:

> We have gone astray ... in what we expect of our educational system ... it must be redirected to be an integral part of our economic system; its job is to supply to the world of employment the human skills that are – and will be – needed (quoted in Chitty, 1990, p.39).

Like any other mode of educational discourse, the language of the new vocationalism is not neutral: to accept and employ its vocabulary is already to express an allegiance to a particular conception of education, a particular view of society and a particular understanding of the relationship between the two.

What this means is that the dominant position of the vocationalist discourse in the contemporary debate about the relationship between school and work actually sets the terms within which that debate can proceed. Challenging the discourse of the new vocationalism is thus not a prelude to the debate about the relationship between school and work but an indispensable dimension of the debate itself (Connolly, 1974). It is for this reason that the meaning of the central concepts of the discourse of the new vocationalism has itself been the subject of conflict and disagreement between those holding rival political views about what the role of education in society should be. It is thus no accident that disagreement about the legitimacy of the distinction between 'education' (as the general development of knowledge and understanding) and 'training' (as the acquisition of specific vocational skills) has been at the heart of the contemporary debate. In *Better Schools* (DES, 1985) it was asserted that 'education and training cannot always be distinguished but they are complementary' (p.25). In the following year, Lord Young announced in a radio interview that the distinction had officially been obliterated: '... the difference between education and training is very slight ... Training is merely the practical application of education' (Chitty, 1989, p.37).

The discourse of the new vocationalism does not simply give expression to the educational opinions of contemporary individuals or social groups; it is also the discourse through which a particular political perspective on education can be persuasively articulated and expressed. Like any other educational discourse, the discourse of the new vocationalism encapsulates a general political ideology – a socially structured and historically sedimented form of consciousness in terms of which the relationship between education and society is tacitly understood and some particular view of the relationship between school and work is seen to be obvious and self-evidently true. In much of the contemporary debate, the political perspective underlying the discourse of the new vocationalism has remained unarticulated and undisclosed and hence has served to foreclose any more fundamental debate about the relationship between education and society. One way of making this perspective more visible and explicit – and hence of widening the debate – is to give some consideration to Feinberg's claim that, 'specific modes of educational discourse ... grow out of the perceived needs of existing societies' and that the dominance of any specific educational discourse reflects the success of some social or political group in persuading or coercing others to interpret and respond to those needs in a particular way (Feinberg, 1983, p.227). Because the origins of a specific mode of educational discourse can be traced to historically perceived social needs, argues Feinberg, any judgement about its contemporary significance must be based on some understanding of the role it now plays in maintaining and reproducing a particular form of social life.

Two paradigms of education

On this basis, Feinberg distinguishes 'two major social functions of education, two paradigms that can begin to provide an understanding of the possibilities that exist for progressive change' (1983, p.228). In the first of these paradigms the social function of education is primarily economic and vocational. It is the paradigm of education that involves:

> those areas that provide deliberate instruction into a code of knowledge, a set of principles and techniques designed to further the participation of an individual in the market through the mediation of skills that possess an exchange value.... It would include not only all those performances that involve simple rote procedures in which one has been instructed, but also those performances that involve the ability to deal with contingencies through the application of well-grounded scientific understanding. Hence, this category would include not only the simplest kind of vocational training, but education into a craft or profession as well, and it is primarily concerned with the transmission of technically exploitable knowledge (p.228).

The social function of Feinberg's second paradigm is primarily political and cultural. Its purpose is to provide:

> those forms of instruction primarily intended to further social participation as a member of the public through the development of interpretive understanding and normative skills. This form of instruction is often called general education. It is that component of education that prepares students for a common life regardless of the nature of their vocation and it is often thought that because general education projects a life in common ... it requires a common curriculum.... It is ... that form of instruction that involves the development of free persons ... who are ... capable of making unmanipulated judgments on the basis of reason.... General education, as education for participation in a public, ideally implies a community of equals, active partners engaged in a process of self-formation. Its ideal is a process ... where arguments are heard and judged on their own merits and where all have equal access to the debate (pp.228–9).

As Feinberg implies, these two paradigms sustain different modes of educational discourse and legitimize particular views of society. But they also galvanize and give credibility to a whole range of specific assumptions about such things as how schools should be organized, the content of the curriculum and the role of the teacher. For example, within the discourse endemic to the paradigm of general education, the primary function of education is to reproduce those forms of social life in which free and equal individuals can collectively participate in public debate about the common good of their society. Its view of society is thus democratic and egalitarian and it draws much of its inspiration from the ideas and ideals expressed by Dewey (1916). It is the view of education that exercised a decisive influence on the Education Act of 1944 and it was the driving force behind the comprehensive reorganization of secondary education in the 1960s.

In this paradigm, then, education is intimately related to the educational needs of a democratic society and it is invariably invoked in support of the idea of community schools to which children of different class, race, gender and religion can all belong and which provide the kind of educative environment and cultural milieux conducive to a form of communal life in which there is a shared concern for the common good. This paradigm of general education also offers support and justification for proposals for a 'core' curriculum based on some conception of the common culture which all future members of a democratic society need to acquire and share. For this reason, curriculum is organized so as to promote the active development of general understanding, social intelligence and cultural awareness, and curriculum content is selected on the basis of its value as an intellectual resource for analysing prevailing social norms, evaluating dominant political institutions and understanding contemporary cultural practices. Curriculum space is thus given to such subjects as social studies, economics and civic education.

It also sees a primary task of the teacher as that of organizing the conditions under which pupils can formulate and resolve social, moral and political problems in ways which involve collaborative enquiring and democratic debate and the development of a shared concern for the common good. Learning proceeds through discussion and joint problem-solving activities rather than through a passive reproduction of what is taught. It thus eschews those authoritarian teaching methods (such as direct instruction and the inculcation of facts) which breed undemocratic social attitudes (such as passive obedience and narrow self-interest) in favour of teaching methods (such as open discussion and enquiry based learning) which foster the qualities of mind (such as reflective understanding and critical thinking) and social attitudes (such as social responsibility and a concern for public issues) which membership of a democratic society both presupposes and requires.

Within the educational discourse of Feinberg's second paradigm – the paradigm of vocational education – the primary function of education is to contribute to the regeneration and modernization of industry and so advance the economic development and growth of modern technocratic society. It thus envisages a meritocratic society in which all individuals have equal opportunity to compete for economic rewards on the basis of their talent, skills, efforts and achievements. It is sharply suspicious of the way in which 'general education' conveys anti-industrial values, and so fails to equip pupils adequately for the world of work. It is particularly critical of traditional distinctions between 'education' and 'training', 'high-status' academic knowledge and 'low-status' 'technical knowledge' and proposes a form of education which provides the knowledge, attitudes and skills appropriate to future workers, producers and consumers in a market economy.

Curriculum knowledge is thus evaluated on the basis of its instrumental value and emphasis is given to the practical application of knowledge and the acquisition of marketable skills. For this reason, vocationally relevant subjects, particularly science and technology, are given pride of place and other subjects, such as literature and history, are organized in ways which minimize their cultural and political function and maximize their market value. Subjects which may promote critical discussion and debate about contemporary society, such as social studies, tend to be marginalized and pupils are taught about 'the world of work' in ways which ensure that critical questions about the norms and values infecting this 'world' are not seriously addressed. Teaching is not about realizing or promoting a particular view of education and society but is itself a practical skill based on that body of technical knowledge which can most effectively and economically produce – or 'deliver' – predetermined learning outcomes in accordance with the requirements laid down in a given curriculum specification.

The essential features of these two paradigms of education are presented diagrammatically in Table 11.1. Although this table represents these two paradigms as isolated and independent, it is obvious that they rarely, if ever, emerge in a pure or undistorted form and that in practice they always merge and overlap.

Table 11.1 *Two paradigms of education*

	Vocational Education	*General Education*
Political orientation	Technocratic	Democratic
Social function of education	Economic regeneration	Democratic participation
Political & social values	Meritocratic	Egalitarian
Guiding educational metaphors	'Relevance' 'Enterprise'	'Participation' 'Collaboration'
Policy exemplars	TVEI	1944 Education Act
Type of school	Technical colleges	Comprehensive community schools
School organization	Managerial	Democratic
Curriculum organization	Differentiation of subjects. Grouping on basis of vocational needs. Weak division between classroom and world of work.	Differentiation of subject matter around common activities. Weak division between classroom and community.
Curriculum knowledge	Technical knowledge and practical skills	Critical knowledge, cultural awareness, and social understanding
Teacher's role	Managerial, maximizing learning outcomes	Co-ordinator organizing learning around common tasks
Teaching methods	Practical instruction	Projects, group work, collaborative enquiry

Educational policies, whether of the state or the school, are invariably the negotiated outcome of a process of conflict, disagreement and compromise between individuals and groups advocating one or other of these paradigms; the outcome reflecting the political dominance of the educational discourse favoured by one of these groups. Similarly, although these different discourses are employed to advance the educational aims and political interests represented by one or other of these paradigms, any educational policies which are produced will, as they are translated into practice, inevitably be reinterpreted and modified as they are mediated through the educational discourse of teachers and as they are enacted within the structure of meaning that characterize the culture of schools. It is for this reason that the actual character of either 'general' or 'vocational' education at any one time always reflects how the tensions and contradictions between them have been reconciled and resolved as their conflicting principles and practices have been absorbed and integrated into the discourse, organization and practice of schools.

Once the relationship between 'general' and 'vocational' education begins to be understood in this way, certain conclusions about the contemporary debate about education and the world of work begin to emerge. The first and most obvious conclusion is that the contemporary debate is part of that much wider debate about the social function of education: a debate about which existing patterns of political, economic and cultural life ought to be reproduced and which ought to be modified or transformed. In this sense the debate about 'general' and 'vocational' education is just one aspect of that continuously evolving historical debate through which the relationship between education and society has been, and continues to be, redefined.

The second is that to enter the debate about 'general' and 'vocational' education is not simply to argue for or against the particular curriculum subjects that one or other prescribes. It is also and always to argue for or against the paradigmatic framework of political assumptions embedded in the discourse through which this subject matter is interpreted and in terms of which either its political function or market value is emphasized. For example, to employ the discourse of general education is not only to assume that subjects such as the humanities, literature and the liberal arts should be directed towards the development of the qualities of mind that democratic social life requires. It is also to argue that vocational subjects should always incorporate opportunities for reflectively understanding and critically examining the cultural norms and values of the world of work. Conversely, to employ the discourse of vocational education is always to assume that the subject matter of general education should be taught and learned in ways which emphasize its market value and that vocational education should be restricted to providing the knowledge and skills required for successful market participation.

This last conclusion suggests another: within the different discourses of general and vocational education the meaning of 'education for the world of work' will be interpreted in different and conflicting ways to reflect differences in how the core concepts of 'vocational' and 'work' are being understood. The difference between the ways in which the concept of 'vocational' is interpreted in these two discourses is well known. In 1917, Dewey pointed out that its meanings:

> vary from the bread and butter conception which identifies 'vocational' with a pecuniary aim to the conception of the calling of man in fulfilling his moral and intellectual destiny. With the first idea it is not difficult to attack the growing trend towards the vocational as a source of all our educational woes; with the latter it is easy to glorify this trend as a movement to bring back the ideal of liberal and cultural education from formal and arid by-paths to a concrete human significance (quoted in Silver and Brennan, 1988, p.14).

Although within the contemporary debate Dewey's distinction between the 'bread and butter' conception of the vocational and the conception which emphasizes 'the calling of man' is widely understood, the way in which the different educational discourses attach different meanings to the concept of 'work' is less clearly articulated. Uncovering those different meanings is, however, readily available in recent philosophical enquiries which have sought to distinguish two forms of human action: those forms of productive activity which make those who perform them more fully human and those which do not. These philosophical enquiries usually proceed by drawing a distinction between 'work' and 'labour' and the arguments that they have deployed can be summarized as follows (Arendt, 1958; Herbst, 1973).

Work, labour and education

Both the concept of 'work' and the concept of 'labour' refer to forms of purposive human activity that call for a certain discipline, that are directed towards the production of some object or artifact and that can be done more or less competently and conscientiously. However, what is central to, and distinctive of, the concept of 'work' is that it implies a necessary intrinsic connection between its process and product, that is, between what is produced and how it is produced. Work is not simply an instrumental means of production but is itself always constitutive of the product. It is for this reason that the product of work – say, a chair – can be described and evaluated by describing and evaluating the quality of the process – that is, the craftsmanship of the joiner – through which it was produced. In this sense, a judgement about the quality of the chair and a judgement about the process of its production are one and the same.

To engage in work is thus to engage in a form of productive activity which is informed and directed by those values, principles and standards of excellence intrinsic to the activity and constitutive of good workmanship. It is the fact that it is governed by such principles and standards that makes it a distinctively human and humanizing form of productive activity. It is in and through work that people express themselves and their human identity and give meaning to their lives. It is in this sense that we can talk about 'living to work'.

In contrast to work, 'labour' is an essentially instrumental activity only contingently related to the object it produces. In itself, labour is devoid of any intrinsic value with which the labourer can identify. Thus distinctive of labour is the absence of those standards of workmanship to which the labourer can aspire and of any concern for the quality of the finished product to which he or she can relate. People labour rather than work only because of the material rewards that it brings: the labourer does not 'live to work' but 'works to live'. In principle, human labour, unlike work, can be supplanted and replaced by robots or machines. In principle, and often in practice, labourers need neither know nor care about the products to which their labours contribute. Herbst (1973) gives a good example:

> Labour ... is the price that we pay for whatever adventure the reward of labour will buy. A typist who neither understands nor cares for the material which she is typing ... accepts the inconvenience of having to perform an uncongenial task ... for the sake of the activities and amusements which her wages ... bring within her reach. If she could obtain those advantages without having to type that is better, but typing is better than forgoing the advantages (pp.59–60).

Work gets transformed into labour when the standards of excellence which the worker aspires to achieve are displaced by standards of productivity, profitability and efficiency to which the process of production must conform. Moreover, such transformations are endemic in a society where objects of work which were previously produced to be used and enjoyed are replaced by commodities which are produced to be used up, or consumed. In a society in which consumption is the greatest good and the ever-expanding production of commodities is an overriding political aim, work is quickly deprived of the cultural resources and economic conditions which it presupposes and requires. In such a society, the distinction between work and labour inevitably appears obsolete and the conception of work as a distinctively human and humanizing activity becomes fragmented and begins to disappear. In such a society:

> ... we produce in order that we may consume and we consume for the sake of the satisfactions to be derived from doing so; thus our satisfactions alone are an end and everything else, the goods themselves, the productive process of which they are the fruit and the labour which is experienced in the process are but means. Viewed from this standpoint nothing has intrinsic value but human satisfactions and the best life is that in which the capacity for consumption is maximised and the opportunities do not lag behind (Herbst, 1973, p.66).

In a society in which work has been transformed into labour, both vocational education and general education are also transformed. Vocational education is no longer about developing the pupils' potential for engaging in work and quickly becomes a means of instilling the knowledge, attitudes and skills required of efficient labourers. General education is no longer about initiating pupils into a range of intellectual and practical disciplines in which the values and excellences intrinsic to activities of work can be systematically learned and pursued. Instead, it is increasingly seen as a list of esoteric academic subjects whose relevance to the educational needs of future members of a highly skilled and well-trained labour force is difficult to discern.

Thus, the final conclusion to emerge about the contemporary educational debate is that it should not be understood as a debate about the extent to which education should prepare individual pupils for the world of work. Rather, it should be understood as a debate about the extent to which education should subserve, and the extent to which it should subvert, the particular 'world' of work' which the consumer society has created. If the contemporary debate were to be conducted in these terms, certain key questions would inevitably have to be addressed. Is it possible or desirable to pursue the social aim of general education in a society in which public participation is increasingly being reduced to market participation (Feinberg, 1983, p.232)? How can the contradictions between the educational needs of a democratic society and the educational demands of a market economy be resolved? To what extent do the ethos and ideology of a consumer society undermine the discourse of general education and legitimize forms of educational discourse which conceal the dehumanizing character of labour and deny the humanizing character of work? Insisting that questions like these be seriously confronted would not only help to dispel the illusion that there can be an uncontested, value-neutral discourse through which the relationship between education and work can be discussed, it would also help to transform the contemporary debate about education and work into a genuinely democratic debate about the present shape and future direction of society. If educational debate is thus transformed it will neither be confined to that agenda of questions for which the consumer society demands answers nor constrained by the view of education and society that the discourse of the new vocationalism has legitimized and sustained.

References

Arendt, H (1958) *The Human Condition*, Chicago, IL: Chicago University Press.

Chitty, C (1989) *Towards a New Education System: The victory of the new right*, London: Falmer Press.

Connolly, K (1974) *The Terms of Political Discourse*, London: Martin Robertson.

DES (1985) *Better Schools*, London: HMSO.

Dewey, J (1916) *Democracy and Education*, Ontario: Collier-MacMillan.

Feinberg, W (1983) *Understanding Education: Towards a reconstruction of educational inquiry*, Cambridge: Cambridge University Press.

Forster, FWE (1870) cited in *Hansard*, cciii, 746, July 22.

Herbst, P (1973) 'Work, labour and education', in Peters, R S (ed.) *The Philosophy of Education*, Oxford: Oxford University Press.

Huxley, T H (1893) *Science and Education*, London: Macmillan.

Jones, K (1989) *Right Turn: The Conservative revolution in education*, London: Hutchinson Radius.

Kazamias, A M (1966) *Politics, Society and Secondary Education in England*, Philadelphia: University of Philadelphia Press.

Silver, H and Brennan, J (1988) *A Liberal Vocationalism*, London: Methuen.

Weiner, M (1981) *English Culture and the Decline of the Industrial Spirit 1850–1980*, Cambridge: Cambridge University Press.

12 The Changing Nature of Work: Responses from Education

William Richardson

This chapter sets out to examine three basic questions about the relationship between education provision and workplace change in Britain in the 1990s. These are:

- What are the basic drivers of curriculum change in British education provision for the 14–19 age group?
- What are the basic drivers of skills demand in British employment and what characterizes patterns of skill utilization in the labour market?
- What is the nature of the relationship between curriculum change and changes in workplace skills?

Evidence about the first two questions is the subject of specialized research literatures in each field and these are reviewed here. Such analyses, however, are rarely related to each other. As a result, policy-makers and practitioners, when considering the third issue, assume the importance of the relationship between curriculum change and workplace change, but are rarely in possession of the tools needed to understand the nature of the relationship. The chapter concludes by probing various analyses of the quality of the match between curriculum change and changes in work skills, and by posing the question: what kind of match is most appropriate?

Forces driving change in British education provision for the age group 14–19

For most of the period since 1944, it has been the social policy goals of education – particularly its promotion of greater equality of opportunity – that have fuelled arguments for and against change in school and college provision in Britain (Finch, 1984). Although education policies of successive Conservative governments since 1979 have largely broken the post-war consensus over the social ends of educational change, teachers in publicly-maintained schools remain strongly committed to this agenda.[1]

Over the longer perspective, however, it may be argued that the renewed focus on efficiency in educational policy-making during the 1980s is a reversion to the norm of education's principal function as an effective allocator of young people to adult work roles (Blackman, 1992; Reeder, 1981). The editors of a recent collection of essays have tried to suggest, however, that whilst this task may remain constant, fundamental changes in the organization and distribution of work in industrial economies will have an inevitable impact on the structure (both curricular and institutional) of education provision (Brown and Lauder, 1992).

According to these arguments, it is economic pressures rather than social policy imperatives that have driven educational change for most of this century and, especially, since the mid-1970s. This is a complementary perspective to that of historians (Field, 1988) and commentators (eg, Cockburn, 1987; Davies, 1986; Fiddy, 1985; Wallace and Cross, 1990) who have related specific changes in vocational education to youth (un)employment policy. Moreover, political economists such as Finegold have been able to demonstrate persuasively that, since the breakdown of the post-war Keynes/Beveridge economic welfare state, Britain's education system has undergone urgent economic and political scrutiny and that it is these influences, determined crucially by institutional relationships, that have dictated the motivation and pace of change (Finegold, 1992a).

Nevertheless, these economic and political pressures remain, to some extent, disguised in debate among educationalists by the technical discourse which dominates specialized issues such as curriculum, assessment and accreditation. One result is that teachers, especially, can find it hard to identify the long-term dynamic of education policy change and, consequently, to influence the pace and direction of such change (Walker and Barton, 1987). This issue, in turn, raises the question of how various professional interest groups – educational or political – seek to control the policy process.

Such tensions are all well illustrated in the conduct of the debate during 1988–92 about changes in the provision of education and training for 16–19-year-olds in England and Wales.[2] Despite all participants being able to agree on the need for policy change – low participation rates beyond the minimum school-leaving age being seen as detrimental to Britain's economic well-being – discussion has been combative and polarized. Furthermore, a wide range of disparate forces bearing upon the policy debate may be identified, all of which play their part in the 'mobilisation of opinion' (Nettl, 1967, pp.172–74). Amongst the most prominent are the roles played by: interest groups; 'opinion formers'; empirical research studies; government bodies; select committees; political parties in opposition; senior civil servants; and the party in government (Richardson, 1991).

Such policy debate appears more politically polarized in Britain than, for example, in America (Boyd, 1992, forthcoming). As a result, it may be questioned whether the British policy process is able to effect necessary change and modernization in the face of a general belief that education provision in Britain needs to change in response to the changing nature of adult work.[3] Specifically, a consensus has arisen over the last decade about the economic need to boost the overall skill level of the workforce through more effective schooling and through increased participation in education and training after the age of 16 (DES/DE, 1991; IMS, 1984; OECD, 1985).

This policy prescription is very wide, however, and more specific interpretations of how to raise young people's skill levels through curriculum change take a number of different forms. In the school curriculum, consolidation of a decade of disparate intervention is being attempted through the cross-curricular theme of economic and industrial understanding, including work experience (Jamieson, this volume, Chapter 10). In the post-compulsory curriculum, such change will be focused upon the emerging general national vocational qualification (GNVQ) (Jessup, 1992, forthcoming).

For the age group 5–16, teachers face the conundrum of how to integrate such teaching and learning into the subject-based National Curriculum – should they so wish. In sixth form and further education courses, the lack of systematic accreditation for non-academic study and experience has remained a barrier to change. In an attempt to solve this latter problem, and to challenge the dominance of academic courses over subordinate vocational study, two broad curriculum developments have gained consider-able support since 1989: the organization of coursework (through 'units', 'modules' or 'credits') according to a plan drawn up for each individual; and the promotion of greater personal effectiveness for students around a set of 'core skills' (Baker, 1989; FEU, 1992; IPPR, 1990).

Ironically, although these two ideas have come to enjoy wide consensus among educational policy groups, progress on both may yet be impeded by a mixture of political ideology on the part of government and uninformed opinion within education circles. Widely supported moves to introduce a modular curriculum framework through credit accumulation remain inhibited by the government's rearguard protection of A-levels, at a time when the last blockage – the cautious bodies representing independent schools – have acknowledged the need for such developments (*The Times*, 1992). The promotion of core skills, meanwhile, was subject to three contradictory official stances by government during 1988–90. Moreover, the findings of two empirical studies have demonstrated the greater effectiveness of the problem-solving element of core skills provision when it is the subject of specific course time rather than being 'permeated' through subject-based or occupationally-specific courses – an opposite finding to the view currently espoused by all the major educational bodies, including the model proposed for the GNVQ framework (Jessup, 1993, forthcoming; Richardson, 1991, pp.47–8).[4]

Despite such contradictions – illustrative of the muddled post-16 education policy process more generally (Spours, 1993, forthcoming) – it seems clear that a mixture of core skills, credit accumulation and individual learning plans for students will form the basis of the response of educationalists to the challenge of securing increased participation and attainment for the majority of the post-16 population.

It is notable that, in contrast to the hopes vested in the comprehensive reorganization of schools in the 1960s, there is widespread agreement within education that the engine of change should be curricular rather than institutional reform (Richardson, 1991, pp.38–41). Indeed, the appeal to many commentators of such changes is that curriculum change is thought to be more powerful, potentially, than the deleterious and unpredictable effects ascribed to the institutional reforms introduced by the Conservative government since 1988 – changes such as the creation of grant-maintained schools and City Technology Colleges (see Chapter 7, this volume).

Proponents of curricular reforms (FEU, 1992; Hodkinson, 1989; IPPR, 1990) argue that their designs are sufficiently far-reaching to form an important element in overcoming the widely acknowledged problems of low quality in British vocational education provision (Prais and Wagner, 1983; Steedman, 1988; White, 1988) and to tackle head-on the question of how to generate 'parity of esteem' between academic and vocational qualifications in England and Wales (DES/DE, 1991).

Furthermore, it is clear from these and other policy prescriptions that the rise of interest in core skills and modular curriculum structures are responses to two viewpoints widely held by educationalists. First, changes in work organization require higher levels of skill to be attained by all young people as they pass through formal education and, second, curriculum reform can meet such needs. What, however, is the basis of either assumption?

Forces driving change in skills demand and utilization

The recent origins of the widespread assumption that advanced industrial societies will uniformly demand rapidly increased levels of workplace skill from all of their citizens lies in the popularization of ideas about 'post-industrialism' during the late 1960s and early 1970s.

The popularizers have been both sociologists such as Alvin Toffler and Daniel Bell, and management educators such as Peter Drucker and, more recently, Charles Handy (Handy, 1984; Kumar, 1992). Their best-sellers have reached far larger numbers of educationalists than more critical academic studies bearing on similar themes (eg, IMS, 1984; OECD, 1985) and have been influential among educators responsible for skills-related curriculum innovation (Crompton, 1987; Tomlinson, 1992).[5]

Moreover, macro-economic modelling of labour market change appears, at first sight, to underline an inexorable increase in skill levels within advanced industrial economies, including that of Britain. For example, studies by the Institute for Employment Research (1991) indicate occupational changes during the period 1971–2000 as shown in Figure 12.1.

Such general trends are commonly explained by reference to strong forces which drive changes in national economies' skills needs. These forces include the increasing pace of technological change and the integration of world markets. Both developments have the effect of diminishing national governments' ability to control their domestic economies whilst focusing transnational

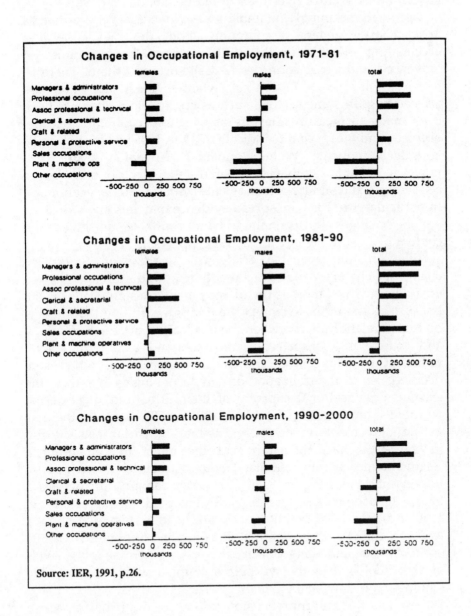

Figure 12.1 *Occupational employment in Britain, 1971–2000*

corporations' location decisions on comparative variables which include the trade-off between national skill levels and unit labour costs (Finegold, 1992a, pp.11–18). In turn, this international dynamic of corporate decision-making diminishes national governments' control over their domestic labour markets.

Despite the seemingly unambiguous evidence, several problems arise from a general assumption about the inexorable and accelerating increase in the skills base of the economies of 'advanced' industrial countries (AICs), such as Britain. There is, for example, the question of whether such demands are accelerating. In some sectors, such as engineering, attempts have been made to measure the rate at which specific skills become obsolete, and these seem to indicate that the 'half-life' of such skills is, indeed, reducing (Walton, quoted in Finegold, 1992b). This, however, is not to say that change in the skill levels of other jobs is accelerating at a similar rate or evenly within regional economies. In particular, there is widespread evidence that, in some industrial sectors, changes in technology have routinely de-skilled the content of existing jobs (Kumar, 1992, pp.54–5).

Although the extensive academic literature on workplace change is characterized by contention and disagreement, two areas about which there is broad agreement are significant for the issues explored in this chapter. The first is the finding that there is no causal relationship between the availability of new technology and change in workplace organization and skill deployment; rather, it is managers in individual organizations who make decisions about the utilization of new technologies 'based on the existing organisational capacity of their firms and the external incentives they face' (Finegold, 1992a, p.18). Second, there is general agreement among specialists that industrial restructuring in the AICs has, thus far, had the effect of cementing a 'segmentation' within national labour markets characterized by pockets of co-existing low-skill, low-wage labour and high-skill, high-wage labour (Ashton *et al.*, 1987; Finegold, 1992a, p.28; King, 1990, pp.150–51; McNabb and Ryan, 1990). This is despite a widespread belief in Britain that, in common with other AICs, the economy is experiencing an across-the-board increase in the levels of skill deployed in the workplace coupled with an inexorable elimination of low-skill jobs.

How has this misapprehension arisen? Beyond the impact in Britain of best-selling sociology and management texts, two further reasons are the desire of both employer interest groups and politicians to create a climate of exhortation about training, and acceptance of market-driven mechanisms for promoting changes in provision.

In private discussion, however, English Training and Enterprise Councils (TECs) will aver that their main problem is lack of leverage over employers who do little to stimulate increases in skill levels – a current manifestation of the dismal picture revealed in 1989 by official government research on national trends (TA/ DE, 1989). In the absence of a statutory duty upon employers to provide training, exhortation and examples of selected high-skill companies are the main weapons both of government and the employers' lobby. Such exhortation, bolstered by journalism which stresses the glamorous and futuristic whilst underplaying the reality of the current situation, serves to reinforce popular misconceptions and disguise the highly variable levels of skill demand in the British labour market.

In the political context, the question of transnational corporate investment provides an example of how a picture of relentlessly increasing skills demand can be oversimplified. Research evidence suggests that the predominant effect of inward investment has been to reproduce existing structural weaknesses and strengths within the British economy (Knell, 1992, pp.1–2; Peck and Stone, 1991). The arrival of Nissan in the North East is a prominent example of the ambiguous effects of inward investment on skills demand. Despite the inflated claims of politicians, the 'Nissan effect' has been to create 4,000 jobs at a single car assembly plant without producing a major stimulus to the secondary sector of component suppliers. Consequently, while the car assembly jobs are relatively highly skilled within their industrial sector, the government promise of higher-level skill creation in the regional economy has largely failed to materialize, the added-value components required for car assembly currently being predominantly imported from suppliers in Japan and Germany.[6]

Some analysts have doubts that Britain can generate any relative progress on raising skills demand in employment in the absence of fundamental change to the incentives facing policy-makers in government and firms (Finegold and Soskice, 1988). The barriers seem formidable and reinforce the argument being developed here: that the forces of demand for increased skill in the British economy remain highly uneven and that an expectation of rapid, widespread skills creation across all sectors of employment, at all occupational levels, is not to be taken at face value.

The overall picture that emerges from a review of literature on the forces driving change in skills demand and utilization is composed of three elements: the utilization of available technology by managers is unpredictable; the dynamics of industrial restructuring create polarized skills demands in regional economies; and the capacity of the British government or employer interest groups to counterbalance the existing weaknesses and strengths of the economy, and so effect an even demand for increased skills, remains weak.

The match between curriculum change and skills change in the workplace

All commentators are agreed that Britain's relatively poor industrial performance during the period 1970–90 has been accompanied by a set of structural changes in work organization as rapid as any since the onset of industrialization and the mass production of goods. Such consensus, however, can serve to disguise several fundamental problems of analysis as well as policy prescription concerning the implications of changes in work organization for the educational preparation of young people. In the remainder of this chapter, some of these difficulties are explored further.

One problem is the tendency of commentators to overstate the subordinate role of education to the labour market. Specifically, the impact upon curricula of the same socio-economic forces which drive employment change (but which remain separate from it) is ignored in analyses such as that of Ashton (1992). The view that schools are unchanging systems with teachers and pupils impervious to social, economic and cultural changes beyond employment change, is implausible. By this reading, the process of schooling, including curriculum, remains static until forced to change by pressures arising from structural alterations in the labour market. More than this, 'the conservatism of educators steeped in the academic curriculum', reinforced by the divisive élitism of the public schools (*ibid*, pp.196,193), is held to be the main force which inhibits a proper correspondence between schooling and the economy.[7]

Although it seems likely that the interplay of economic and social forces which dictate educational change is considerably more complex than that of a causal relationship between occupational change and curriculum design, a further problem of analysis arises in the difficulty of assessing the strength of other variables in the relationship. The role of the teacher is clearly important. Whilst a number of studies have shown how British teachers mediate existing inequalities through schooling (eg, Ball, 1981), there has been no systematic investigation of teacher attitudes to curriculum reform. Similarly, research is awaited on the specific impact on schooling of the information-rich, technology-driven teenage culture of the last two decades and the new consumer markets it has spawned.[8] Evidence from ethnographic studies of individual British schools, however, portrays differentiated peer groups which anticipate the segmentation of the labour market (Ball, 1981; Hargreaves, 1967; Lacey, 1970; Oppenheim, 1955; Turner, 1983; Willis, 1977; Woods, 1979). The implication here is that it is the stratified social relations within the school which determine curriculum strategies, and not the latter which determines the former.[9]

Taken together, these influences suggest a far more complex nexus of forces influencing the education-economy relationship than Ashton's analysis allows. Seen in this wider context, the unwitting implication of his prescription for correcting imbalances between labour market requirements and education provision – the resurrection of a thoroughgoing policy of comprehensive schooling, the 'discouragement' of private schools and re-introduction of apprenticeships in industries 'where transferable skills are not necessary' – is that the organization of education and training will be exposed more fully to the economic and social conservatism of 'market changes' in employment (Ashton, 1992, pp.193,197). This, however, would merely serve to reproduce the central problem he is attempting to solve: 'the defining characteristic' of the British system in socializing 'each new generation for their (sic) future position in the class structure and domestic division of labour' (*ibid*, p.180).

A third problem evident in the education-economy literature is that most analysts are unfamiliar with the complexity and subtlety of that side of the equation which is not their own specialism.[10] Ashton, for example, seems less secure when moving from labour market analysis, where he and his colleagues at Leicester have a formidable record, to education policy analysis. This may be because he is directly influenced (*ibid*, p.185) by those whose position, when assessing the question of the educational implications of late twentieth century economic change, lies in the conservative mainstream of educational progressivism. This approach has recently been restated by Brown and Lauder (1992). It maintains that, whilst industrial restructuring over the last 20 years has been momentous, what has not changed is the need for 'struggle' with the 'inherent logic of capitalist development' (*ibid*, p.2).

Despite this unpromising start, the discussion by Brown and Lauder points usefully to ways in which a number of current changes in British education provision for the age group 14–19 seem to mirror some of the changes in skill deployment characteristic of employers in their search for flexibility (Finegold, 1992a, pp.23–8). The emphasis is on those changes which seek to promote the 'transferable social and conceptual skills' of individuals – integrated core studies, records of achievement, and delayed specialization of course choices by students (Brown and Lauder, 1992, p.28).

As with Ashton's policy critique, the main shortcoming of the assumptions underlying this kind of analysis – and with the prescriptive changes that they engender – is a severe underestimation of the complexity of the school-economy relationship. In this case, however, it is the economic changes outside education which are severely underestimated. The problem is illustrated by difficulties surrounding the concept of student 'empowerment' as a basic educational response to increased skill demands in the labour market (*ibid*, p.30). If the term empowerment holds any meaning, it is often the opposite of that meant by those deploying it. Disarmingly, for young people it can be seen as an empty expression which fails to disguise the incoherence and muddle of the post-16 system of education and training (Richardson, 1991; 1993a, forthcoming). As one 16-year-old said to her careers adviser, 'When you tell me I'm empowered, that's really saying "You're on your own chum"'.[11] Among professional interest groups the inversion in meaning can be equally disarming, with TEC officers promoting the empowerment of young people alongside radical educationalists. The former are likely to have in mind the promotion of students as more effective individual consumers bestowed, for example, with 'real purchasing power' through training credits (DE, 1992, p.3); the latter would seek to see students as an organized, 'collective intelligence' better able to engage in the struggle with capitalism (Brown and Lauder, 1992, pp.27,2,30).[12]

This breadth of meaning applied to a single concept is illustrative of a clear tension between those economic and social pressures which stimulate teenagers to become active consumers (choosing, for example, to leave school at 16 for a job offering no training) and those which point to the need for more young people to remain in the education and training system to an older age, attaining higher levels of qualification. Brown and Lauder ignore the former and concentrate on the latter. Like Ashton, their prescription involves institutional changes such as the 'need' for schools 'to discard streaming in favour of mixed ability teaching' (*ibid*, p.30), measures which are designed to bring about equality of opportunity but which, in theory and practice, seem more likely to reinforce social disadvantage with specific economic disadvantage (Ball, 1981; Bernstein, 1990; Bourdieu and Passeron, 1977).

As a response to some of the problems discussed here, a rather different interpretation of the relationship of employment change to educational change stresses the duty of education and training to reproduce faithfully segmented labour market conditions. Bash *et al.*, (1985) summarize this position in the following way:

> ... the stratification of the labour market is such that public and private employers actually require young people with different skills at different levels. Industry, commerce, the professions and service facilities need some young people with a high level of specific specialised skill. They also need people with low-level skills or virtually no skills at all. If schools do not produce unskilled and unqualified young people, then they will fail to meet one of the demands of the labour market (p. 136).[13]

This interpretation of the response required from schools to labour market change (or, rather, continuity) shares some of Ashton, Brown and Lauder's assumptions about how the education-labour market relationship in Britain works in practice, but arrives at a proposed solution which is the exact opposite of what they have prescribed (see also, O'Keeffe, 1979). One practical strength of an argument which ascribes to education the role of more accurately reproducing stratification in the labour market is that schools and colleges are accustomed to operating within such a framework. Moreover, it is arguable whether they can assume any other role without major political intervention of a kind most unlikely in the post-Keynes/Beveridge era. Furthermore, this line of argument has the benefit of allowing policy-makers to work with the system as it is in order to effect incremental change, whilst not relying on one predominant policy instrument – institutional reform – to alter the deeply entrenched forces which lead to social and economic reproduction of an unwanted kind through education.

Nevertheless, an interpretation of the policy implications of the education-economy relationship which stresses enhanced social and economic reproduction suffers from a powerful and obvious drawback. It fails to acknowledge the ethical aspiration of virtually all teachers, and the official stance of education policy-makers, to use education to intervene in, and disrupt, what has, historically, been a causal relationship in Britain between social origins and labour market destinations (Halsey *et al.*, 1980). Furthermore, the promotion of equality of opportunity through education appears to continue to enjoy widespread, if relatively superficial, support among parents of school-age children, professional groups and employers.

Concluding comments

This discussion has reviewed four problems inherent in recent analyses of the appropriate response of education to industrial restructuring and workplace change: an overstatement of the subordinate role of curriculum design to external economic pressures; the problem of identifying how non-economic variables generate curriculum change; the absence of an analytical framework which gives equal weight to the complex findings of the two specialist literatures involved; and the problem of reconciling the efficiency/equality balance in education policy.

That these issues should have proved problematic illustrates the extent to which education is seen by analysts as a passive instrument, only able to respond to external social and economic pressures. Moreover, this is a perspective reinforced powerfully by theories and empirical studies of how successfully education achieves a social and economic reproduction of adult society in successive generations of pupils (Ball, 1981; MacLeod, 1987, pp.9–22).

This state of affairs points to a central paradox in current policy and to the critical question at the heart of the education-workplace relationship. At a time when policy-makers are agreed that the traditional function of education – that of allocating pupils and students to an established pattern of labour market destinations – is economically retrogressive, recent policy has stressed reforms in education which, through market disciplines, will enable it *more closely* to mirror labour market demands. As this chapter has sought to demonstrate, there is no clear evidence that such demands (or other elements of current public policy) can create in Britain the widely anticipated 'high-skill economy' of popular literature.

Viewed in this light, the key question for educationalists becomes: can education policies ever create conditions in which supply pressures are at least as powerful in labour market formation as the skills demands of employers? At present, on the basis of the evidence reviewed here, the answer to this question is unknown. Strikingly, however, various educational developments currently underway in Britain are attempting to generate skills supply pressures and so create a better match between curriculum objectives (as opposed to responses) and the dynamics of workplace change. This is the goal of such initiatives as: the design of modular courses which allow for credit accumulation and transfer; the routine recording of students' achievement beyond that formally accredited; the identification of accreditable 'core skills' within general national vocational qualifications (GNVQs); and the promotion of education-business partnerships.

The difficult task facing each programme is to ensure that curriculum change is not passively and predominantly deter-mined by employers' immediate skills demands, but remains the subject of its own objectives: the development of individual students' knowledge and skills on a sufficient and continuing scale to ensure their deployment at a higher level than that which would have been generated by employers' short-term skill demands alone.

This is a formidable proposition, and a range of problems stand in the way of its achievement. These relate both to potential weaknesses within individual initiatives as well as to the pressure of countervailing policies which promote a passive relationship between education and the labour market. Predominant amongst the weaknesses displayed by individual initiatives is a subordina-tion of curriculum objectives to programme objectives. Business-education partnerships, for example, suffer from being highly reactive to employers' immediate, self-interested demands (Woolhouse, 1991, p.4); the Compact initiative, meanwhile, has suffered from being ill-focused and an amalgam of employment, social and educational policy. Moreover, the dissemination literature generated by both programmes has been prescriptive and lacking in critical sophistication (Richardson, 1992b, forth-coming).

Meanwhile, there are several countervailing external influences which retard the effective development of skills supply pressures through curriculum change. First, the education policies of large companies are usually driven at the strategic level by employers' public affairs concerns rather than their work organization needs. The result is that the education-skills issue is not driven by line managers in middle management (Finegold and Richardson, 1991). Second, considerable doubts remain as to whether the national vocational qualifications structure will serve to increase skills demand; indeed, the likelihood is that the new system will certificate existing and historical skills needs in employment which by international standards have been, and remain, sub-standard (Steedman, 1992). Third, despite 20 years of public criticism of the education system, analysis of what employers say they want from it reveals a picture of incoherence, reinforced by a lack of knowledge and understanding (Keep, 1988; Wellington, Chapter 4, this volume). Fourth, there remains an interlocking set of institutional components in the skills-creation system which continues to suppress both the supply and demand for skills in Britain (Finegold, 1992c). These problems are compounded by other factors: the role of ideology in government policy decisions about education and training; a lack of tools to measure the relationship between curriculum change and increased skills-supply pressures; and a vacuum, in the public sector, of management theories and practices which are sufficiently power-ful to overcome the routine imposition of inappropriate private sector practice (Keep, 1992).

The list of difficulties seems daunting, but need not distract from the central strategy being pursued by many educationalists: that of stimulating skills-supply pressures through such curricu-lum initiatives as credit accumulation and transfer, the wider recording of students' achievement and the identification of accreditable 'core skills'. These activities are, in turn, being bolstered by the expansion of the further and higher education sectors by government through selective alteration of the incentives available to the managers of institutions.

Finally, some straws in the wind suggest that the traditionally deferential role of the mainstream curriculum to the low-level skill demands of employers may be changing. British Telecom, for example, is to publish a report based on a systematic survey of 160 of its managers' perceptions of workplace change and how this is being matched in the school and college curriculum (BT, 1993, forthcoming). Meanwhile, the Rover Group is developing a 'partnership degree' in engineering. The curriculum of this post-16 programme will be based upon an analysis of future skill demands to be generated within the firm's flexible design and manufacturing organization; furthermore, the programme will offer students the opportunity to progress to degree-level study. Both projects recognize the potential of curricula focused on personal effectiveness to stimulate skills-supply pressures and so reinforce changes in workplace organization.

Such developments may come to form part of the survival strategies of Britain's leading companies as they compete for skilled labour. This, of course, is not to say that curriculum change will influence the mass of employers in a similar way, or be able causally to exert skills supply pressures upon them. The paradox for educationalists is that, by working with selected companies to effect new relationships between the curriculum and skill utilization, the power of the labour market to impose segmented aspirations upon the majority of young people may remain unchanged.

Acknowledgements

I should like to thank Ellen Renner, Guy Whitmarsh and David Finegold for a number of useful comments on a draft of this chapter.

Notes

1. The policies of the Thatcher period had, however, been anticipated in the Black Papers of 1969–77 and by the Labour government of 1974–9. From 1977, the DES followed Prime Minister Callaghan's lead and began to raise doubts about whether the goals of education policy were sufficiently attuned to the need of the economy (see DES, 1977; TES, 1977).
2. This question is more fully explored in Richardson (1991; 1993a, forthcoming).
3. Americans, however, would point to different constraints on effective policy-making in their system, such as the relative weakness of the federal government to bring about change. In both countries it is the policy process itself which inhibits the effectiveness of educational reform (Finegold et al., 1992).
4. The NCVQ literature is unclear as to how 'core skills' will be taught in GNVQs but, at a presentation at Brunel University in February 1992, Gilbert Jessup was clear that they would be 'permeated' in students' occupationally-related studies.
5. For John Tomlinson's leading role in promoting the education-industry relationship see Tomlinson (1986).
6. This picture is not accurately reflected in Garrahan and Stewart's (1992) studies. In their hostility to the multinational itself, they underplay the levels of skill in Nissan jobs in Sunderland and so deflect attention from their main argument – that specific incidences of inward investment are no substitute for regional economic policy

in tackling industrial decay and low-level skills demand in regional economies.

7. The determination of Conservative governments since 1988 to impose a traditional curriculum on schools in England and Wales suggests that politicians can see the lack of correspondence as being due to the detrimental influence of an undisciplined, progressive teaching force, rather than its predominant conservatism.

8. This is a more sophisticated version of the teenage affluence which generated research interest in the 1960s and early 1970s. See Wallace and Cross (1990, pp.1–3) for a discussion of how, during the 1980s, research interest in 'youth' switched from interpretations of their roles as consumers to their struggle with unemployment. With my colleague Guy Whitmarsh I hope, during 1993, to return to the issue of contemporary teenage culture and its effect on schooling.

9. This pattern may be complicated by high levels of youth unemployment as evidenced in Brown's (1987) study in South Wales.

10. An interesting exception is the discussion by Wellington (1987, pp.174–5) of information technology education.

11. Reported at a conference on careers education and guidance, University of Warwick, November, 1991.

12. Government ministers and civil servants appear to find the term 'empowerment' threatening: their preferred word is 'entitlement' (eg, DE, 1992, p.3). The same is true for some TEC staff.

13. I owe this reference to Karin Hutchinson.

References

Ashton, D (1992) 'The restructuring of the labour market and youth training', in Brown, P and Lauder, H (eds) *Education for Economic Survival: From Fordism to post-Fordism?* London: Routledge.

Ashton, D, Maguire M and Spilsbury, M (1987) 'Labour segmentation and the structure of the youth labour market' in Brown, P and Ashton, D (eds) *Education, Unemployment and Labour Markets*, London: Falmer Press.

BT (1993, forthcoming) *Matching Skills . . . a question of demand and supply*, London: British Telecom.

Ball, S (1981) *Beachside Comprehensive: A case-study of secondary schooling*, Cambridge: Cambridge University Press.

Baker, K (1989) Speech: 'Further Education: A new strategy', London, DES, 15 February.

Bash, L, Coulby, D and Jones, C (1985) *Urban Schooling: Theory and practice*, London: Holt, Rinehart and Winston.

Bernstein, B (1990) *The Restructuring of Pedagogic Discourse, Volume IV: Class, codes and control*, London: Routledge.

Blackman, S (1992) 'Beyond vocationalism', in Brown, P and Lauder, H (eds) *Education for Economic Survival: From Fordism to post-Fordism?*, London: Routledge.

Bourdieu, P and Passeron, J-C (1977) *Reproduction in Education, Society and Culture*, London: Sage.

Boyd, W (1993, forthcoming) 'Choice and market forces in American education: A revolution or a nonevent', in Finegold, D, McFarland, L and Richardson, W (eds) *Something Borrowed, Something Blue? A study of the Thatcher government's appropriation of American education and training policy*, Wallingford: Triangle.

Brown, P (1987) 'Schooling for inequality? Ordinary kids in school and the labour market', in Brown, P and Ashton, D (eds) *Education, Unemployment and Labour Markets*, London: Falmer Press.

Brown, P and Lauder, H (eds) (1992) *Education for Economic Survival: From Fordism to post-Fordism?*, London: Routledge.

Cockburn, C (1987) *Two Track Training*, Basingstoke: Macmillan.

Crompton, C (1987) 'A curriculum for enterprise: pedagogy or propaganda?', *School Organisation*, **7**, 1 , 5–11.

Davies, B (1986) *Threatening Youth: Toward a national youth policy*, Milton Keynes: Open University Press.

DE (1992) *Training Credits Directory*, London: Department of Employment.

DES (1977) *Education in Schools: A consultative Document*, Cmnd 6869, July, London: HMSO.

DES/DE (1991) *Education and Training for the 21st Century*, London: HMSO.

FEU (1992) *A Basis for Credit? Developing a post-16 credit accumulation and transfer framework*, London: Further Education Unit.

Fiddy, R (ed.) (1985) *Youth Unemployment And Training: A collection of national perspectives*, London: Falmer Press.

Field, J (1988) 'Unemployment, training and manpower policy in inter-war Britain', *British Journal of Education and Work*, **2**, 1, 39–50.

Finch, J (1984) *Education as Social Policy*, Harlow: Longman.

Finegold, D (1992a) 'The Low Skill Equilibrium: An institutional analysis of Britain's education and training failure', unpublished D.Phil thesis, University of Oxford, Hilary Term.

Finegold, D (1992b) 'Economic changes driving education reform', in Richardson, W (ed.) *Work Related Teaching and Learning: Education and business in partnership*, Coventry: University of Warwick, Centre for Education and Industry.

Finegold, D (1992c) *Breaking out of the Low-skills Equilibrium*, Briefing Paper No. 5, London: National Commission on Education.

Finegold, D and Richardson, W (1991) *Making Education Our Business*, Coventry: University of Warwick, Centre for Education and Industry.

Finegold, D and Soskice, D (1988) 'The failure of British training: analysis and prescription', *Oxford Review of Economic Policy*, **4**, 3, Autumn, 21–53.

Finegold, D, MacFarland, L and Richardson, W (1992) 'Introduction: Policy borrowing in education and training', in Finegold, D, MacFarland, L and Richardson, W, (eds) *Something Borrowed, Something Blue? A study of the Thatcher government's appropriation of American education and training policy*, Wallingford: Triangle.

Garrahan, P and Stewart, P (1992a) 'Lean Production and the "Movable Feast": Training for What?', paper presented to VET Forum Conference, University of Warwick, June.

Garrahan, P and Stewart, P (1992b) *The Nissan Enigma: Flexibility at work in the local economy*, London: Mansell.

Halsey, A, Heath, A and Ridge, J (1980) *Origins and Destinations*, Oxford: Clarendon Press.

Handy, C (1984) *The Future of Work*, Oxford: Basil Blackwell.

Hargreaves, D (1967) *Social Relations in a Secondary School*, London: Routledge.

Hodkinson, P (1989) 'Crossing the academic/vocational divide: personal effectiveness and autonomy as an integrating theme in post-16 education', *British Journal of Educational Studies*, **37**, 4, 369–83.

IER (1991) *Review of the Economy and Employment 1991: Occupational assessment*, Coventry: Institute for Employment Research, University of Warwick, October.

Institute for Manpower Studies (1984) *Competence and Competition*, London: MSC/NEDO.

Institute for Public Policy Research (1990) *A British Baccalaureate; Ending the division between education and training*, London: IPPR.

Jessup, G (1993, forthcoming) 'Towards a coherent post-16 qualifications framework', in Finegold, D, Richardson, W and Woolhouse, J (eds) *The Reform of Post-16 Education and Training in England and Wales*, London: Longman.

Keep, E (1988) 'What do employers want from education? A question more easily asked than answered', unpublished paper presented to the VET Forum, University of Warwick, May.

Keep, E (1992) 'Schools in this marketplace? Some problems with private sector models', in Wallace, G (ed.) *Local Management of Schools: Research and experience*, (BERA Dialogues Series No.6), Clevedon: Multi-lingual Matters.

King, J (1990) *Labour Economics*, London: Macmillan.

Knell, J (1992) 'TNCs and the dynamics of human capital formation: evidence from West Yorkshire', Leeds: School of Business and Economic Studies, University of Leeds, May.

Kumar, K (1992) 'New theories of industrial society', in Brown, P and Lauder, H (eds) *Education for Economic Survival: From Fordism to post-Fordism?* London: Routledge.

Lacey, C (1970) *Hightown Grammar*, Manchester: Manchester University Press.

MacLeod, J (1987) *Ain't No Makin' It*, London: Tavistock.

McNabb, R and Ryan, P (1990) 'Segmented labour markets', in Sapsford, D and Tzannatos, Z (eds) *Current Issues in Labour Economics*, Basingstoke: Macmillan.

Nettl, J (1967) *Political Mobilization: A sociological analysis of methods and concepts*, London: Faber and Faber.

OECD (1985) *Education and Training after Basic Schooling*, Paris: Organisation for Economic Cooperation and Development.

O'Keeffe, D (1979) 'Capitalism and correspondence: a critique of Marxist analyses of education', *Higher Education Review*, **12**, 1.

Oppenheim, A (1955) 'Social status and clique formation among grammar school boys', *British Journal of Sociology*, **VI**, 228–45.

Prais, S and Wagner, K (1983) 'Some practical aspects of human capital investment: training standards in five occupations in Britain and Germany', *National Institute Economic Review*, **105**, 46–65.

Peck, F and Stone, I (1991) *New Investment and the Northern Region Labour Market*, Newcastle: Newcastle Polytechnic.

Reeder, D (1981) 'A recurring debate: education and industry', in Dale, R, Esland, G, Ferguson, R, and MacDonald M (eds) *Education and the State: Volume 1, Schooling and the national interest*, London: Falmer Press

Richardson, W (1991) *Education and Training Post-16: Options for reform and the public policy process in England and Wales*, Coventry: Warwick VET Forum Report No. 1, University of Warwick.

Richardson, W (1993a, forthcoming) 'Overview of the debate', in Finegold, D, Richardson, W, and Woolhouse, J (eds) *The Reform of Post-16 Education and Training in England and Wales*, London: Longman.

Richardson, W (1993b, forthcoming) 'Employers as an instrument of school reform: Compacts in Britain and America', in Finegold, D, MacFarland, L and Richardson, W (eds) *Something Borrowed, Something Blue? A study of the Thatcher government's appropriation of American education and training policy*, Wallingford: Triangle.

Spours, K (1993, forthcoming) 'Qualification reform: analysis and conclusions', in Finegold, D, Richardson, W and Woolhouse, J (eds) *The Reform of Post-16 Education and Training in England and Wales*, London: Longman.

Steedman, H (1988) 'Vocational training in Britain and France: mechanical and electrical craftsmen', *National Institute Economic Review*, **126**, 57–70.

Steedman, H (1992) 'A gap in post-16 strategy', *Times Educational Supplement*, 8 May, 14.

TA/DE (1989) *Training in Britain*, Sheffield: Training Agency and Department of Employment.

TES (1977) 'Light the green paper and retire', *Times Educational Supplement*, 22 July.

Times, The (1992) 'Colleges and schools call for A-level shake up', 12 February.

Tomlinson, J (1986) 'Changes in education', in Jamieson, I and Blandford, D (eds) *Education and Change: Can you afford to ignore it?*, Cambridge: Hobsons Limited.

Tomlinson, J (1992) 'The education agenda of the 1990s', in Richardson, W (ed.) *Work Related Teaching and Learning: Education and business in partnership*, Coventry: University of Warwick, Centre for Education and Industry.

Turner, G (1983) *The Social World of the Comprehensive School*, Beckenham: Croom Helm.

Walker, S and Barton, L (eds) (1987) *Changing Policies Changing Teachers*, Milton Keynes: Open University Press.

Wallace, C and Cross, M (1990) 'Introduction: Youth in transition', in Wallace, C and Cross, M (eds) *Youth in Transition: The sociology of youth and youth policy*, London: Falmer Press.

Wellington, J (1987) 'Employment patterns and the goals of education', in *British Journal of Education and Work*, **1**, 3, 163–77.

White, M (1988) 'Education policy and economic goals', *Oxford Review of Economic Policy*, **4**, 1–20.

Willis, P (1977) *Learning to Labour*, Farnborough: Saxon House.

Woods, P (1979) *The Divided School*, London: Routledge and Kegan Paul.

Woolhouse, J (1991) 'Partnership principles', in Gibbs, R, Hodge, R and Clough, E (eds) *The Reality of Partnership*, Harlow: Longman.

Concluding Remarks:
The Vocational Imperative –
Which Way Now?

J J Wellington

Recurring Themes

One of the features of this book is that there have been several issues and themes, taken up by various authors, which seem to be central in examining the debate over the vocational imperative and the purpose of education. They are summarized below without repeating them at length:

- One of the results of rising unemployment, particularly youth unemployment, is to increase the level of questioning of the function of education. The implicit promise in schooling (Watts, 1983), ie, work hard at school to get a job after it, is increasingly questioned and to some extent undermined. However, paradoxically, the emphasis on vocational education is reinforced and strengthened.
- This strengthening results in vocational initiatives aimed at restoring the implicit promise in education. Initiatives such as Compact and TVEI have been intended to serve this purpose, ie, restoration of faith, morale and belief in schooling. This process has been accompanied by the introduction of training programmes which act as a buffer between compulsory education and the world of employment or unemployment.
- Vocational initiatives, however well-intentioned, are often overtaken by events outside their remit and their control. The contexts (economic, social, political and technological) in which initiatives occur play a vital role in their impact. This, in turn,

makes the evaluation of a single initiative extremely problematic.

- One initiative in education may well undermine another. The importance of the institution is paramount. A vocational initiative from one source may well be negated by activity or legislation from another.

- New structures and mechanisms for bringing about change in education have been created which are associated with terms like the contract culture, the biddable curriculum and contract-compliance mechanism. Those in education seem to have adapted to these new procedures, demands and structures with remarkable ingenuity and creativity.

- It is vital to consider critically the language used in the debate on the vocational imperative. The discourse of education has changed dramatically to include many terms and metaphors which previously belonged to other realms of discourse. Thus we have witnessed the commodification of education in which the language of the retail and service industries ('producers', 'consumers', 'marketeers' and even 'punters') now enters the debate on education and training to accompany the earlier introduction of terms like 'enterprise', 'competence' and 'transferable skills'. Language plays a vital role in shaping pupil identities, in creating or constraining equal opportunities, in determining the curriculum and in changing modes of assessment. We need to be critically aware of such language in order to further the debate.

- The education-employment relationship remains as complex as it ever has been. For education and training, there is no clear causal relationship between workplace change and curriculum development. For the individual, the interface between education and the labour market is often unclear.

- This complex interface includes one of the perennial paradoxes of vocational education: in practice, vocational qualifications are less valuable in gaining employment than general or academic ones. This often results in disguised or deferred vocationalism, in which an academic route is followed in order to achieve eventual labour market success. This is a key factor undermining vocational education and preserving the academic/vocational divide. It may also undermine the future plans and targets of the NVQ programme.

- Neither in practice nor in theory is the distinction between a vocational and a liberal education an absolute one. We have witnessed a convergence of the aims of liberal and vocational education. Acknowledgement of this convergence may be the best way forward in considering the future of education and the world of work.

Visions of the future of work: a review of yesterday's tomorrows

One of the vital issues in the debate on education for employment concerns the question of the purpose and future of work itself. Chapters in this book have considered unemployment and employment patterns, skill changes in the workplace, the impact of technology on employment and the issues of de-skilling and the polarization of skills. Tentative conclusions have been put forward. There are, however, more ambitious and more visionary discussions of the future of work which help to stimulate debate and provoke discussion, even if those brave enough to make them are likely to be proved hopelessly wrong. The literature is full of past predictions – what could be termed 'yesterday's tomorrows'.

Robertson (1985), for example, talked of the SHE future for employment and work: sane, humane and ecological. In his view, which to be fair is more a hope than a prediction, work would become a purposeful activity, organized and controlled by people themselves. In this future there will be a breakdown of traditional distinctions between employment and unemployment, leisure and work. Paid employment would no longer be the dominant form of work. Such changes will be accompanied by two 'paradigm shifts': from a scientific and economic view of nature to an ecological and spiritual view, and from growth and expansion in economics to sufficiency and balance.

In a similar vein, Schumacher (1979), in his description of 'good work', talked of the three purposes of work in the future as being: to provide necessary goods and services; to enable everyone to use and thereby perfect their gifts; to do so in the service of and in cooperation with others. Subsequent authors have often drawn upon Schumacher's work in considering the future of work in relation to new technology. Shallis (1984) for example, in discussing the 'silicon idol', talks of the need for the appropriate use of information technology in society, both at work and in education. Many other visions of the future of work have included a forecast of the impact of new technology, though perhaps of a less humane nature. Mackintosh (1986) put forward the notion of a new IT infrastructure for the whole of Europe, the 'Eurogrid', which would stimulate growth in demand for and supply of IT resources and services. This in turn would lead to the intelligent use of information in business, government and the home. He describes the scheme in detail and goes on to analyse the consequential demands on the education system to provide the required personnel, including the need for a doubling of IT graduates by 1995. Mackintosh is not alone in putting forward a vision of the future which depends on information technology. Gershuny (1984) talked of the need for development in IT which could only come about by the creation of an appropriate infrastructure, including extensive communications networks. This would lead to a huge growth in service employment, in (for example) the production, distribution and maintenance of software and make consequent demands on education and training. These somewhat deterministic predictions will clearly not become reality in the timescale envisaged by their authors, although they have provided important food for debate.

More cautious discussions of future work are perhaps less stimulating but more worthy of close consideration in the debate over education for employment. Thus Gill (1985) predicted that future work patterns will include: less paid employment; shorter life working hours; fewer manual jobs; new forms of organization in the workplace; a blurred boundary between leisure and work; and a weaker trade union movement. These changes in turn will lead to a higher demand for technically qualified people and an increased demand for education at all levels. Tolley's (1984) discussion argued likewise that future working patterns will move away from the old 50 years/50 weeks/50 hours model to 30 years/ 30 weeks/30 hours, a shift similar to that predicted by Handy (1985) in presenting his future of work. With the benefit of hindsight, we can see that some of these patterns have become reality. Similarly, Watts, in 1983, put forward six definitions of work which are still valuable a decade later:

1. formal paid employment generating wealth;
2. formal paid employment;
3. aspects of the formal economy including self-employment;
4. other economic activity including the informal economy;
5. voluntary work;
6. any application of productive effort, eg, housework, DIY.

Watts argued that category 1 is sure to decrease in the future; subsequent figures have shown this to have happened and still be happening. Education should surely take account of this and adapt the work-related curriculum to take account of all aspects of work.

There is still work to be done

One of the most important messages which emerges both from the literature in this area and from everyday experience is that, despite interesting visions of the future and predictions of fewer jobs and shorter working hours and years, there is still a lot of work that remains to be done. This phrase is taken from a vitally important publication by Mukherjee (1974) for the MSC, as it was at that time. He argued then that despite the current unemployment figure – approximately 0.6 million – there were still many jobs in the community and society which needed to be done. How clear this is two decades later. Mukherjee argued for a vast community industry or public employment programme which would both create work and reduce the social, psychological and economic impact of unemployment. This would go hand-in-hand with a massive training programme. Looking back, we have the training programmes but not the jobs. Experience has shown clearly that training programmes do not create jobs. Roberts (1984), writing in a similar vein a decade later, argued that there is plenty of 'work that is currently being left undone'. He listed: 'schools, social work, highways, sewers, railroads, homes, hospitals and prisons'. Roberts argued that the solution must involve a threefold initiative of education, training and jobs. As stated earlier, we have had the training but not the jobs, a situation referred to by Gleeson (1989) as the paradox of training. This is analogous to providing, in information technology, software without the hardware to exploit it.

The realization that there were, and still are, important jobs to be done, must lead to the dismissal of the so-called 'leisure alternative' as a possible scenario for the future, and with it the hackneyed notion of 'education for leisure' as a possible goal for the future. Roberts (1983) dismissed it then by arguing that the answer to unemployment is not leisure, it is the provision of occupations in employment, education and training. This view still holds good. Work (however defined), and the purposes it serves for the individual, are surely as important now as they ever have been. An excellent analysis by Jahoda (1983) which involved studies of both unemployment and employment, suggested that work or employment can serve five important functions:

1. it imposes a time-structure on a person's day;
2. it enlarges a person's social horizon;
3. it provides a sense of purpose and a feeling of participation in collective effort;
4. it can give a person a place in society, providing identity and status;
5. it provides regular, often enforced, activity.

Jahoda's analysis of work still remains accurate to a large degree. In addition, of course, its central function for many is to provide an income. The purpose of work and, to some extent, it will be argued, education for it, remain remarkably constant despite the rapid social, employment and technology changes that have been witnessed.

Education for the future

The purpose of work has remained largely unchanged. In many ways the requirements of education have shown similar constancy. The analysis by the Central Policy Review Staff (1980) relating education to industrial performance came to this opinion:

> ... we think there is some truth in the view that the qualities now emphasised in educational theory such as resourcefulness, an enquiring mind, and enthusiasm are at least as appropriate for the jobs that will be available over the next twenty years as the rather dour and old-fashioned virtues of obedience and discipline which were emphasised by some employers in the past (para. 6).

Much of the evidence presented on the needs of employers since that time, summarized in Chapter 4, has supported their opinion. Thus in the field of information technology, where one might expect the greatest changes to take place, studies have shown that communication skills are ranked highly as are personal qualities such as drive and enthusiasm (Angell, 1987). Angell's study was based on a survey of 1,300 companies involved in the IT industry who surprisingly rated computing skills *per se* of less importance than interpersonal skills. A similar large-scale study by the IMS (Connor and Pearson, 1986) showed that there is an increased requirement for good interpersonal skills amongst staff as IT becomes more sophisticated. Studies such as these have been discussed at length in earlier chapters. The main aim in this concluding section is to summarize and reinforce the view that the aims of education in a technological world should include traditional worthwhile qualities. This was summed up neatly by one employer in the retail industry in a study reported in 1989:

> Although we've made major advances in the last few years, to be quite honest it hasn't affected the sort of person we're recruiting. From a branch point of view, we need the same skills now, even though we've got the computers there, as we did 10 or 15 years ago. What they need to do is interpret data ... and they've been interpreting data, albeit in a different format, for 10 years. I wonder why there is this emphasis to teach kids about computers? How many of them, when they leave school, are actually going to get hands-on experience?
> We're looking for people who will treat customers as human beings ... mix well with their colleagues ... communicate well with customers (Wellington, 1989, p.126).

A model of education for the future needs to be broad enough to encompass a wide range of aims, abilities, qualities, skills and knowledge. A narrow view of education and vocational preparation based, for example, solely on competence may not be either educationally desirable or vocationally significant. This section cannot do justice to the current debate on competence, which may well have an important place in the future of education. But we do need to pose the question: can a model of education – the new emerging model (Jessup, 1991) – based solely on competence and outcomes be broad enough for the future? Where do tacit knowledge, intuition, personal qualities, latent abilities and the process of education, for example, come into a model which focuses solely on outcomes? How does reflective practice or 'knowing-in-action' (Schon, 1983) fit into this vision? Does the emerging model of education herald a new form of behaviourism?

There are also dangers in giving extensive responsibility for the creation of new modes of vocational education, training and assessment to employers. Do employers have a strong enough track record to be entrusted with this role? Do they want it? Can they take a sufficiently broad, balanced and long-term view of the future to create an adequate new model of education?

As Reeder (1979) has pointed out, the controversy over the role of education in a modern industrial society is a long-standing one. It is certain to continue. This book has attempted to at least consider the recent history of that controversy, to examine the discourse involved in it and to clarify some of the central issues. It has also attempted to uncover some of the recurrent themes in the debate. One of those themes is the view that there has been, and should be, an increasing convergence of the aims and methods of liberal and vocational education. Indeed, the maintenance of an opposition or a polarization of liberal versus vocational education will not help in creating a framework for education in the future. Vocational preparation must form an integral part of general education, and vice versa.

References

Angell, C (1987) *Information, New Technology and Manpower*, Boston Spa: British Library.

Central Policy Review Staff (1980) *Education, Training and Industrial Performance*, London: HMSO.

Connor, H and Pearson, R (1986) *Information Technology Manpower into the 1990s*, London: Institute of Manpower Studies.

Gershuny, J (1984) 'The future of service employment', in Marstrand, P (ed.), *New Technology and the Future of Work and Skills*, London: Francis Pinter.

Gill, C (1985) *Work, Unemployment and the New Technology*, Cambridge: Polity Press.

Gleeson, D (1989) *The Paradox of Training*, Milton Keynes: Open University Press.

Handy, C (1985) *The Future of Work*, Oxford: Basil Blackwell.

Jahoda, M (1983) *Employment and Unemployment: A social/psychological analysis*, Cambridge: Cambridge University Press.

Jessup, G (1991) *NVQs and the Emerging Model of Education*, Lewes: Falmer Press.

Mackintosh, I (1986) *Sunrise Europe: The Dynamics of Information Technology*, Oxford: Blackwell.

Mukherjee, S (1974) *There's Work To Be Done: Unemployment and manpower policies*, London: MSC/HMSO.

Reeder, D (1979) 'A recurring debate: education and industry', in Bernbaum, G (ed.), *Schooling in Decline*, Basingstoke: Macmillan.

Roberts, K (1983) *Youth and Leisure*, London: Allen and Unwin.

Roberts, K (1984) *School Leavers and Their Prospects*, Milton Keynes: Open University Press.

Robertson, J (1985) *Future Work*, Gower: Maurice Temple Smith.

Schon, D (1983) *The Reflective Practitioner*, Gower: Maurice Temple Smith.

Schumacher, E F (1979) *Good Work*, London: Cape.

Shallis, M (1984) *The Silicon Idol*, Oxford: Oxford University Press.

Tolley, G (1984) 'What will the world of work demand from education and training in the future?', in Tucker, J (ed.), *Education, Training and the New Technologies*, London: Kogan Page.

Watts, A G (1983) *Education, Unemployment and the Future of Work*, Milton Keynes: Open University Press.

Wellington, J J (1989) *Education for Employment: The place of information technology,* Windsor: NFER-Nelson.

Glossary

AOTs	Adults other than teachers
BIC	Business in the Community
BTEC	Business and Technology Education Council
CBI	Confederation of British Industry
CGLI	City & Guilds of London Institute
CITB	Construction Industry Training Board
CP	Community Programme
CPVE	Certificate of Pre-vocational Education
CRAC	Careers Research and Advisory Centre
CTC	City Technology College
DE	Department of Employment
DES	Department of Education and Science
DTI	Department of Trade and Industry
EAS	Enterprise Allowance Scheme
EATE	Enterprise Awareness in Teacher Education
EBP	Education Business Partnership
EEI	Enterprise and Education Initiative
EHEI	Enterprise in Higher Education Initiative
EITB	Engineering Industry Training Board
ET	Employment Training
FEU	Further Education Unit
ILB	Industry Lead Body
IMS	Institute of Manpower Studies
ITECs	Information Technology Centres
ITO	Industry Training Organization
LEAs	Local Education Authorities
LEC	Local Enterprise Council (Scottish version of TEC)
LEN	Local Employers Network
MSC	Manpower Services Commission
NAFE	Non-advanced Further Education
NCET	National Council for Education Technology
NCVQ	National Council for Vocational Qualifications
NEDO	National Economic Development Office
NROVA	National Record of Vocational Achievement
NVQ	National Vocational Qualifications
OTF	Occupational Training Family
PIC	Private Industry Council

PT	Project Trident
ROAE	Record of Achievement and Experience
RSA	Royal Society for the Encouragement of Arts, Manufacturing and Commerce
RVQ	Review of Vocational Qualifications
SATRO	Science and Technology Regional Organizations
SCIP	School Curriculum Industry Partnership
SCSST	Standing Conference on Schools' Science and Technology
SIC	Standard Industrial Classification
SILO/EILO	Schools/Education Industry Liaison Officer
TA	Training Agency (a division of the Employment Department which assumed the residual functions of the TC)
TC	Training Commission
TEC	Training and Enterprise Council
TEED	Training, Enterprise and Education Directorate (a new division of the Employment Department which replaced the TA)
TUC	Trades Union Congress
TVEI	Technical and Vocational Education Initiative
UBI	Understanding British Industry
VET	Vocational Education and Training
WRFE	Work-related Further Education
WRNAFE	Work-related Non-advanced Further Education
YE	Young Enterprise
YOP	Youth Opportunities Programme
YT	Youth Training
YTS	Youth Training Scheme

South East Essex College
of Arts & Technology
Carnarvon Road Southend-on-Sea Essex SS2 6LS
Tel: (01702) 220400 Fax: (01702) 432320 Minicom: (01702) 220642

Education for Employment – Chronology

1974 MSC established by Employment and Training Act
1975 MSC publishes *Vocational Preparation of Young People*
1976 Callaghan's Ruskin College speech
1978 Youth Opportunities Programme (YOP), until 1983
1981 *New Training Initiative* (NTI) – White Paper and MSC
     Document
1982 TVEI launched
     DES proposal for CPVE
1983 14 TVEI pilot projects begin
     One-year Youth Training Scheme (YTS) launched
1984 *Training for Jobs* White Paper
1985 'Mini Enterprise in Schools Project' (MESP) launched by the
     DTI
1985 CPVE introduced
     TVEI now running in every LEA
1986 National Council for Vocational Qualifications (NCVQ)
     established
     CTC plans announced by Kenneth Baker
     Two-year YTS introduced
     GCSE introduced
     'Enterprise in YTS' launched by MSC
1987 TVEI extension
     MSC launches EHE programme
1988 Compact initiative launched nationwide
     Education Reform Act (ERA)
     First CTCs open
     MSC reabsorbed into Department of Employment
     MSC becomes Training Commission
     TECs announced in White Paper, *Employment for the 1990s*
1989 LECs launched in Scotland
     'Enterprise Awareness in Teacher Education' (EATE) project
     begins
1990 YT (Youth Training) replaces YTS
1991 NCVQ completes its review

Index